WOMEN IN NURSING

A Descriptive Study

Directed by

Lisbeth Hockey

Director of Nursing Research Unit
Department of Nursing Studies, University of Edinburgh

HODDER AND STOUGHTON
LONDON SYDNEY AUCKLAND TORONTO

ISBN 0 340 20425 7

First printed 1976

Printed and bound in Great Britain for
Hodder and Stoughton Educational,
a division of Hodder and Stoughton Limited,
Mill Road, Dunton Green, Sevenoaks, Kent
by Morrison and Gibb Ltd, London and Edinburgh

Foreword

'Women in Nursing' has a rather special significance for the nursing profession for a number of reasons. It is the first Report produced by a team of research workers in the Nursing Research Unit under the leadership of the Director, Miss Lisbeth Hockey. This achievement is undoubtedly noteworthy in a profession where knowledge of the research process and its implications is still in the developmental phase. For this reason too the research team was young, talented and motivated but its membership changed a number of times during the study thus requiring experienced guidance and direction.

Most nursing research in the United Kingdom to date has been carried out by individual workers. Although many of the studies undertaken are undoubtedly of value, most of them need replication or validation; and they have not necessarily been related to subjects which nurse practitioners themselves see to be of top priority. 'Women in Nursing' was, in fact, 'customer' based before that principle became the approved policy of the Chief Scientist Organisation. It also set out to offer an opportunity for nurses to learn systematically about the research process on a broad front, as some members of the Unit's team are nurses and some are graduates of other relevant disciplines.

Although the main objective of the Report is to provide specific feedback to the profession in Scotland on the subject of its own choosing, advantage has been taken of the existence of such a Unit to achieve additional outcomes of the study.

As one of the principal purposes of the Unit is to educate nurses for research as well as to undertake studies, the Report is presented in such a way that all research-minded nurses, and there are now many of them, can use it, and its Appendices, as a guidebook of 'do's and don'ts' in the research process. Hopefully some of them will be encouraged to investigate for themselves many of the further possible studies highlighted in many of the chapters. These suggestions include the need to study more closely the actual role and function of nurses and how they should give care; the facilities, both professional and personal, required for an effective nursing service and the processes of communication especially between nurses and their patients.

One of the exciting outcomes of this team based research is that the existence of the Unit has enabled the Director with her team of co-workers to lay plans for future studies on some of the principal outcomes of 'Women in Nursing'. Thus, perhaps for the first time in this country, the impetus and knowhow gained from this customer-orientated study will be used to undertake further research in areas specifically indicated by it. For instance, there is undoubtedly a great need for further investigation into the role, attitudes and preparation of nursing auxiliaries. This study is now in an advanced stage of planning. Similarly, further investigation of nurse-patient interaction is clearly indicated and opportunities of working in this area are being investigated. As the related studies develop from this parent investigation, more opportunities will also be available to nurses to become attached to the research team to learn about research methods under the guidance of those who are themselves rapidly acquiring expertise.

Finally, it must be recorded that this Report is the result of the foresight, leadership and meticulous attention to detail of Lisbeth Hockey who has achieved an unbelievable volume of work since the establishment of the Unit in October 1971. Those working with her including research and secretarial staff, have also been a dedicated group of pioneers frequently taking on work started by others and developing it further themselves. But they have gained experience as richly as they have given of their own talents.

No study of this dimension could be undertaken without the fullest and most generous cooperation of the nursing staff of all categories involved in it, who gave of their time and thoughts to provide the total data for analysis. It is another example of the interrelatedness of the Department of Nursing Studies and its Research Unit with nursing colleagues working in the National Health Service.

Margaret Scott Wright

Director's Acknowledgments

This report is the result of many people's concerted effort. Gratitude must first be expressed to all the members of the nursing staff who agreed to be interviewed in the pilot and main studies. They gave time and thought to the project which could not have been undertaken without their help.

A number of colleagues contributed to the work, some for longer and some for shorter periods.

I would like to acknowledge especially the help of John Bond in getting the study off the ground. He took major responsibility for the supervision of coding and processing of most of the data; he also contributed creatively to the development of the Unit during its first two years of life.

Elizabeth Broumley, Erica Lowry and Sara Parkin together with John Bond undertook most of the interviews. They were helped with the coding by a team of temporary part-time coders. Helen Murray joined the Unit at that stage and also gave valuable help with data processing.

Hend Abdel-Al worked for a short period on some of the analyses as did Melissa Woelfel Hardie who, as research associate for 10 months, also helped in other ways.

Staff changes in the course of a group study are bound to be traumatic. The team who eventually saw the work through to its completion, giving loyal support and expending much creative effort were Helen Murray, Ethel Sutherland and Kate French. Eric Anderson gave computing support in the latter stages, assisted in the graph plotting by Craig Stott. Erica Thomas contributed significantly at all stages of analysis, drafting and checking and Jenny Wright helped willingly with the many inevitably tedious but important tasks.

Mr Peter Fisk, Department of Statistics, and Dr Margaret Gilmore, Department of Nursing Studies, advised on some of the statistical presentation.

The drafts were read and constructively commented on by Dr Albert Pilliner, Director, Godfrey Thomson Unit for Academic Assessment, and Miss Annie Altschul, Senior Lecturer, Department of Nursing Studies.

As Unit Secretary, Fiona Wilson carried a great deal of responsibility throughout the whole period of the study; her conscientious help, commonsense, patience and efficiency are readily acknowledged. Most of the arduous typing was ably undertaken by Muriel Armstrong and Patricia Jeffrey.

I would like to place on record my appreciation of the constant support, advice and encouragement given by Professor Margaret Scott Wright, Head of Department of Nursing Studies.

The Unit's Steering Committee gave valuable counsel.

To all colleagues who helped in major and minor ways, I am grateful.

Financial support provided by the Scottish Home and Health Department is gratefully acknowledged.

Contents

FOREWORD   5

DIRECTOR'S ACKNOWLEDGMENTS   7

CHAPTER 1   INTRODUCTION   11
Choice of topic; Census conducted by the Scottish Home and Health Department; Objectives of study; Staff; Synopsis of content; Presentation.

CHAPTER 2   STUDY DESIGN AND METHOD   17
Exploratory work; The pilot study; Choice of areas; Sampling; Tools for data collection; Organisation of interviews; Non-response.

CHAPTER 3   STUDY AREAS   23

CHAPTER 4   TOP MANAGERS AND THEIR POLICIES   28
Recruitment—pupil and student nurses, trainees in the community services, qualified staff in hospitals, community nursing staff; Establishments; Facilities for staff; Attachment of community nursing staff; Absenteeism and sickness absence; Personal data.

CHAPTER 5   WOMEN AS NURSES   46
Age distribution; Qualifications; Staff stability and mobility; Type of hospital and area; Part-time employment and marital status.

CHAPTER 6   NURSES AS WOMEN   65
Family background; Marriage; Households and family structure; Single parent families; Living with older/dependent relatives; Arrangements for children; Income; Housing; Travel to work; Social life.

CHAPTER 7   CAREER PATTERNS   93
Occupational choice; Pre-nursing experience; Breaks in service; Reasons for break in nursing career; Reasons for return; Effects of break; Future plans; Career patterns.

CHAPTER 8   JOB SATISFACTION   118
Theoretical background; Development of research tool; Distribution of scores among study population; Skill utilisation.

CHAPTER 9 PART-TIME NURSING 133
Definition of part-time work; Part-time nursing; Part-time nurses in the study.

CHAPTER 10 WORKING HOURS 145
Overall picture; Hospital nursing staff—administrators, sisters, staff nurses and midwives, learners; Community nursing staff—district nurses, health visitors, combined duty nurses, domiciliary midwives.

CHAPTER 11 NURSING AUXILIARIES 164
Definition; Nursing auxiliaries in the research areas; Nursing staff's contact with nursing auxiliaries; Allocation; Nursing staff's opinions about nursing auxiliaries; Reasons for opinions concerning levels of responsibility; Presence at formal ward reports; Better care for patients/clients.

CHAPTER 12 NURSES' VIEWS ON PATIENT CARE 180
Time for patients; Use of time; Important care elements; Patients whose care could be improved; Possible improvements in patient care; Conclusions.

CHAPTER 13 CONCLUDING DISCUSSION 194
APPENDIX 1 STATISTICAL APPROACH 199
APPENDIX 2 THE DEFINITION OF SOCIAL CLASS 208
APPENDIX 3 COMMENTS ON INTERVIEWING SCHEDULES AND GUIDE TO INTERVIEWERS 215
APPENDIX 4 SUPPLEMENTARY TABLES 219
APPENDIX 5 ATTITUDE SCALES 222
APPENDIX 6 NURSING QUALIFICATIONS—A PROBLEM OF CLASSIFICATION 239
APPENDIX 7 GLOSSARY 245
REFERENCES 249

CHAPTER ONE
Introduction

This chapter is intended to indicate the factors which led to the decision on the choice of the research topic, to describe the framework within which the study was undertaken and to give a synopsis of the Report's structure and content.

CHOICE OF TOPIC

Any choice of topic for research must be related to policy, need or interest or a combination of two or all of these; to this extent, therefore, any choice has an inherent and inevitable bias.

As such bias cannot be avoided it would seem reasonable to aim at a research environment in which desirable factors are optimised, that is where the interest of the research worker can be linked with the need of the consumer and where controlling policy facilitates this.

The study of which this is a report was the first undertaken in a new unique Research Unit.* There was, therefore, no precedent to follow and no foundation on which to build; a situation which appeared to make the selection of the first research topic both easy and difficult. The selection seemed easy because there was no pattern to be followed. It proved difficult because there were many potential projects from which to select but little or no knowledge of consumer need and no staff whose research interests could show the way, at least in the initial stages of development.

The Steering Committee which drafted the Unit's constitution gave it a broad two-sided commission—to undertake research and to engage in educational activities designed to help the profession in awareness and use of research. The research remit was left deliberately broad, specifying merely that the Unit's programme should be concerned with current nursing problems. An identification of such problems was essential but such an exercise, systematically undertaken, would itself have constituted a major research project. It was decided, therefore, to make an initial assessment of nursing problems simply by talking to a variety of nursing personnel at various stages of their career in different parts of the country and of the Health Service. It was thought that:

(i) the results of such informal discussions would reveal a variety of problems, some of which might be related and could be woven into the design of a major study;

---

* The Nursing Research Unit in the Department of Nursing Studies of the University of Edinburgh is the first such Unit within a British University.

(ii) such an approach would achieve maximum utility for the nursing profession;

(iii) staff with an interest in the selected study could be recruited;

(iv) the results of the study might open the way for a long term research programme and, to some extent, direct the Unit's policy.

Discussions with nursing staff were arranged, some organised and formal, others spontaneous and informal, some in a one-to-one situation, others in groups. Reports of the discussions were made and the analysis exposed the following problem areas:

Shortage of nursing staff.

Shortage of auxiliary and secretarial staff.

Resentment between full- and part-time staff.

Resentment between enrolled and registered nurses.

Communication difficulties between grades of staff.

'Absenteeism'.

Travelling and accommodation difficulties.

Inadequate in-service training for promotion.

Insufficient 'breaking-in' period for nurses returning after a break in service.

Insufficient clinical teaching of students/pupils.

Inflexibility of working hours.

Poor use of skills for trained staff.

It became obvious that a study of some aspect of the staffing of services was needed but its objectives, scope, design and focus remained to be decided.

The following arguments and ideas played a part in the final direction of the study.

Demographic trends suggest that in the future more ancillary and nursing staff will be married women.[1] As the nursing services are needed 24 hours a day throughout the week, this trend suggests several implications. Modern consumer society holds certain expectations and values about the way time is allocated between work and life outside work or leisure. For example, traditionally, individuals claim the right of two days off a week at the week-end and at present there is some pressure to extend the week-end by a further day. In addition, many individuals are campaigning for fewer working hours per week. The majority of people work between the hours of 0800 and 1800 and recent public debate has highlighted the problem of working during unsocial hours. This concern suggests that there are certain periods in the week when the majority of the population would choose not to work; at the week-end, on public holidays, during the early morning, at nights or in the evenings.

There is as yet little or no evidence to show whether nurses generally wish to follow society's work and leisure pattern. It is possible that they are content to fit their working hours to meet the needs of the service or that they prefer to work during nights or week-ends when husbands are at home, thereby meeting the needs of their families.

What is certain is the need for 24-hour nursing coverage for seven days a week

---

[1] Bond, J., (1972) The Role of the Married Nurse: One aspect of the staffing of the health services at socially unacceptable working hours, *Working Paper 2*, Nursing Research Unit, Edinburgh University.

at least in the hospital service. Discussions suggested that many chief nursing officers have difficulties in staffing services at socially unacceptable hours. Some hospitals have adopted, or experimented with, new work patterns to reduce work loads during these hours.

Week-end discharge was tried in one such hospital where it was decided to experiment on the basis that laboratory and investigative services only operated a five-day week.[2] Other hospitals have opened five-day wards[3] for surgical patients on the basis that care at the week-end following discharge is given by the district nursing service. However, as one recent survey has shown that district nurses tend to reduce the amount of nursing care over the week-end,[4] continuity of patient care may be interrupted. It has been indicated that many married nurses prefer to work in the community nursing services because the work patterns tend to be less rigid and can be more easily combined with family commitments. It is common practice for district nursing staff to have every other, or every third, week-end off duty and in the health visiting service it seems comparatively rare to provide even an emergency service at the week-end.

During the exploratory work it became increasingly obvious that many of the staffing problems were in some way related to female nursing staff, many of whom work part-time because of domestic commitments.

Thus, it was finally decided to undertake a study of the staffing of nursing services, both in hospital and in the community, and to focus attention on the problems experienced and created by female nurses. The decision to omit male nurses from the study was, moreover, re-enforced by the knowledge of the on-going valuable work on male nurses at the University of Hull.[5]

CENSUS CONDUCTED BY THE SCOTTISH HOME AND HEALTH DEPARTMENT (SHHD)

Soon after the initial plans for pre-pilot and pilot work were made the Nursing Division of SHHD commissioned a staffing census to obtain information on qualified nursing manpower in Scotland.

It seemed opportune to collaborate with the team conducting the census in order to complement rather than duplicate the information to be obtained. It was, moreover, deemed essential to assure the nursing profession that the objectives of both studies differed and that the findings of both were expected to be helpful in creating a detailed picture of the current staffing situation as well as providing information about specific problems, possible suggestions as to their solution and pointers to further research. The SHHD Census differed from the Research Unit Study in four main ways:

---

[2] Ross, S. K., Munsin, B. J., Ireland, J. T. and Adams, J. F., (1969) Home for the Weekend, *Health Bulletin*, Vol. XXVII, No. 4, pp. 38–39.

[3] Hutchinson, A. S. and Kane, J., (1967) Short stay on 5 day ward, *District Nursing*, 10, p. 145.

[4] Hockey, L., (1972) *Use or abuse? A study of the state enrolled nurse in the local authority nursing services*, Queen's Institute of District Nursing, London.

[5] Brown, R. G. S. and Stones, R. W. H., (1973) *The Male Nurse*, Occasional Papers on Social Administration No. 52, G. Bell & Sons, London.

First, it was a national census whereas the Unit Study was undertaken in selected areas.

Secondly, it included all qualified nursing staff, whereas the Unit Study included female nursing staff and female learners, that is, student and pupil nurses, and excluded male nurses.

Thirdly, the SHHD Census was a postal survey whereas the Unit Study used personal interviews as the method for data collection.

Fourthly, the SHHD Census covered a broad area of enquiry whereas the Unit Study attempted to get more detailed information in a narrower field.

However, some questions were deliberately intended to elicit similar information. These were mainly factual questions on respondents' present age, school leaving age, marital status, etc., and helped to assess the representativeness of the sample.

OBJECTIVES OF STUDY

As stated earlier, it was hoped that the Unit's Study would help to throw some light on problems expressed by the profession. Sections on the employment of part-time nursing staff, on auxiliary personnel and on job satisfaction were included as these featured in the preliminary discussion.

It was also hoped that the first Unit Study would not only provide data on which further studies could be built but that it would also point the way to such studies. The final chapter discusses topics for further study which appeared to emerge.

STAFF

For a variety of reasons the Unit staff team had to be built up over a prolonged period of time, the last member not being appointed until the field work was well under way.*

The first complete team consisted of two nurse graduates, one non-graduate nurse with a change of person after the completion of the field work and two non-nurse graduates—a sociologist with experience in health service statistics and, for eight months only, a social psychologist. There was, therefore, an inevitable break in continuity between the data collection and analysis stages. Although further staff changes occurred since, members of staff were fully involved throughout all stages of the study and this Report is the result of collaborative effort.

SYNOPSIS OF CONTENT

The following chapter describes the design and method of the study. The pilot study is presented and the reasons for the second pilot study are explained. The remainder of the chapter deals with the main study and includes the choice of areas, organisational aspects, sampling of respondents, tools for data collection, method of data analysis and response rates.

Chapter 3 presents a brief geographical sketch of the study areas, providing some demographic details and poses the problems of anonymity in research.

---

* The Unit constitution makes provision for a team consisting of a Director, two Research Associates and two Research Assistants, supported by a secretariat.

Owing to the small number of top managers in the study they were treated as a completely separate group of respondents. An 'open interview' method covering predetermined topics was used for the collection of information from this group and all interviews were conducted by the same person. Chapter 4 deals with this part of the study.

The main part of the Report presents the analyses of the data obtained from the personal structured interviews with nursing staff. Whilst Chapter 5 views the respondents as a work force discussing the implications of their personal attributes such as age and marital status for staffing of nursing services, the focus in Chapter 6 is on nurses as women in society, who, however, hold various posts in the nursing service.

Occupational choices and career patterns are discussed in Chapter 7 which is followed in Chapter 8 by a brief discourse on job satisfaction including the respondents' views on the utilisation of their skills.

Part-time employment and its implications for nursing form the topic of Chapter 9, preparing the way for a detailed analysis of the hours worked by different types and grades of staff presented in Chapter 10.

As indicated earlier, one of the main reasons for the broad framework of the survey and the lack of clearly defined topics for investigation was the attempt to identify problem areas for further study. The last two chapters show the results of questions relating, first, to the employment of auxiliaries and, secondly, to aspects of patient care. The considerable number of auxiliaries in the nursing services suggests that any study of the staffing structure of nursing cannot ignore this grade of personnel and some of the more specific problems related to their employment are discussed in Chapter 11.

To date, nursing research into direct patient care in the clinical area is sparse. It is felt that a Unit specifically established to conduct nursing research should attempt to make a contribution in this field, but it was hoped that the focus of patient centred research might be suggested by the nursing staff. Respondents were, therefore, asked to identify types of patients whose care should be improved and their answers are shown in Chapter 12.

Appendices 1–4 are intended to give more detailed information on specific points than would be appropriate in the body of the text.

Appendix 5 is included to show the development of one of the data collecting tools used in the study, namely, the attitude scale.

Appendix 6 explains the series of steps leading from raw data on nursing qualifications to their presentation in manageable categories.

The purpose of Appendix 7 is to help readers who are not acquainted with British nursing to understand its structure and its related terminology, as far as these are relevant to the study. It also includes a glossary of other specific terms and a list of abbreviations.

PRESENTATION

This study was the first project undertaken by the Unit's core staff team; as explained earlier some members were appointed after the study had been designed and, inevitably, there were several staff changes over the period of the study between design and preparation of the final manuscript. Moreover, the period of the study coincided with the Unit's initial growth period and a proliferation of demands on its resources. The study was also intended as a learning situation for the research assistants; in fact it proved to be a learning situation for the whole team in evolving a satisfactory method of conducting a multidisciplinary study and in discovering the resources as well as constraints of the unique setting of the Research Unit within a large University. All these factors tended to retard the research process a little and also to cause some fragmentation of thought in presentation.

This report is intended to give the main information about the study design, method and findings, but it should not be regarded as the definitive account of this investigation. A base-line study of this nature, designed not only to obtain fundamental knowledge but also to lay the foundations for further research, accumulates and generates a vast amount of data. The choice is between presenting an exhaustive account which, because of the length of time taken, would be more of historical than contemporary interest, or, alternatively, presenting the main facts of the study and then following up with a series of papers on further aspects, going into greater detail, and in some cases expanding and refining the previously published results. The latter course has been chosen. Two papers on particular aspects of the book have already been published,[6, 7] another accepted for publication[8] and others are being planned.

As one of the Research Unit's ascribed functions is to teach research methods the report was written, at least in part, with this objective. It, therefore, contains some detail on certain aspects of the research process which may be helpful to a novice researcher; some of the appendices have also been included for this reason. Weaknesses, mistakes and problems are presented as honestly as possible in order to warn others. The experienced researcher is at liberty to ignore those sections which are considered too elementary.

    [6] Bond, J., (1974) Knowledge and opinions of nurses—Reorganisation, *Nursing Times*, Vol. 70, No. 13, pp. 460–462.
    [7] Bond, J., (1974) The construction of a scale to measure nurses' attitudes, *International Journal of Nursing Studies*, Vol. 11, pp. 75–84.
    [8] Woelfel, M., (1975) Geriatric Care: opinions of a sample of nurses, *Nursing Times*, Occasional Papers, Vol. 71, No. 26.

CHAPTER TWO
Study Design and Method

EXPLORATORY WORK

Members of the nursing profession actively engaged in the clinical or administrative provision of nursing care are best able to identify problem areas which merit attention. In order to gain information on current problems preliminary discussions were held with both hospital and local authority nursing staff, some involving only senior members of staff with administrative responsibility, others providing the opportunity for gathering opinions from a wider cross-section of nurses of varying grades. In spite of deliberate effort to create a relaxed informal atmosphere at the discussion meetings, many students and pupil nurses appeared inhibited by the presence of senior staff and it might have been more helpful to have organised small group discussions involving only nursing staff of similar status. However, twelve areas of concern were identified as outlined in Chapter 1.

THE PILOT STUDY

Any research project within a hospital group or local authority nursing service obviously increases the administrative workload and may temporarily affect staffing levels. The testing of tools for the collection of information is ultimately less satisfying to the participants in a pilot study than are the results of a main study to those involved. The vital contribution of pilot areas was stressed and where ready access and support were afforded, this was much appreciated.

Pilot work was conducted in order to test the interview schedule which was to be the principal tool for the collection of data. Initially, attitude scales for inclusion in the schedule were developed and tested, and pilot work used for validation. This process is described in Appendix 5.

The first stage of the pilot work commenced in May 1972 and involved personal interviews with members of the nursing staff in one large city hospital and the adjacent local authority. To ensure that all grades of hospital staff were represented 71 nurses were selected by means of a sample stratified by grade, drawn from a staff list of female nurses. A simple random sample of 42 local authority nurses was selected and contact made by letter. A 100 per cent response rate was achieved from the community nursing service but the 43 per cent response rate from hospital nurses was disappointing. There were many people from whom no reply was received and considerable difficulty was encountered in arranging interviews; this gave valuable warning of the problems which might be experienced in the main study arising from inadequacy of internal post systems in hospitals and absence due to sickness or holidays. A further complication in the pilot study arose from confusion with the postal survey conducted shortly before by the Scottish Home and Health Department referred to in Chapter 1. In all, 76 interviews were conducted at that stage, 34 with hospital nurses and 42 with community nurses.

The pilot study then entered the next stage as it was obvious that a greater number of interviews was required for further refinement and restructuring of the interview schedule. It also became apparent that some further topics were central to the study and these were included.

For the extension of the pilot study a hospital group was used in which the Salmon[1] structure had been implemented. It comprised a psychiatric hospital, a large general hospital and four smaller hospitals scattered over a fairly wide rural area. On this occasion 101 nurses were selected by means of a simple random sample and the response rate was 78 per cent. A quota sample of 21 staff of different designations was drawn from the surrounding local authority nursing service and the response rate was again 100 per cent. In total 100 nurses were interviewed. Final revision of the interview schedule was then undertaken.

CHOICE OF AREAS

It was decided to undertake the study in four hospital groups and their adjacent local health authority areas. In order to ensure at least one common denominator among the very different hospital groups the four groups were selected from those where the Salmon structure had been fully implemented. Geographical location was an important factor in selection and a crude north, south, east, west spread was achieved, with two areas of a rural nature and two urban areas. The total number of nurses in these four groups was approximately 3000.

In order to achieve a similar setting for both the local authority and the hospital nurses, local authority nursing services surrounding those hospital groups were then selected. However, the city authority around one hospital group was large and had been extensively used in a recent study.[2] Therefore, an adjacent area with similar characteristics was substituted. For three areas there was only one local authority community nursing service associated with the hospital group, but the area covered by the fourth hospital group was served by four separate community nursing services. Three were county authorities and one a small burgh authority. The total number of nurses in the seven local authorities was approximately two hundred and sixty.

The person in charge of each nursing service selected was approached by letter and the study described in outline. Participation was invited and members of the Unit staff made visits, where requested, to explain the study and details of organisation further.

---

[1] Ministry of Health and Scottish Home and Health Department, (1966) *Report of the Committee on Senior Nursing Staff Structure* (Chairman: B. L. Salmon, Esq.), HMSO, London.

[2] Hockey, L., (1972) *Use or Abuse? A study of the state enrolled nurse in the local authority nursing services*, Queen's Institute of District Nursing, London.

SAMPLING

As explained in Chapter 1, the study was restricted to female nursing staff and three samples were drawn. Staff lists arranged in alphabetical order served as sampling frames. Each hospital and community nursing service was sampled separately with the exception of the four local health authority areas, whose community services between them, served one hospital group; these were combined into one for this purpose.

Because numbers of administrators were comparatively small, the total population of staff employed in an administrative capacity was invited to participate. A simple one-in-five random sample of nurses from ward sister to pupil nurse was drawn from the hospital staff lists.

The method of sampling was adopted after carefully examining the possibility of stratification by grade of staff which would have ensured adequate representation of all grades of staff but would have been based on the untested assumption that staff grade was the most important factor. Also, such a stratification would have ignored other variables like hospital size or area of work. After the random sample was drawn, calculations were made as to its reliability by comparing the number of staff of each grade in the sample with the number in the total hospital population (Appendix 1). As the number of community staff was so much smaller a three-in-five sample was drawn from the local health authority staff lists in order to achieve an adequate size for useful analysis.

The method of sampling makes it possible to generalise from the sample to the nursing population from which the sample was drawn. Wider applicability of the findings cannot be taken for granted and the occasional use of the present tense is not intended to imply it.

TOOLS FOR DATA COLLECTION

It was decided that the Unit's director should interview all top managers, that is chief nursing officers and principal nursing officers in hospitals and their equivalents in the community nursing service. Interviews were almost completely unstructured but covered some predetermined topics which related mainly to matters of policy. Basic statistical information on staff numbers and composition was gained by use of a standardised form.

The pilot work revealed a difference between the orientation of nurses in administrative posts and that of nurses directly involved with patient care. For this reason staff from ward sister to pupil nurse and health visitors, district nurses, midwives and combined duty nurses were grouped under the title 'fieldworkers'. Personal interviews were conducted with fieldworkers using a structured interview schedule with some open-ended questions and opportunity for additional comments. An interview schedule similar in most respects was used for administrative staff other than top managers, a few questions being omitted and replaced by others which demanded some knowledge of organisational details. The same interview schedule was used for hospital and community nurses, with one section on area of employment adapted accordingly. Where ranking or selection of answers was required, the respondents were handed cards showing the alternatives, thereby ensuring that all possible answers had an opportunity of being considered.

ORGANISATION OF INTERVIEWS

Four members of staff were available for the structured interviews and two pairs were formed each of which was responsible, with secretarial help, for the organisation and interviewing within one rural and one urban area. Each pair consisted of a nurse who had gained interviewing skills during the pilot work and a research associate who had had previous experience of survey interviewing. It was thought that the presence of someone with insight into both the constraints and the terminology of nursing might be helpful.

Initial contact was made with the nurses in the sample by a personal letter outlining the proposed study and the function of the Nursing Research Unit, and inviting participation. A form for completion was attached and there was space for respondents to state their reasons for refusal. Letters to community nurses were sent to their home addresses. Every effort was made to avoid giving an impression of compulsion by stressing the voluntary nature of the enquiry. Confidentiality and ultimate anonymity were assured. To facilitate organisation a liaison officer was appointed in each hospital group, and letters were distributed in the manner most appropriate locally. The efficiency of the system and the subsequent arrangement of interviews was almost entirely dependent on the energy and goodwill of the liaison officer together with other administrative staff who facilitated communication.

Emphasis was laid on the availability of interviewers at all times and the very real desire to avoid the creation of any staffing difficulties. Interviews lasted from 30 minutes to 2 hours and, with hospital nurses, were conducted during duty hours. Nurses on night duty were interviewed at some convenient time during the night. Community nurses were given the opportunity to be interviewed either at home or at their place of work.

The fieldwork for the main study took place between mid-January and mid-April 1973.

NON-RESPONSE

Once the initial communication had been sent out, the unreliability of the original hospital staffing lists became apparent. The swift turnover of staff in hospitals inevitably meant that there were many changes between the time the list was received and the arrival of the first letters. A number of letters was returned marked 'left'. The reasons for the return of others 'not known' was harder to understand. It was, therefore, decided to replace nurses, whose first letter was returned unopened to the Unit within two weeks, by the next name on the sampling frame. This did not destroy the random nature of the sample and ensured that sample numbers were maintained. Replacement was not continued beyond this stage, despite the return of further letters.

As in the pilot study, there was some doubt as to whether communications were reaching the selected sample and it was also recognised that letters are often put aside with the intention of reply but are then forgotten. For these reasons it was decided that two follow-up letters should be sent with an appropriate interval between each. A reply was made to anyone expressing some reservation after the first or second letter with further explanation and, where appropriate, reassurance of the interviewer's availability at any time. An invitation to reconsider the original decision was given. Many nurses initially refused to take part in the study because they were on night duty or away from work; for them a standard letter was used, partly in order to maintain standard procedure, but occasionally a more personal letter was required. No further action was taken if three letters elicited either no reply at all or a refusal to participate.

The overall response rate was 84 per cent. This can be separated into the response rates from each of the three samples.

TABLE 2/1
Response rates

	Hospital administrators		Hospital fieldworkers		Community nurses	
	No.	%	No.	%	No.	%
Nurses interviewed	125	91.9	448	79.0	146	91.8
Non-response:	11	8.1	119	21.0	13	8.2
Refused*	3	2.2	58	10.2	8	5.1
Other non-response**	8	5.9	61	10.8	5	3.1
No. of nurses in sample	136		567		159	

* Includes nurses who gave no reason for refusal. Reasons for refusal are presented in detail in Appendix 1.
** Includes nurses who had left or retired before the first letter was received and those from whom there was no reply to any communication.

ANALYSIS OF INFORMATION

It is appreciated that social survey research cannot lay claim to the same degree of precision and reliability which can be expected of research in the physical sciences. The sources of raw data—people—are not amenable to the kind of manipulation central to the laboratory tradition; the data themselves include not only matters of fact, but also opinions; moreover the methods of data collection and interpretation cannot preclude human error.

These weaknesses, however, are relative to the scientific paradigm, and they are neither absolute nor incapacitating. The social survey is a well-understood and established method of collecting realistic social data, and one which embodies strengths of subtlety and suppleness which many other research methods lack.

For the reasons stated, it was considered inappropriate in this study to exhibit complex statistical operations and their results in the report as this would imply high claims to precision which might not be justified. Statistical tests were, however, used to determine priorities in the discussion of results and to establish a justifiable terminology. For instance, the term 'significant' is used when a finding has reached a level of at least 95 per cent confidence and a finding which does not reach that level is deemed 'not significant'. The statistical tests used in the analysis are described in Appendix 1.

Numerical values are deliberately expressed to one decimal point only, again as a safeguard against conveying an impression of unwarranted mathematical precision.

Data from the interview schedules were coded with the assistance of temporary part-time staff trained and supervised by the interviewers. Each schedule was independently coded by two people and a comparison was then made. Discrepancies or uncertainties were deferred for careful discussion before a final decision was made by those who had been involved in the interviewing. The information was transferred to 80 column punch cards and then to magnetic tape. Most of the analysis was carried out using SPSS (Statistical Package for the Social Sciences)[3] programs on an IBM 370/158 computer. Some data were analysed with the aid of the Unit's electronic calculators.

Data obtained from the open interviews with top managers were examined and analysed by the interviewer.

[3] Nie, N., Bent, D. H. and Hull, C. H., (1970) *Statistical Package for the Social Sciences*, McGraw-Hill, New York.

CHAPTER THREE
Study Areas

The purpose of this chapter is to sketch, albeit crudely, the background against which the study was undertaken, thereby setting the findings into the context of the physical, demographic and occupational factors which characterise the four research areas in Scotland.

Anonymity and confidentiality are problems which confront many research workers. They are important issues with ethical implications and, therefore, should be given serious consideration. A promise of anonymity such as that 'no individuals' names will be mentioned in any report' and that 'no person will be identifiable' must be honoured. A breach of confidence by one researcher may easily spoil potential research for another. Sometimes, a promise, such as 'no names will be mentioned' is honoured literally but, because an area is small, the person mentioned as Miss X can be recognised. In such a case anonymity is little more than a pretence and it might be better not to publish any points which might make identification possible without obtaining explicit consent from the person in question.

In this study the problem of anonymity lay in the possibility of identifying the research areas. It would have been possible to describe them as A, B, C, etc., without mentioning their names. However, reference to certain characteristics of an area such as jute industry in a Scottish town awaiting the opening of a new District General Hospital would identify Dundee without difficulty. Both facts, namely, jute industry and the new hospital were considered relevant as background material for the study. The options were, therefore, either to omit such relevant facts altogether or to obtain consent to mention the areas by name thereby making no false pretence at anonymity. The latter course was adopted and the relevant top managers were sent a draft of the proposed area description with a request to make comments if they wished to do so.

However, in the body of the report which gives research findings, the areas are concealed. Hospital groups are referred to as A, B, C, D, and AA, BB, CC, DD are applied to their adjacent local authority areas, the alphabetical order being un-related to the order in which the areas are described and direct area comparisons are rarely made.

The area descriptions are intended rather to highlight the background differences between the four areas in which the hospital groups and the adjacent local author-ities were located.

The only two phenomena common to all four areas were that they had implemented a management structure for hospital nursing staff recommended by the Salmon Committee, and, like every other health authority in the United Kingdom, they were attempting to provide a health service for their population, both in hospital and in the community.

As explained in Chapter 2, the areas were deliberately selected to represent a geographical scatter; this in itself has social and economic implications, as industries tend to be related to geographical location, often tied to natural resources or transport facilities. Demographic characteristics, vital statistical data and administrative size are other interrelated factors which accentuated the differences between the four study areas. The findings of the accumulated data can, therefore, be taken as being roughly representative of a country of known contrasts. At the same time it must be emphasised that the areas were not randomly selected with statistical rigour and no claim for generalisation to the whole of Scotland can be made.

Some caution is recommended in the interpretation of all staff/bed and staff/population ratios. The figures are based on whole time equivalents of nursing staff, not total number of personnel, but such calculations may easily be imprecise especially when many part-time staff work short shifts.

AREA I
The hospital group comprises 16 hospitals serving the scattered population of the south west of Scotland. The area lies along the north coast of the Solway Firth and includes the counties of Dumfries, Kirkcudbright and Wigtown. A general hospital, a maternity hospital and a large psychiatric hospital are situated in the county town of Dumfries. The remaining hospitals in the group are for the most part comparatively small, five of them have under 20 beds, and many function as general practitioner units. The total number of beds in the group was 1858 in March 1973 and the ratio of all nursing staff to beds was 27:100, or one nurse to approximately 3.7 beds. A district general hospital is under construction and, when opened, will centralise many of the dispersed services. Four local health authorities cover the area, the population of which is approximately 143 000. The ratio of qualified community nursing staff to head of population was 1:1781, or 56 nurses per 100 000 people.

The area is a rural one with agriculture being the main industry. A small part of the lowlands is used for arable farming, but milk is the principal product. The coastal plain rapidly gives way to moorland used for the rough grazing of sheep.

The south west tends to be self-contained with a strong regional consciousness. The small towns act as service centres for the surrounding agricultural areas but do not provide many opportunities for employment. The area has consequently suffered from migration and only in the Dumfries–Annan region has there been a moderate population growth. Many people are forced to seek further education and training away from the south west and are often lost to the area at this stage.

Given the rural nature of the area—relieved only by some coal mining in the Sanqhuar–Kirkconnel area—it is not surprising that with the exception of tourism there are few opportunities for female employment outside the main towns.

The number of employed women is low compared to the rest of Scotland,* and it seems that the south west has an untapped reserve of female labour. However, travel is difficult as distances are considerable and public transport infrequent. The factories in the small burghs, engaged in tweed, hosiery and leather industries, appear to employ many women and have achieved this in part by supplying transport to collect workers from outlying areas. The recruitment of women for community work, such as the home help service, is difficult and may become more so, if tourism is expanded and there is more seasonal employment available for local women in hotels and restaurants.

The main focus for female employment in the area is Dumfries (population 29 380), and it is here that the three largest hospitals—general, maternity and psychiatric—are situated. Dumfries is also the local centre for light industry. Knitwear, plastics, clothing, chemical and milk processing industries have been developed and offer, together with the hospitals and the normal urban service industries, the greatest scope for female employment in the entire area.

AREA II

The hospital group serves the county of Moray and the west part of Banffshire, whereas the local health authority in the area covers Moray and Nairn. A joint county council administers major local government services. The hospital group comprises six hospitals, five of which are units with less than 100 beds and one a larger psychiatric hospital. The total number of beds in the group was reported as 428 in March 1973 and the ratio of nursing staff to beds was 31:100, or one nurse for approximately 3.2 beds. The local health authority serves a population of approximately 61 000 and the number of qualified community nursing staff per head of population was 1:1891, or the equivalent of 53 nurses per 100 000 people.

Moray and Nairn are north eastern counties of Scotland which border the southern shore of the Moray Firth. Although administered as one unit at the time of the study, the two counties are to separate with the re-organisation of the Health Service and of local government, Nairn joining the Highland region, while Moray goes in with Grampian. The County of Nairn has maintained a separate identity with its orientation towards Inverness for specialist medical services and cultural and business interests. The administrative and commercial centre of the area is the town of Elgin with a population of around 16 400, and Nairn Burgh with a population of roughly 8000 acts as a subsidiary centre for the County of Nairn. The area is predominantly rural with a scattered population and so faces the same sort of problems with transport which were mentioned in the discussion of south west Scotland. The southern moorland is mainly used for sheep, but to the north the coastal plain has rich soil suitable for intensive farming and is devoted mainly to wheat, barley, oats, beef and dairy farming. However, market gardening has developed over recent years and this does offer opportunities of employment to local women. Market gardening is complemented in this respect by Baxter's canning and preserves factory.

Most of the other local industries—distilling, trawling, salmon fishing, forestry

* But similar to the other rural area in the study.

and the saw mills—employ mainly men. However, the woollen mills and tourism are the other two sources of income locally and they offer competition for female labour to the hospital and community nursing services.

AREA III

Area III comprises four hospitals, three of which are situated in the Govan district of Glasgow and one at Cowglen. One large general hospital covers all clinical specialties, two small hospitals are devoted to gynaecology and general surgical convalescence and one hospital is for geriatric and young chronic sick patients. The total number of beds in the group was reported as 1592 in March 1973 and the ratio of all nursing staff to beds was 27:100, or one nurse to approximately 3.7 beds.

Glasgow, extending for six miles on either side of the Clyde, is the largest city in Scotland and the industrial and commercial capital. The city had pre-industrial importance as a market and international port, but its real expansion came with the industrial revolution. This brought the rapid development of heavy industry—iron, steel, cotton, heavy engineering and, predominantly, ship-building.

As a result of the Irish famine and troubles, together with the Highland clearances, the industrial expansion of the city attracted large numbers of migrants. Approximately one-third of the Glasgow population is of Irish descent, and the cultural links with the Highlands are also extremely strong.

This century has seen the gradual decline of the heavy industries and diversification into light engineering, paper and printing, foodstuffs, textiles, vehicle and component manufacture. There are also many opportunities for employment in the service industries as well as in the two universities and various colleges of further education.

The Govan area is in many ways a microcosm of the problems affecting the centre of Glasgow. Its shipyards are declining rapidly under the onslaught of foreign competition, there is high unemployment, and the slum clearance and road building programmes have meant a dramatic decline in population. In 1961 the population was around 26 000 whereas in 1971 it had gone down to just over 17 500. The poor quality of this disrupted environment is a matter for grave concern, and, in association with the migration from the area, exerts an important influence on hospital staff recruitment.

The adjacent local health authority serves the municipal burgh of Paisley, the county town of Renfrewshire. Paisley is seven miles from the centre of Glasgow and is integral to the industrial Greater Glasgow area in which one-third of Scotland's population resides. The urban environment is in many respects similar to that of Glasgow although dereliction is less marked.

The town was originally famous for linen and lawn manufacture, though these cloths were superseded by cotton. The thread mills, a major source of female employment, still command a world market. The other local industries that use female labour are the jam, marmalade and tobacco factories. The remaining commercial concerns in the town—engineering, timber yards and a small amount of ship-building—have labour forces that are almost entirely male.

The local health authority serves a population of approximately 95 000 and the ratio of qualified community nursing staff to head of population is 1:2375, or 42 nurses per 100 000 people.

AREA IV

The hospital group is situated in the city of Dundee and serves approximately the same area as the local health authority. It comprises nine hospitals, the majority of which are large units covering all fields of nursing except mental illness. The opening of a newly built district general hospital was awaited; the hospital became operational in early 1974. The total number of beds in the group was reported as 1592 in March 1973 and the ratio of all nursing staff to beds was 45:100 or one nurse to approximately 2.2 beds. The local health authority serves a population of approximately 182 200 and the ratio of qualified community nursing staff to head of population was 1:1516 or 66 nurses per 100 000 people at the same period.

Dundee, situated on the north shore of the Firth of Tay, is Scotland's fourth largest city and second most important commercial centre. Its prosperity was founded originally on its harbours and the processing of local products—jam-making, saw-milling and brewing but the staple industry of the city became the processing of imported jute. Indeed, the city is largely famous for 'Jam, Jute and Journalism'. But although these products have predominated, the city's industries have become more diversified. Jute processing, like local ship-building, is of less importance than formerly, but light industries, making electrical goods, watches, cash registers and so on, have opened up on the new industrial estates, and are offering greater opportunities to women.

The social environment in Dundee, measured in such things as quality of housing or the violent crime rate, has long been a cause for concern. The high density housing erected to meet the sudden population increase of the industrial revolution turned into the slums which the city has had to deal with in this century. Many areas of the city centre are being improved by extensive demolition and re-building programmes, but parts of the city retain both physical and social manifestations of the legacy of the industrial revolution.

Not surprisingly, part-time employment was significantly higher in the urban than in the rural areas and so was the proportion of married nurses. However, part-time nursing forms the whole concern of Chapter 9.

CHAPTER FOUR
Top Managers and Their Policies

It is reasonable to assume that staffing policies in any organisation are likely to influence not only the staffing structure in the composite sense but also the views and opinions of individual staff members; in the case of long-term employment in an organisation, even attitudes may be affected by managerial policies. It is also possible for staff to be attracted to an organisation whose policies are known to be acceptable. It was, therefore, considered essential to obtain some information from the top managers in the research areas. For the purpose of this study these included all nursing officers who had responsibility for policy formulation in their fields of activity, whether service or education.

As explained in Chapter 3 the study was undertaken in four areas in Scotland, each area including one hospital group and the 'adjacent' local authorities served mainly by these hospitals. In three of the four hospital groups the 'adjacent' area was represented by just one local authority; in the fourth, the area served by the hospital group was divided among four local authorities. The study included, therefore, four hospital groups and seven local health authorities.

As all hospital groups had implemented the senior nursing management structure recommended by the Salmon report, there was one chief administrative nursing officer post in each group; in three she ranked as Chief Nursing Officer, in the fourth as Principal Nursing Officer. The picture in the local authorities was slightly different in that four of the seven authorities had appointed Directors of Nursing Services who were responsible for the administration of the district nursing, midwifery and health visiting services; in one of the remaining authorities the three services were administered separately, each by its own Principal Nursing Officer; another had one Nursing Officer who took responsibility for the district nursing and health visiting services whilst a senior midwife undertook the day-to-day administration of the dwindling domiciliary midwifery service. The last local authority was too small to warrant the appointment of a Director of Nursing Services and, although one person was in charge of the three local authority nursing services, she also had a small case load and for the purposes of this study ranked as Nursing Officer below the level of a Principal.

In addition to the top administrators, two hospital groups had four Principal Nursing Officers each, one had three and the smallest group had only the top administrator who, as explained earlier, ranked as Principal Nursing Officer.

It is not easy to determine a suitable yardstick by which to compare the span of control between top managers in nursing. It is usual practice to express the size of a hospital in the number of beds and the size of a community area in the number of the population. Many other variables must, undoubtedly, be relevant in assessing managerial responsibility and the number of staff is of major importance. However, it is utlimately the patient or client for whom nursing services are provided and, therefore, factors with management meaning are the number of beds and the number of population for whom both preventive and therapeutic care should be available.

Table 4/1 shows the number of top managers (Chief and Principal Nursing Officers) in the four hospital groups in relation to the number of beds.

TABLE 4/1
Hospital top managers in research areas

Hospital groups	Number of top managers	Number of beds*	Number of beds per one top manager
A	5	1592**	318.4
B	5	1592**	318.4
C	1	428	428
D	4	1858	464.5

* Figures provided by top managers in 1973.
** The identical data are more likely to be due to coincidence than policy.

Table 4/2 presents comparable information for the community nursing services in the study, expressed in terms of numbers of top managers in relation to the number of population.

TABLE 4/2
Local authority top managers in research areas

Local health authority areas		Number of top managers	Number of population*	Number of population per one top manager
AA		1	95 000	95 000
BB		3	182 000	60 606
CC		1	60 633	60 633
	DD¹	1	58 714	58 714
	DD²	1	27 500	27 500
DD	DD³	1	27 251	27 251
	DD⁴**	0	29 041	—

* Figures provided by top managers in 1973.
** This health authority was administered jointly by a medical officer and a senior nurse who also carried a case load.

It can be seen from Tables 4/1 and 4/2 that there is more uniformity between the hospital groups than between the local authority areas in the ratios of managers in nursing to number of consumers of the service. This finding is not surprising as the community services are less clearly defined and less easily determined, in terms of consumer demand, than is the hospital service. The nursing needs of domiciliary patients are not always known to nursing management and the need for preventive care for the total population is varied, debatable and rarely translated into demand.

As shown in Tables 4/1 and 4/2 there were 23 Chief or Principal Nursing Officers in the study areas, 15 employed in the hospital service and 8 by local health authorities; because of this small number, it was decided to involve them all in the study by inviting them to be interviewed. It was further decided to arrange unstructured interviews with this group rather than administering the general structured schedule. This decision was made for two reasons:

(a) Only the senior nursing personnel were able to provide information about policy issues which was important as background material for the study whilst other topics covered by the structured schedule were irrelevant for them.

(b) This group of staff was too specific to be included with the general sample of respondents and too small for separate statistical analysis.

All nursing officers who met the study criteria of being responsible for policy formulation, accepted the invitation to participate. Two of the respondents in top management positions were men; one headed a relatively autonomous educational establishment; the other was in charge of a psychiatric hospital and agreed to be interviewed after some initial reluctance because none of the other male administrators in the hospital were included. Although both interviews were taken full cognisance of, the former was finally excluded from the detailed analysis as it was less concerned with the staffing of the nursing services which was the primary focus of the study; it raised other important and valuable issues in terms of educational policies. It is important to re-iterate that all these open-ended interviews were conducted by one person and that additional statistical details were recorded by the respondents on purpose-designed forms.

The interviews dealt with specific predetermined topics which were selected on the basis of the exploratory discussions. They included:

recruitment

establishment

facilities provided for staff

policies on the employment of auxiliaries and part-time workers

policies regarding the attachment of nursing staff to general medical practice
    (local authority administrators)

absenteeism, sickness and staff turn-over

In addition the respondents were asked for some personal data and for their views on certain matters.

RECRUITMENT

It became clear that recruitment methods differed between those used for trainees and qualified staff and also between those used for hospital and local authority staff; they are, therefore, described separately.

Recruitment of pupil and student nurses

Recruitment includes the whole process from publicising available training opportunities, to the appointment of selected candidates. In two of the four hospital groups the recruitment of trainees was left entirely to the Principal Nursing Officer responsible for the School of Nursing; in the other two it was shared between that officer and the Chief Nursing Officer or someone acting up for her.*

Even this comparatively small study showed that recruitment is a local rather than a national concern and the choice of recruitment methods was related to local circumstances. In fact, in one group it seemed that no active steps had to be taken to attract trainees as applications came in spontaneously; other areas, however, had to use a combination of methods.

The most frequent method of publicity was advertising, but whether the national or the local press was preferred seemed to depend on the type of area. Understandably, a small remote area would be mainly dependent on local school leavers and the local advertisement was more suitable. Large centres of industry, offering a wide range of amenities, could well expect entrants from afar off, especially if the hospital was one of national repute. Two of the groups in this study *appeared* to fall into this latter category but no systematic investigation of reasons for the choice of any particular School of Nursing was undertaken.

All Principal Nursing Officers (Education) mentioned the importance of career guidance for school leavers, and two respondents in this group had themselves secured regular access to at least one school's final classes for the purpose of conveying information about nursing. The 'Open Day', with special invitations to local schools, featuring the work of nurses and opportunities in the profession, was the other most frequently used publicity method. Regional Nursing Officers** were said to be contributing to recruitment efforts in a variety of ways including publicity on a regional basis, talks to career officers and re-direction of candidates and staff.

One Chief Nursing Officer thought that the most effective way of securing trainees for nursing was to project an acceptable image of the profession in the local community. To this end she was an active member of several groups encompassing a range of interests, such as golf clubs and women's institutes:

'It's no good being seen hob-nobbing with any one narrow group in a small community like ours.'

Several respondents mentioned that they readily accepted invitations of Church Groups and Clubs to speak about nursing as a career.

A pre-nursing course organised by a technical college in one area was said to have beneficial as well as adverse effects on local recruitment. On the one hand it attracted school leavers to nursing but on the other hand it gave local girls who completed the course an urge to apply for training away from their home area.

As far as selection was concerned it was practice in all four groups for the

---

* All Chief Nursing Officers in the study areas were women.

** As the data collection took place before the reorganisation of the health service, Regional Nursing Officers were still in post.

Principal of the School to interview candidates with the appropriate educational requirements, either in conjunction with another member of the teaching staff or with the CNO or a deputy appointed for the purpose.

Recruitment of trainees in the community services

Clearly, the recruitment problem in the community field is different from that in the hospital, in that it is directed to qualified nursing staff.

Advertisements in the nursing and local press were used as main recruitment methods, but almost all nursing officers expressed concern about the difficulty in recruiting health visitor students. They tended to be recruited before undertaking the statutory training and then seconded for the course. The offer of facilities for training appeared to be the most important aid to recruitment of health visitors. Only one of the local authorities in the study had a health visitors' course available within its own administrative area, which meant that staff in the other areas, once recruited, had to be sent away to a College which was not only acceptable to them but was also prepared to offer a vacancy.

As the district nursing qualification is not a requirement for licence to practise district nursing, the offer of training facilities was not used as an encouragement to recruitment. In two of the authorities unqualified district nursing staff were only accepted in exceptional circumstances. However, in the other areas where unqualified staff were acceptable, the district nursing qualification appeared to play no part whatever in recruitment, and no deliberate effort or offer was made to send unqualified applicants for training on secondment.

In all areas recruitment of trainees in the midwifery service was the responsibility of the midwifery training school.

Recruitment of qualified staff in hospital

Within this group of staff recruitment methods differed for the grades of staff nurse/ward sister and nursing officers, the method for the appointment of senior nursing staff being prescribed by the Scottish Nursing Staffs Committee.

It was usual for most staff nurses and ward sisters/charge nurses to be appointed by promotion from within the group. In none of the four groups were newly registered nurses requested to remain on the staff for a specified period as is the practice in some teaching hospitals. Two PNOs (Teaching) and several other PNOs stressed the need for all student nurses to be given some advice on their career towards the end of their training period and they had put routine interviews into practice. One said:

'I think it's worth seeing them all, although a lot of them have already made up their minds. I stress that "staffing" is important but I try not to push them too hard.'

and another:

'I try to see them all to find out what they want to do. I think it is important for both sides.'

Advertising in the professional and local press was the most frequent method of making vacancies known and it was common practice for advertisements to be formulated by the Regional Board and displayed alongside other vacancies in the Region. Not all respondents agreed wholeheartedly with this policy although they saw the reasons for it. One said:

'It makes sense to get some uniformity but I would like to use my own wording.'

and another:

'I think if we were to advertise in our own way stressing a specific point we might do better.'

Although all hospital groups had implemented the Salmon management structure not all Unit Nursing Officers seemed to carry major responsibility for recruitment of clinical staff. Several PNOs were involved in the appointment of these grades, sometimes because they felt the SNOs had not sufficient experience in selection or because they had been asked by the SNO to give help and advice. Some PNOs considered that they should always be consulted on the appointments of qualified staff. In one group SNOs and ward sisters dealt with staff nurse selection and the CNO shared the appointments of ward sisters with the PNO.

In all groups, the appointments of more senior grades of staff, i.e. Senior Nursing Officer and Principal Nursing Officer, were made in conjunction with the Chief Nursing Officer, sometimes assisted by the Regional Nursing Officer and/or a member of the Management Committee.

Probably because of the comparatively recent implementation of the Salmon structure most senior appointments other than the CNOs themselves had been made by assimilation from grades of existing staff. No problem in filling these posts had arisen, although there were some doubts voiced about the suitability of the appointments. There was some apprehension about the recruitment of senior staff in the future when vacancies due to retirement were bound to occur. Several respondents felt that a rapid staff turnover in the clinical grades was more beneficial than harmful as it ensured new and up-to-date methods in clinical care; in senior grades, however, where policy had to be implemented and staff attitudes had to be attuned to innovations in management, some continuity was considered to be essential and a rapid turnover in these grades was, therefore, to be avoided if possible.

Based on the General Nursing Council establishment all Schools of Nursing in the study seemed to have some unfilled tutor vacancies; some were filled temporarily by nursing officers with an interest in teaching as 'unqualified tutors'; others were open, pending the return of staff seconded to take the Tutor's Diploma.

In two areas, Technical Colleges providing courses allied to nursing were reported to contribute to the tutor shortage as they attracted qualified tutors by better conditions of service. The Chief Nursing Officer in one of these areas was optimistic about this competitive element being removed by the revised salary structure, which brought the tutor grade in the Health Service up to and above the Further Education salary levels.

Where an effort to fill vacancies with qualified tutors was considered necessary, the pattern followed that of other senior staff, in that the CNO and PNO (Teaching) shared the task of selection.

W.N.—3

Three of the four CNOs mentioned the appointment of auxiliary staff as a specific problem, and in this they were supported by several PNOs. As auxiliary staff were not usually recruited to any specific department of the hospital, the PNO herself, or one of the SNOs assisting with the central administration tended to deal with the auxiliary personnel. Although there appeared to be no shortage of female applicants their suitability was often questionable. Male auxiliary staff were said to be difficult to recruit, as other job opportunities for men offered greater attraction. The nursing auxiliary forms the topic discussed in Chapter 11.

One would normally expect to find that recruitment problems were linked with the availability of other career opportunities. However, this competitive element applied mainly to auxiliary rather than to nursing staff; where it was relevant to nursing staff at all, it was concerned with the initial recruitment of trainees rather than the recruitment of qualified nursing staff. Only two respondents mentioned that male nurses were sometimes attracted to more remunerative non-nursing work. For qualified female staff the competition between the hospital and local authority services appeared more pertinent than competition from occupations other than nursing.

Recruitment of community nursing staff

In none of the local authority areas did the recruitment of district nursing staff present a serious problem. The nursing officer of one of the industrialised areas seemed to express the general opinion when she said:

'We get many applications from district nurses;—most are married, most prefer the hours in the community and like working on their own.'

Another district nursing administrator, fully endorsing the sentiment of her colleague, added:

'Plenty of RGNs apply so there is no need to get enrolled nurses.'

Even for occasional night work registered nurses were available although they were not necessarily qualified district nurses.

In all areas, problems were voiced about the recruitment of health visitors and difficulties were experienced in sparing unqualified health visitors for health visitor training. Health visitors for whom secondment to a training school had been provided, were in most cases required to work for the sponsoring authority for an agreed period; it was hoped that they would remain on the staff for longer than the contract required. The system was described by one respondent to work well in theory but to have disadvantages in practice. In the first place it was necessary to plan a year ahead and there was no guarantee that the seconded trainee would be successful or, given that the contract period could not easily be enforced, that she would actually return to the area. Secondly, this respondent felt that it was psychologically undesirable for people to work in an area because they were compelled, or at least felt compelled, to do so. This was one of the reasons why many local authorities had, in fact, discontinued the contract as a routine practice.

There was only one administrator responsible exclusively for district midwifery. Her view, in line with that of other top managers with responsibility for the midwifery service, was that the only competition for domiciliary midwives came from the hospital service. However, they all felt that midwives fell into two categories; first, the career midwife anxious to practise who, owing to the rapid fall in domiciliary confinements, would be attracted to the hospital service; and secondly, the category consisting of married midwives with home commitments, who welcomed the diminished likelihood of night calls and, at the same time, felt that their qualifications were being utilised. There was a constant supply of the latter group and recruitment was easy.

In all areas, posts tended to be advertised in the local and professional press, although spontaneous enquiries from qualified nurses occasionally met needs in the district nursing service, thereby sometimes making advertisements unnecessary.

The management structure in the community nursing service[1] had not been generally introduced and there was a variety of patterns in use regarding selection processes. In three areas the Medical Officer of Health appeared totally responsible for this duty. The difficulties which were frequently expressed about the recruitment of health visitors have already been mentioned.

If there was one general, rather than local, recruitment difficulty in the hospital nursing service it was in highly specialised areas, particularly neurosurgery; intensive care and thoracic surgery were other specialised units which did not seem to attract nursing staff. Reasons for this were not systematically explored in this study, but some observations made by respondents may well merit further investigation. One CNO, talking about her worry of staffing a neurosurgery unit, said:

'The reason might be the intensity of medical care in that sort of area; patients tend to be of great interest to the doctors which limits nursing initiative.'

Similar views were expressed by other respondents.

Two PNOs, who were concerned about difficulty in recruiting qualified staff to intensive care and thoracic surgery respectively, implied that these were specialised areas where student and auxiliary labour could not be deployed to the usual high extent, thereby accentuating the overall dearth of well-qualified clinical nursing staff:

'It shows more there as we can't use students in the same way.'

'Intensive care units are hardly suitable for auxiliaries. We try to have all trained nurses apart from one or two third-year students. But staff nurses are generally thin on the ground.'

In one small hospital group the staff nurses were particularly 'thin on the ground'. This was thought to be due to the long-term tenure of senior staff who, once safely settled, did not seem anxious to move. Newly qualified staff recognising their limited career prospects either left the area or the profession.

---

[1] Department of Health and Social Security, Scottish Home and Health Department and Welsh Office, (1969) *Report of the working party on management structure in the local authority nursing services* (Chairman: E. L. Mayston, Esq.), HMSO, London.

ESTABLISHMENT

Recruitment and establishment are interrelated, one being dependent on the other. Thus there is little point in setting an establishment far beyond feasible recruitment possibilities and it is clearly irrelevant to worry about recruitment problems where the establishment has been reached. In relation to this topic an attempt was made in the interview to elicit answers to the following questions:

1 Who determines the establishment and by what criteria?
2 How often is the establishment re-assessed, and how easy or difficult is it to make a change?
3 What is the present general staffing position in relation to the present establishment and is any particular part of the service more difficult to staff than another?

'Establishments' seemed to have different meanings for different respondents. For some it meant the minimum and for others the optimum number of staff, although actual figures were rarely mentioned and statements like 'below' and 'above' establishment were not related to given numbers. The nursing officers were, of course, aware of this; some considered it best to keep the staffing situation under constant review and adjust as necessary:

'I think it is best not to be tied, the situation changes all the time.'

Others expressed a desire for an objective yardstick on which their employment policies could be based:

'If we had a minimum figure laid down we could have a better lever to get what we need.'

One respondent, however, felt that a minimum prescribed establishment would be dangerous as it would be difficult to get permission to exceed it. She did not seem to think that a maximum figure would help as it would soon become the minimum:

'If we were told we could have, say, twenty extra staff, we would either get them, in which case we would rearrange care to use them fully and we could then not do without them anymore; or, more probably, we couldn't get them anyway. It is bad for an organisation to be always "below establishment". It means understaffed and projects a bad image.'

The Chief Nursing Officers of the three major hospital groups seemed to share the general opinion that it was more advantageous to have a budget for staff than a specified number. This was thought to allow more flexibility and adjustment of ratios in different grades of both qualified and unqualified nursing manpower. One respondent mentioned that she could also adjust the domestic/nursing staff ratios which was helpful. Two CNOs calculated their own establishment for submission to the Management Committee, one indicated that the permitted staff quota was given by the Regional Board and the fourth CNO implied that this was the concern of the Management Committee.

Although only four Chief Nursing Officers were involved every possible alternative for the calculation of establishments was mentioned, none proving completely satisfactory.

The Urwick–Orr formula, the Aberdeen formula and various systems based on patient dependency were quoted:

'I use the Aberdeen guide line but it doesn't work altogether.'

'The Oxford formula used to be all right but it takes a lot of adjusting.'

'We just go by the work load and the senior nursing officers watch it.'

Although budgets were redrafted annually in all areas, only one respondent appeared to calculate her budget systematically on the basis of an annual adjustment of her establishment. In the other cases the budget tended to be related to staff in post. In areas considered to be understaffed, the problem was one of recruitment and an increase of the budget would have been of little use. In the better staffed areas the establishment and staff in post were, in any case, similar.

In all four research areas, the community nursing officers seemed to have had to defend their case for even one additional staff member more often than their hospital colleagues; this may be related to the smaller total number of staff in community nursing where each individual member represents a larger proportion of the total.

Most respondents identified staffing problems in particular parts of their service; these are, of course, inextricably linked with recruitment. Specialised units were consistently mentioned as being particularly difficult to staff, even on a temporary basis.

Two Chief Nursing Officers mentioned psychiatric units as their main problem areas which seemed related to the known general decrease in numbers of male nurses. Community nursing officers were consistent in their experience that the health visiting service posed most staffing problems, which may well be related to the pattern of health visiting; as a preventive service it is geared less to expressed demand than to perceived need which is, by definition, subjective and closely linked with the interests and ambitions of staff.

FACILITIES FOR STAFF

The Chief and Principal Nursing Officers were asked specifically about a range of facilities provided and for their comments on the need for these. It was hoped to relate this information to comparable data received from the nursing staff. The exploratory and pilot work had suggested that there might be discrepancies between the views of management and staff concerning the desirability of facilities provided for the staff. This study did not, on the whole, find this to be the case, except in isolated instances. It is, nevertheless, considered appropriate to present at least some of the results of this part of the enquiry, as an illustration of the thought, reasoning and problems surrounding the provision of special facilities for nursing staff.

Details on many provisions were obtained but, for simplicity, they have been condensed into two main groups—Educational and Practical facilities.

Respondents were asked to make their comments on specific facilities, but the open ended nature of the interview gave them the opportunity to raise others. Educational facilities included the provision of in-service training, 'back-to-nursing' courses, opportunities to acquire further qualifications and to attend refresher courses. Practical facilities include help with transport, housing, telephone, the provision of changing and rest rooms, and also of creches or nurseries. In view of the organisational differences between hospital and community nursing services it is necessary to discuss them separately.

EDUCATIONAL FACILITIES

Hospital Nursing Services
All four Chief Nursing Officers appreciated the need for some form of on-going professional development, although they did not totally agree on how this could best be provided and the Principal Nursing Officers' views were similarly divided.

The main trend of opinion seemed to be that more senior members of staff should attend courses outside their own group and that the hospital group itself should provide some in-service training for junior members of staff. However, precisely the opposite view was also voiced, suggesting that senior personnel should have regular multidisciplinary educational activities within the group, and junior members of staff should be 'sent away' to courses.

There was agreement on the need to keep clinical specialists up to date by encouraging attendance at specialised national events, such as conferences for theatre sisters or courses on 'progress in renal dialysis'. Five respondents mentioned the need to send senior paediatric nursing staff to London as courses at the Hospital for Sick Children were both helpful and popular. All stated, or implied, that methods of nursing sick children tended to change more rapidly than in other nursing areas and two linked this comment with a reference to the trend to keep sick children in their own homes, thereby reducing opportunities for hospital nursing experience. Paediatric nursing would, therefore, seem to be one specific area of care which can be expected to benefit enormously from the integrated health service, by giving child patients and their parents continuity of care, and by widening the experience of paediatric nurses. These are the objectives of the Child Health Service described in 'Nurses in an Integrated Health Service'.[2]

Other specialised areas of experience for which staff were often sent to courses in London and other parts of England were ophthalmic and orthopaedic nursing. The Moorfields Eye Hospital in London and Stoke Mandeville Hospital were mentioned in this connection. Secondment for such special courses usually preceded the offer of a post in the specialty and thereafter promotion or its prospect.

'Back-to-nursing' courses, though strongly agreed with in principle, were, on the whole, not considered practicable. One large hospital group organised a course centrally at least twice a year, drawing participants through advertisements in the local press. The CNO of that group stressed that they must ensure the applicants were not on the 'black list' so recruitment had to be carefully carried out. She explained that there were some qualified nurses in the area who had held

[2] Scottish Home and Health Department, (1972) *Nurses in an Integrated Health Service, Report of a Working Group appointed by the Scottish Home and Health Department*, HMSO, Edinburgh.

several posts and had their employment terminated as they had not been reliable. With her colleagues she had attempted to keep a register of unsatisfactory staff members which was referred to as the 'black list'.

The 'back-to-nursing' course was paid for by the hospital if employment followed, otherwise expenses had to be borne by the participant. Application and evaluation forms were completed and a 'follow-up' was undertaken six months later.

Understandably, in smaller groups and more sparsely populated areas, 'back-to-nursing' courses are not possible as there would not be sufficient applicants at any one time. The solution in one such area was described:

'When mothers have brought up families, they will 'phone and state their case saying that they haven't been in hospital for a while. They may come as enrolled nurses, although they are perhaps registered, for a month on trial. They are put in a white coat for a bit so nobody gives them too much responsibility. We had one who preferred to go on like this. Some like week-ends and other odd hours.'

Figure 4/1 shows that the provision of 'back-to-nursing' courses had the second largest number of 'votes' as being an encouragement for qualified nurses to return to nursing. It was exceeded only by flexibility of working hours and, as the above quotation suggests, this was heeded in practice whenever possible.

In the teaching departments, efforts were made to send tutors to more than the statutory courses and also to conferences and study days; the importance of such further educational experiences was not disputed by any of the respondents in teaching posts, but the usefulness of available courses was questioned. One Principal Nursing Officer said:

'It's good to get away for a while even if one doesn't learn anything new. I suppose we benefit from each other's company a bit.'

Community Nursing Services

Statutory refresher courses for domiciliary midwives were, of course, observed; health visitors in all areas seemed to be given the opportunity of attending courses and study days on special aspects of their work such as health education. However, arrangements for district nursing staff's refresher courses tended to be less systematic:

'Sometimes we get them away to a national course or they attend the hospital study days. Married women prefer this.'

In all areas there were close relationships between the hospital and community nursing services and a variety of mixed educational activities were reported. One respondent implied that it was impossible to isolate one specific subject of importance within a district nurse's work on which to focus attention. She thought that national courses were useful up to a point, but not always relevant to the needs of an area. For that reason local study days for nursing staff in hospital and community were more sensible, and also helped people to meet each other.

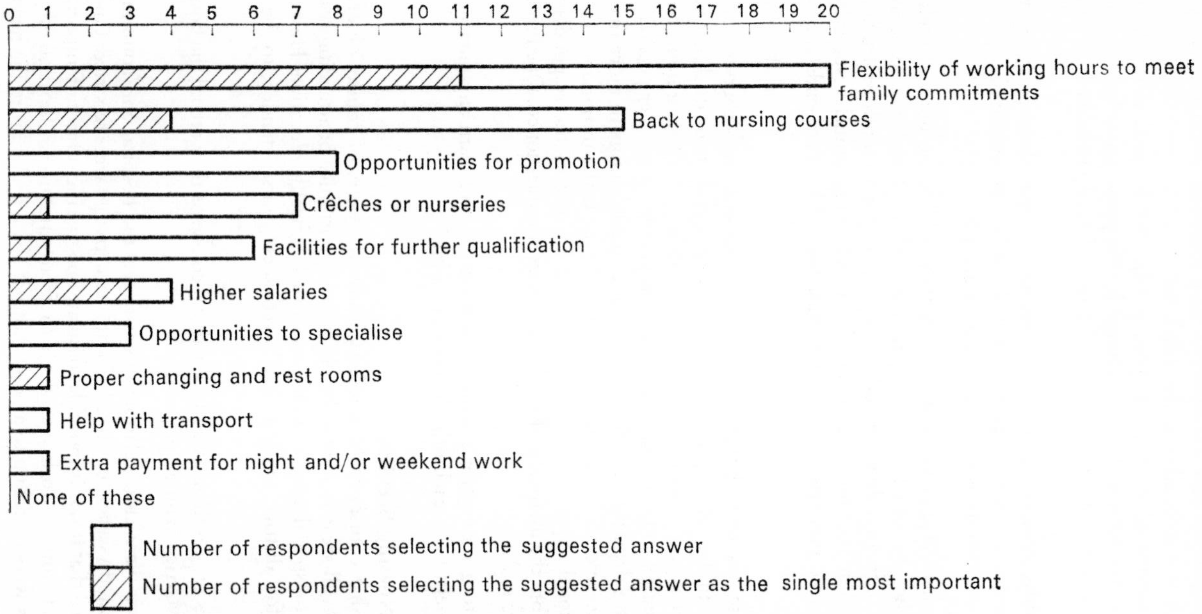

Figure 4/1 Top managers' views★ on incentives for encouraging inactive nurses back to nursing.
★*Question 60* Which three on this list do you consider the most important? Which one of these that you have chosen do you think is the most important?

In another area local Rcn* meetings were relied on to keep district nursing staff in touch with developments. Courses held in Edinburgh for staff preparing for group attachment were considered useful, but it was not easy for everybody to be sent to one.

As formal courses for qualified nurses returning to community nursing were not available, new members of staff were usually initiated into the work by a colleague. This was considered just as necessary for younger recently qualified people as for those who had not been working for some time. Four respondents mentioned that they usually encouraged the 'returning district nurses' to spend a short while in hospital, and attempted to send returning health visitors on a suitable course somewhere. Midwives were in any case not allowed to practise without recent experience and their induction was, therefore, compulsory.

Management courses at all levels were mentioned by both hospital and community nursing respondents. As these courses were seen as a necessary pre-requisite for promotion, opportunities to attend were given when possible.

PRACTICAL FACILITIES

There was a wide measure of uniformity in the provision of those practical facilities about which information was requested. On the whole, facilities considered to be needed were provided. In the hospital services, staff in outlying hospitals had some help with transport, either in the form of mileage allowance or a hospital car or bus. Those who were required to be on call had telephones provided and/or rental paid. Financial help for professional telephone calls was given where it was considered appropriate and the same applied to car allowances. There were differences in the amount of mileage allowances and in the concession given to staff using local authority owned cars for private purposes. Two respondents said that rates were under review and the desirability of a nationally applicable arrangement was expressed by several:

'At the moment they look for the place that can give them the best "extras"; it would be good if local differences were done away with.'

An opposite view was held by a nursing officer who, by virtue of being in an acceptable popular area, had no staffing problems:

'It would be fair if people in bad areas could be given extras in terms of houses, cars and better conditions generally. We must give them a bit of bait.'

This suggestion would, of course, be in line with systems available within the field of general medical practice where doctors get inducements for work in 'designated areas'.

The only real regret voiced by several hospital nursing managers was the lack of housing for married staff. In contrast, one community nursing administrator took a firm stance against tied housing:

'I don't think it (tied housing) is a good idea. Everyone wants to live in their own homes. They get priority for council houses.'

---

* Royal College of Nursing and National Council of Nurses of The United Kingdom.

Nurses' homes were not always fully used, although there was a general trend for single staff to request hospital accommodation as it was cheaper. No doubt, the lifting of conventional restrictions for residents within nurses' homes is a considerable contributory factor in this development. Whilst freedom was possibly considered worth the payment of a high rent outside hospital, there was an increasing attraction for many nurses in reducing their cost of living. All respondents said that restrictions in nurses' residences were virtually non-existent and those which did exist facilitated harmonious communal living and included such consideration in the use of joint equipment, of privacy and of quietness during the night.

In one (the northern) area of the study the proximity to the recently developed industrial boom, with its rapidly rising housing prices and scarcity of accommodation caused the nursing officer to say:

'I have often come back to residential problems, I wonder if a block of flatlets for *any* member of staff (not just nurses) wouldn't help. We have staff from far away—doctors and nurses. They can't get reasonable property quickly and sometimes have to go to boarding houses.'

Predictably and understandably, the provision of creches or nurseries was far from general, nor was there general agreement on the need for such provision. Only one of the smaller hospitals in one of the larger groups had a creche for staff's children. The idea had been discussed by several hospital respondents but the majority felt that local authorities should make the provision giving hospital staff preference for usage.

Community nursing administrators were almost unanimous in their preference for employing staff without young children and, therefore, could not see the need for a creche. The reason for their view was related to staffing problems created by illness of children:

'I suppose it is easier in hospital, I would find it difficult to cope if mothers rang up at eight in the morning saying that their child was sick.'

One community administrator also mentioned the conflict a health visitor would have if her young child were in a creche whilst she exhorted her clients to stay at home until children reached school age.

Another facility which, in the view of most Chief and Principal Nursing Officers, called for improvement was suitable changing-room accommodation. This applied particularly to non-resident staff of hospitals. It was somewhat ambiguously, and with unintentional humour, expressed by one Chief Nursing Officer:

'We need much more changing room facilities, especially for female staff, but they must be fully manned all the time as clothing can be pinched.'

Rest room facilities were, in most cases, provided in the nurses' homes and were equally available for resident and non-resident staff. Most respondents considered that continuous shifts reduced the need for rest rooms anyway, but when there was free time such as after a meal, it was good to mix all the staff. Most hospitals had communal coffee lounges, attached to the dining areas, which were freely used by all types and grades of hospital staff. The only instance when community nursing administrators considered the need for a proper rest room justified, was for a nurse 'on duty for late calls' but this was not given priority in demands:

'A slightly more comfortable room for the "on call" people would be helpful but it is not urgent compared with many other things that are needed.'

ATTACHMENT OF COMMUNITY NURSING STAFF
Attachment of community nursing staff was a topic discussed only with the local health authority administrators. Somewhat surprisingly only one respondent expressed unreserved enthusiasm for a policy of attachment but the implementation of such a policy, in her area, appeared to be hindered by the Medical Officer of Health.* She said:

'I'd do it tomorrow, but the MOH is adamant that GPs don't know how to use health visitors.'

Another Nursing Officer in charge of the district nursing service in her area considered attachment a good idea because it would help doctors and nurses to meet each other and discuss the care of the patients. She added:

'Mind you, there's no guarantee that it will work better and it will give everybody a lot of trouble, but it's new and we ought to try.'

Increased travel and more expense were the reasons given by almost all respondents as disadvantages of attachment.

ABSENTEEISM AND SICKNESS ABSENCE
Absenteeism, defined as uncertificated absence from work, was reported to be low by all CNO's except one. This respondent reported high absenteeism especially among part-time staff; she contended that in the case of part-timers, absenteeism and sickness were particularly difficult to differentiate. This respondent and several others looked forward to an occupational health service which would monitor staff sickness and advise on appropriate action. A practical preventive 'ploy' was suggested by one of the community nursing officers who said:

'I don't have anyone who takes a day off because of sleeping in. I say it is better to come in late than pretend to be sick and so they do it.'

Sickness statistics were kept everywhere or, at least, sickness was recorded. It was mentioned by several respondents that one should study this information; mainly it was collected routinely but no one had time to analyse it.

Based on impressions and opinions, non-resident staff were reported to be away from work more often and more than half of the respondents claimed to be able

---

* The data were obtained before the reorganisation of the health service when this post became obsolete.

to name a 'handful of people' who have a tendency to be 'sick'. Clark[3] identified non-residence as a significant factor associated with absenteeism in her systematic study of the problem.

Not a single respondent seemed worried about high staff turn-over, in fact, the opposite seemed more likely:

'People only leave if they get married, get pregnant or husbands move out of the area. Sometimes I feel we could do with a bit more movement.' or

'We are more likely to lose people in junior than in senior posts. This is all part and parcel of the same thing. Senior people are blocking jobs and juniors are quick to see this. In spite of it, few leave as they are often tied to their husband's job.'

PERSONAL DATA

Of the 22 top managers, 14 were between forty-five and fifty-four years of age tending toward the top rather than the bottom end of that age group. Clearly, the numbers are too small to compare hospital with community personnel. Three hospital but no community top managers had been in their present post for less than three years, which can possibly be explained by the later implementation of a senior management structure in the local authority than in the hospital nursing service.

Nine respondents had had some breaks in service of no less than two years, one for marriage, one to look after her elderly mother and the others had either given war service or had worked abroad in a variety of positions. The married respondent and the other respondent whose break was necessitated by home commitments were alone in feeling that their break might have influenced their career in an adverse way as they had to 'catch up'. The nursing officers who had been abroad saw their added experience as an asset.

In view of the general trend toward a shorter working week, the top managers were asked whether their responsibilities would allow them to benefit from an official reduction of working hours. Only one respondent felt that she could benefit as she could delegate more of her work. The others were adamant that working hours had no meaning when one reached a top managerial position:

'We get paid for the work, not the time and most of us take work home anyway'; or

'A shorter week wouldn't mean anything to me, it would merely make me do more work at home'; or

'I wouldn't want it otherwise. When one gets to this stage one must be prepared to do the job even if it doesn't fit the official hours. It's nice to be able to do one's own things occasionally during the day knowing that one works many evenings and week-ends.'

---

[3] Clark, J., (1975) *Time Out? A Study of Absenteeism Among Nurses*, Royal College of Nursing and National Council of Nurses of the United Kingdom, London.

The top managers had the same 'job satisfaction' test administered to them, as all other respondents in the study. However, as the stimulus preceding the test was not identical, comparison is neither possible nor desirable. The test consisted of a battery of positive and negative statements to which respondents were asked to react on a five point scale; they had the options to disagree or agree strongly, to disagree or agree or register uncertainty.

The test results for this group of respondents showed a consistently strong positive tendency. No single negative statement had a strong agreement and the total number who 'strongly agreed' with positive statements or 'strongly disagreed' with negative statements far outweighed the moderate or uncertain stances. Such a result suggesting high job satisfaction, must be interpreted within the limitations of the list itself, which did not seem as pertinent for this group as for the full range of nursing staff. Staff in the position of top managers would have found ways of achieving greater satisfaction in their work by manipulating their own situation than the negative results in this test implied. Although the test was used and validated for a cross section of nursing staff in the pilot study, its appropriateness for top managers only, could be questioned; for this group who have control of their own work situation a more subtly devised tool appears necessary. Polarisation of the nursing profession into those who control and those who are being controlled has become more obvious with the introduction of a nursing management structure. The difference in the result of this simple job satisfaction test between nursing staff in general and top managers in nursing, lends a little support to a hypothesis that some intra-professional differences may be as great if not greater than inter-professional ones. No attempt to test such a hypothesis was made in this study; however, in view of the rapidly changing role of nurse managers in the re-organised health service, further investigation of this nature would appear worthwhile.

CHAPTER FIVE
Women as Nurses

This chapter describes the respondents, other than the top managers, as nursing staff in the study areas. The chapter following focuses on the respondents as private individuals. The distinction is neither easy nor always realistic as private and professional commitments are inevitably closely inter-related. It was one of the main purposes of this study to find out how women fare in their nursing work-a-day life, how they manage and what they think.

As explained in the description of the study method (Chapter 2) two samples were drawn from lists of staff provided by the respective employing authorities: a 1 in 5 sample of hospital nursing staff up to the administrator grade and a 3 in 5 sample of community nursing staff. The total population of administrators was included in the study.

The total staffing picture based on information provided by the appropriate administrators in 1973 is presented in Appendix 4.

Tables 5/1a and b show the population of female staff from which the sample was drawn.

TABLE 5/1a
Hospital population of female staff from which sample was drawn

| | Hospital Groups | | | |
	A	B	C	D
Top managers	5	4	1	3
Administrators	42	54	6	34
Fieldworkers	802	1250	130	662
Total	849	1308	137	699

Numerous variables come into play in a broad study of this type. As the sample constituted a cross section of all female nursing staff it was important to indicate their designation in the first instance. The initial listing showed 38 designations, some of which were represented by only one or two respondents. It was necessary to group the designations and Table 5/2 describes the constituent groups in the designation categories most frequently used for the purpose of cross tabulation. As expanded more fully in Appendix 6, categorisation may present problems in that some detail of information is bound to be lost in the process. Thus, in these categories the distinctions between nursing officers and senior nursing officers, between enrolled nurses and senior enrolled nurses, between basic and post-basic students, between registered and enrolled district nurses are among those sacrificed for most calculations. The precaution was taken, however, to preserve all designation details on the data file so that they can be used for further work.

The crudity of categorisation creates problems of anomalies. For example, the

TABLE 5/1b
Community population of female staff from which sample was drawn

| | **Local Authority Areas** | | | |
	AA	*BB*	*CC*	*DD*
Top managers	1	3	1	3
Fieldworkers★	40	99	32	85
Total	41	102	33	88

★ The inclusion of some administrators in this category is explained on p. 19; for simplicity it is referred to as 'Fieldworkers' in the Tables.

merging of basic and post-basic students as a learner category placed a health visitor student of fifty years of age into a predominantly young group working in hospital. Such anomalies may distort averages and, therefore, have inherent dangers. Where necessary these difficulties are discussed in the text.

AGE DISTRIBUTION

Table 5/3 shows the 5 year interval age distribution of the respondents related to their designation. Percentages across age groups are deliberately omitted from this table as the different sampling distributions adopted for administrators, hospital fieldworkers and community nurses militate against inter-group comparison. The age group up to twenty-four years inclusive is an exception since it contains no administrators and only 3 district nurses who do not distort the picture significantly.

Almost by definition, all respondents under the age of twenty years were students or pupils and, not surprisingly, three-quarters of the learner group were of that age. Post-basic students were, of course, older but only 4 were over thirty years. The older members of the learner group were mostly basic student and pupil nurses, 17 in all, that is 12 per cent of all learners.

The age group 20–24 years, as the largest 5 year group in the sample, is worthy of more detailed consideration. This group is important as far as direct nursing care provision is concerned. Apart from learners it consists almost entirely of staff nurses/midwives and enrolled nurses. It is, in fact, the modal age group of the latter comprising 29 per cent of hospital enrolled nurses, twice as many as any other 5 year age group. Almost one-quarter of the staff nurses are in their early twenties and a contributory factor in making this group so important is its mainly

TABLE 5/2
Designation categories and their constituent groups

Designation category	Constituent groups	
Administrators	Senior nursing officers	34
	Unit nursing officers	78
	Night superintendents	4
	Community nursing officers★	7
	Total	123★★

Hospital fieldworkers

Sisters/teachers	Sisters	95
	Teachers	11
	Total	106
Staff nurses/midwives	Staff nurses	108
	Staff midwives	11
	Total	119
Enrolled nurses	Enrolled nurses	83
	Senior enrolled nurses	6
	Total	89
Students	Basic student nurses	73
	Post basic students	10
	Student midwives	9
	Student health visitors	2
	Total	94
Pupils		51

Community fieldworkers

District nurses	District nurses (registered)	41
	District nurses (enrolled)	7
	Total	48
Health visitors	Health visitors	37
	Senior health visitors	2
	Total	39
Other community nurses	Triple duty nurses†	19
	Domiciliary midwives	11
	District nurses/midwives	8
	School nurses	7
	Other duty combinations	5
	Total	50

★ As not all local health authorities had implemented the Mayston structure, several community nursing officers were top managers for their respective branch of the service.
★★ This includes 10 nursing officers with responsibility for teaching.
† District nurse/midwife/health visitor.

TABLE 5/3

Five year age groups by designation

	Administrators No.	%	Sisters/teachers No.	%	Staff nurses/midwives No.	%	Enrolled nurses No.	%	Students No.	%	Pupils No.	%	District nurses No.	%	Health visitors No.	%	Other community nurses No.	%	Total
Under 20	0	0.0	0	0.0	0	0.0	0	0.0	33	35.5	25	49.0	0	0.0	0	0.0	0	0.0	58
20–24	0	0.0	6	5.7	28	23.7	26	29.2	40	43.0	15	29.4	3	6.3	0	0.0	0	0.0	118
25–29	2	1.6	21	19.8	27	22.9	7	7.9	9	9.7	1	2.0	4	8.3	2	5.3	4	8.0	77
30–34	5	4.1	20	18.9	15	12.7	8	9.0	6	6.5	2	3.9	2	4.2	5	13.2	5	10.0	68
35–39	22	17.9	16	15.1	20	16.9	8	9.0	1	1.1	4	7.8	9	18.8	4	10.5	7	14.0	91
40–44	25	20.3	7	6.6	13	11.0	6	6.7	2	2.2	1	2.0	11	22.9	6	15.8	5	10.0	76
45–49	23	18.7	16	15.1	7	5.9	12	13.5	1	1.1	3	5.9	9	18.8	8	21.1	7	14.0	86
50–54	22	17.9	8	7.5	2	1.7	10	11.2	1	1.1	0	0.0	5	10.4	5	13.2	10	20.0	63
55–59	24	19.5	10	9.4	5	4.2	12	13.5	0	0.0	0	0.0	5	10.4	7	18.4	7	14.0	70
Over 60	0	0.0	2	1.9	1	0.8	0	0.0	0	0.0	0	0.0	0	0.0	1	2.6	5	10.0	9
Total=100%	123		106		118		89		93		51		48		38		50		716*

* 3 people gave inadequate answers.

full-time employment. Relatively few enrolled nurses under twenty-five years of age, just under 1 in 5, and a smaller proportion of staff nurses/midwives, roughly 1 in 9, worked part-time.

In the later twenties there is a sharp fall in the number of enrolled nurses but not in the number of staff nurses/midwives who, however, are more likely to work part time. These data suggest that a higher proportion of enrolled than registered nurses leave nursing during their late twenties, at least temporarily, rather than work part time. It may be that they feel less career conscious than their registered colleagues and, therefore, are more ready to take the risk of a complete break from nursing; career breaks are more fully discussed in Chapter 7. After the age of twenty-five years, registered nurses are likely to move into a variety of other designations, most probably becoming ward sisters. Almost a third of the 25–29 year old group of respondents were staff nurses/midwives and the proportion of sisters was just over a quarter. Two members of that age group had already reached the nursing officer's grade and 10 had moved into community nursing.

Predictably, the number of staff nurses diminishes steadily with increasing age leaving relatively few over the age of forty-five. The decline of sisters in the higher age groups is less marked although, again predictably, there is a marked trend toward administration from thirty-five years onward. Administrators comprise about a quarter of the age group 35–50 years and more than a third of respondents in their fifties were hospital administrators; nurses in their late thirties are also likely to move into the community nursing services. Among respondents in their fifties, slightly more were hospital administrators than community nurses and only one-third were hospital fieldworkers, nearly half of them enrolled nurses.

Figures 5/1a and b are intended to convey the age pattern in the various groups more clearly. In Figure 5/1a the enrolled nurse group shows the sharp fall in their late twenties with a second peak after forty-five years of age. This picture reflects not only the impact of marriage and childbearing but also late entrants into training for enrolment. The main difference in Figure 5/1b is the absence of the second peak for the staff nurses and midwives.

The numbers of staff nurses and of sisters diminish with increasing age, the decline being steeper for staff nurses. As indicated earlier, conventional career patterns, with promotion to sisters or administrators respectively, account for this decline. It is important to note, however, that the numbers of community nurses and administrators in the higher age groups do not compensate for the reducing numbers of hospital fieldworkers. The general picture is one of a steady fall in numbers of nursing personnel with age which is only kept in some check by the second peak among the enrolled nurses group.

This statement is supported by Figure 5/2 which attempts to convey an approximation of the overall age structure of the sample of registered nurses correcting for differences in the sampling ratios.

The pattern in Figure 5/2 is set by the hospital fieldworkers who, as the largest group of the nursing labour force, must be the pace setters. The relatively small deficit in the 30–34 year age group can be taken to be due to family building; as mentioned earlier enrolled nurses seem more ready to take longer breaks for this purpose.

The gradual decline of numbers with increasing age is worthy of note; it may be due to low recruitment of the older nurse or to withdrawal of older nurses from work. As the 30–39 year age group is likely to work part time and the fall in

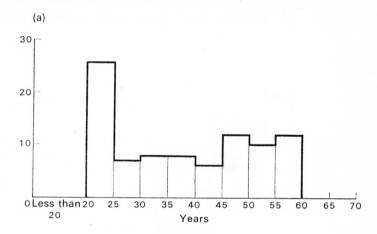

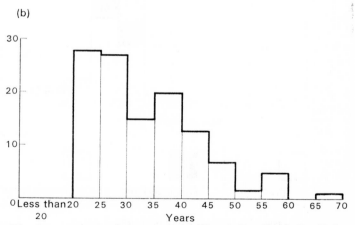

Figure 5/1 Age structure of two groups of hospital staff. (a) Enrolled nurses. (b) Staff nurses/midwives.

numbers from the age of forty years is marked, the importance of adequate recruitment to nursing is obvious.

Part-time work and its implications are more fully discussed in Chapter 9.

At the upper end of the age scale, 6 of the 9 nurses in their sixties were working in the community nursing service; the oldest respondent was a triple duty com-

munity nurse aged sixty-nine, who had retired, but was asked to return to her post
a few months later and was still working full time.

With the exception of 2 student health visitors, all learners were among the
hospital staff; no district nursing students were in the sample of respondents.

Apart from learners the other designation category predominantly confined to

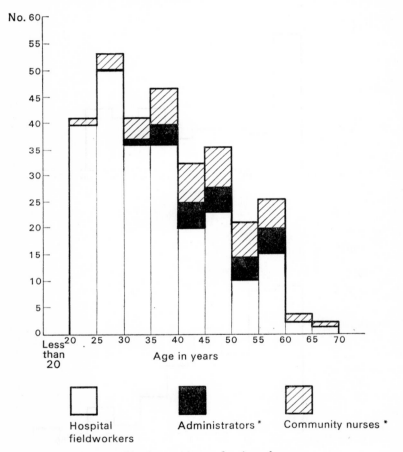

Figure 5/2 Age structure of registered nurses.
★ Adjusted for different sampling fractions.

the hospital field are the enrolled nurses. They represent approximately one-
quarter of all qualified hospital staff other than administrators. Although, as
mentioned earlier, more than a quarter of enrolled nurses were under twenty-five
years of age, roughly a quarter of hospital fieldworkers aged thirty years and over
were enrolled nurses. In a discussion of age structure, enrolment versus registration
appears to have some relevance.

The proportion of enrolled nurses in the community nursing service is much lower than in the hospital service. The community nursing field, as a whole, is more restricted than the hospital field as far as employment opportunities for enrolled nurses are concerned. They are not eligible for health visitor training and they are usually discouraged from training as midwives. The general reduction of domiciliary midwives further accentuates the enrolled nurses' limited work opportunities in that field. The district nursing service is, at least in theory, freely open to enrolled nurses, so much so that a special district nurse training course is available to them. Yet only 1 in 7 of the district nursing staff in the sample of respondents were enrolled nurses; why this should be the case, is difficult to establish with certainty. The continued reluctance of local health authorities to employ enrolled nurses especially with adequate registered nurse recruitment can, however, be taken as playing a major part. Interviews with top managers in this study (Chapter 4) support this suggestion. Other studies have produced similar findings and advanced similar reasons for them; in the most detailed of these, 'Use or Abuse',[1] the data were collected in 1970/71, just about two years before the field work in this project was undertaken.

QUALIFICATIONS

Of the 100 respondents who possessed the state enrolment certificate, 23 had at least one further qualification. Five nurses had proceeded to state registration, 16 enrolled nurses held a second qualification other than registration and 2 respondents had 2 other qualifications. These other qualifications included district nursing for the largest number, midwifery and mental nursing certificates.

The full list of single qualifications as well as the most usual combinations of qualifications held by the nursing staff are presented in Appendix 6.

Table 5/4 shows the number of qualifications for different groups of nursing staff. As can be seen 70 of the 108 staff nurses, 65 per cent, had a single qualification, mostly RGN/SRN. No doubt, this is mainly a function of their youth, about half of them being in their twenties. Predictably, as one moves up the hierarchy the number of qualifications increases. Only 24 per cent of the sisters and 5 per cent of the administrators had just a single nursing qualification.

The small sample of teachers had more qualifications than the sisters and at least as many as the administrators. It is worthy of mention that the health visitors had more qualifications in general than the administrators in the hospital service; by definition they all had at least 2 qualifications but only 10 per cent had this minimum; almost 1 in 5 of the health visitors had 5 qualifications. However, the number of qualifications alone has little meaning as there are important differences in their value. For this reason, as explained fully in Appendix 6, the qualifications were classified using certain criteria.

Qualifications in relation to the respondents' field of nursing are discussed below.

---

[1] Hockey, L., (1972) *Use or Abuse? A Study of the state enrolled nurse in the local authority nursing services*, Queen's Institute of District Nursing, London.

TABLE 5/4
Number of qualifications for groups of staff

| | Number of nursing qualifications | | | | | | | |
	None	One	Two	Three	Four	Five	Six	Total
Administrators	0	6	52	39	19	5	2	123
Teachers	0	0	3	5	1	2	0	11
Sisters	0	23	47	22	3	0	0	95
Staff nurses	0	70	30	8	0	0	0	108
Staff midwives	0	0	8	3	0	0	0	11
Registered district nurses	0	3	15	20	3	0	0	41
Health visitors	0	0	1	24	8	6	0	39
Health visitors combined duty	0	0	5	7	5	6	0	23
Other registered community nurses	0	1	13	8	5	0	0	27
Enrolled hospital nurses	2	76	11	0	0	0	0	89
Enrolled district nurses	0	2	4	1	0	0	0	7

STAFF STABILITY AND MOBILITY

In an attempt to obtain some information on the stability of nursing staff three related questions were asked.* The first question related to the length of continuous employment by the same employing authority; the second to the length of continuous employment in the respondent's present post; and the third to length of time in the present designation.

Answers to the first two questions were comparatively easy to obtain, code and analyse. The third question caused difficulty in spite of the extensive pilot work that had been undertaken. The research team were not unaware of the potential problems inherent in the question but hoped that the interviews would clarify them. In the event, this was not possible in all cases, although it was a question on which probing was freely permitted. The problem lay partly in respondents' breaks from the service and partly in the introduction of new designations with 'Salmon'. The possibility of some misleading answers must, therefore, be kept in mind in the interpretation of the results.

Hospital and community staff showed distinctly different patterns in this context and their answers are, therefore, presented separately.

As can be seen from Table 5/5, more than half (56 per cent) of the hospital

---

* *Question 1.* How long have you been employed by the — — — — — — — — — hospital group/local authority?

Question 8. How long have you been a — — — — — — — — — — — — in this — — — — — — ward/area?

Question 4. How long have you been a — — — — — — — — — — — — ?

administrators★ had been in the continuous employment of their hospital group for ten years or longer and just over 90 per cent had been employed within the group for at least two years.

Qualified hospital staff other than administrators were more likely to have come to their current hospital group within the previous two years, either from employment elsewhere or after a break from service. The percentage of ward sisters/teachers who had worked for ten years or more within their present group was only half that of the administrators who had such a record of stability—28 per

TABLE 5/5
Length of time in present hospital group

	Administrators	Sisters/ teachers	Staff nurses/ midwives	Enrolled nurses	Students	Pupils
Less than 1 year	5	9	24	12	30	23
1 year less than 2 years	5	9	21	6	32	17
2 years less than 3 years	9	15	10	12	18	7
3 years less than 5 years	10	15	24	17	11	4
5 years less than 10 years	22	28	26	23	1	0
10 years less than 20 years	41	19	9	14	0	0
20 years and over	24	11	4	5	0	0
Total	116	106	118	89	92	51

Respondents who gave inadequate answers and/or those to whom the question was inapplicable are excluded from the totals.

cent of the former against 56 per cent of the latter. Nevertheless, they are still a relatively stable element among the nursing staff. Enrolled nurses followed fairly closely with 21 per cent of respondents having given continuous service to the group for ten years or more, while 11 per cent of staff nurses had done so; staff nurses are known to be the more transient grade of qualified nurses.

Clearly, the period of employment by a hospital group includes the training period. Thus, it could be that a staff nurse who stated that she had been in the employment of the same hospital group for six years had been a staff nurse for just the last three of these. Therefore, in terms of mobility of qualified staff, the information obtained in answer to the other questions about length of time in present post is more relevant.

As shown in Table 5/6 half the staff nurses/midwives had held their present post for less than a year; in fact, the largest proportion of qualified hospital staff in all

---

★ Attention is again drawn to the fact that this does not include the top managers.

designations fell within that category, which is indicative of a fairly rapid staff mobility within a hospital. The sharp drop in numbers from those who had been in their present post less than one year (182) and those of 1–2 years' standing (74) deserves further investigation; it can only partly be accounted for by promotion. Some of the loss is almost certainly due to a break away from nursing, be it temporary or permanent.

The small group of staff who had remained static within their present post for ten years or more were enrolled nurses and sisters/teachers. As already mentioned, the promotion prospects for enrolled nurses are limited and for sisters/teachers

TABLE 5/6
Length of time in present post (hospital)

	Administrators	Sisters/ teachers	Staff nurses/ midwives	Enrolled nurses
Less than 1 year	44	30	59	49
1 year less than 2 years	15	19	26	14
2 years less than 3 years	35	25	11	10
3 years less than 5 years	18	12	13	6
5 years less than 10 years	3	10	8	4
10 years less than 20 years	1	6	1	5
20 years and over	0	3	0	0
Total	116	105	118	88

Respondents who gave inadequate answers and/or those to whom the question was inapplicable are excluded from the totals.

promotion tends to imply administration in service or education. It seems that those nurses who either do not achieve or who do not desire an upward mobility in their professional career seek a change in other ways, whether by having a break altogether or by changing posts at the same level. Thus only one-third of the enrolled nurses who had been in that designation for ten years or more had remained in the same post for that length of time. It can, however, also be argued that some nurses who move around for one reason or another, are either less concerned about, or less likely to achieve, professional promotion.

The answers to the question 'How long have you been in your present designation' are shown in Table 5/7. As explained earlier, it was a difficult question to answer, particularly by those respondents who had been away from nursing for a period of time and to a lesser extent by those whose designation had been given a new name or whose jobs had been re-graded in the implementation of the Salmon structure. For example a person might have been a matron of a small hospital for some years but have been re-graded as Senior Nursing Officer. The small number of administrators who had been in their present designation for five years or more is almost bound to be largely due to administrative re-organisation. Not only had the new administrative grade of Unit Nursing Officer been introduced, but the two top administrative grades, namely, Principal and Chief Nursing Officer, are not included in this analysis. The effect of the exclusion of the top managerial grades from this analysis is particularly marked when administrators are grouped according to the type of their hospital. As a direct result of the Salmon management structure the top administrative grade in a small rural hospital would, most likely,

TABLE 5/7
Length of time in present designation (hospital)

	Administrators	Sisters/ teachers	Staff nurses/ midwives	Enrolled nurses	Students	Pupils
Less than 1 year	41	17	21	12	36	25
1 year less than 2 years	14	16	17	13	29	19
2 years less than 3 years	35	14	6	16	20	7
3 years less than 5 years	21	20	19	12	7	0
5 years less than 10 years	3	17	19	21	0	0
10 years less than 20 years	2	15	28	10	0	0
20 years and over	0	7	9	5	0	0
Total	116	106	119	89	92	51

be a person of nursing officer grade and, therefore, be included in this analysis. The top administrator in a large urban hospital, however, would most probably be a person of Principal Nursing Officer grade who was interviewed as one of the top managers and whose answers are presented in the preceding chapter.

Sisters/teachers who had been in their present designation for ten years or more were almost all over forty years of age and were working full time. Most of them had not had a break in service, although they had changed posts. When asked about future plans, some sisters/teachers indicated clearly that they had no promotion ambitions and felt happy in their present job.

Enrolled nurses in the same position of having been at that level for ten years or more, were also likely to be over forty years of age, but two-thirds of them had taken breaks in service and half of them were either working part time or had done so for a while after their break.

Staff nurses and midwives whose answer indicated that they had been in the same designation for ten years or more presented a different picture. More than half were under forty years of age and about 90 per cent were working part time after breaks in service for family building. In fact, many of them had been employed for only a small proportion of this span of time. It could be that these young mothers are not sufficiently career oriented to mind their long-term staff nurse position or that they even prefer a post with less responsibility. However, as interviews with top managers showed, there is some reluctance in giving part-time nursing staff sisters or administrators posts. In either case it is important to keep this group of nurses sufficiently interested and up-to-date, to allow them to make their maximum contribution to the service.

The community nursing services presented blurred boundaries between some nursing officers who had administrative responsibilities in addition to a small case load and some who either acted as practical teachers or who deputised for the more senior administrator on some occasions and for the fieldworkers on others. For the above reasons, those community nursing officers, who did not qualify for the open-ended interview as policy makers, were sampled on a 3 in 5 basis like all community nursing staff. Seven administrators and 137 other community nurses constituted the sample of community nursing staff.

Of the 7 respondents with administrative duties, one had very recently been promoted and moved her area of employment at that time, but the remaining 6 had all served in their area for substantial periods before being appointed to their present administrative positions.

Community nursing staff, other than administrators, also tended to have had long periods of service in their local authority area. About half had been in the same employment for five years or more and roughly one-third ten years or even longer. In this respect the community nursing staff seemed similar to the hospital sisters/teachers.

Apart from the 7 administrators, all of whom had been promoted within the last five years, 54 per cent of the community nurses had remained in their present designation for five years or more.

While this suggests a rather static situation among nursing staff who have moved into community work, the question asking how long the respondent had been in her present post showed that three-quarters of the community nurses had, in fact, changed their district and/or designation or returned from a break in service during the previous five years. A third of all community nurses, 33 per cent, had come to their present post within the previous year. The survey on a wider geographical basis, previously referred to, showed a distinctly lower proportion of community staff, 16 per cent, who had been less than a year in their present post.[2]

As mentioned earlier, the number of qualifications held by individual respondents has little meaning. The number and type of qualifications give certain information about investment of resources in nurse education and the use of learner resources for the staffing of services. The usefulness of these qualifications can only be assessed in relation to the individual's field of work. It was mainly for this reason that respondents were asked some details about their current work and any specialised responsibilities.

---

[2] Hockey, L., (1972) *Use or Abuse? A Study of the state enrolled nurse in the local authority nursing services*, Queen's Institute of District Nursing, London.

Hospital staff provided information about the department or ward in which they were currently working and this is presented in Table 5/8.

Predictably, the majority worked in the general field, in fact just over half. Geriatric departments or wards claimed the largest number of respondents in specialised fields followed by maternity, psychiatry and teaching, in that order.

It can be assumed that the staffing picture presented in Table 5/8 is typical. It shows that the two specialties, psychiatry and geriatrics, reputed to be under-privileged, had, between them, 20 per cent of all the administrators, 24 per cent of ward sisters/teachers and just 15 per cent of all staff nurses. No basic or post-basic

TABLE 5/8
Designation by field of work (hospital)

	Administrators No. %	Sisters/ teachers No. %	Staff nurses/ midwives No. %	Enrolled nurses No. %	Students No. %	Pupils No. %	Community liaison worker No. %
General	40 34.5	44 41.5	80 68.4	42 47.7	67 74.4	25 50.0	0 0.0
Maternity	22 19.0	20 18.9	14 12.0	5 5.7	11 12.2	0 0.0	0 0.0
Psychiatric	6 5.2	10 9.4	7 6.0	18 20.5	12 13.3	4 8.0	0 0.0
Geriatric	17 14.7	16 15.1	11 9.4	23 26.1	0 0.0	21 42.0	0 0.0
Not confined to any one field	21 18.1	5 4.7	5 4.3	0 0.0	0 0.0	0 0.0	1 100.0
Teaching	10 8.6	11 10.4	0 0.0	0 0.0	0 0.0	0 0.0	0 0.0
Total=100%	116	106	117	88	90	50	1

students were working in any geriatric departments compared with 42 per cent of all pupil nurses.

In the general nursing field the ratio of enrolled nurses to sisters was roughly 1:1, in geriatric areas 3:2 and in the psychiatric specialty 2:1. Respondents in the general nursing field were working in a variety of specialisms within it as follows:

Surgical/orthopaedic	73
Medical	69
Outpatient/casualty	15
Operating theatre	11
Other specialties	99
Combined specialties	11
Not confined to any one field	20
	298

Although the group in 'other specialties' contained the largest number of respondents it included many specialised areas none of which was represented by more than 10 people. Examples of those areas are gynaecology, chest conditions, ophthalmics, ear, nose and throat (ENT) and neurology.

Apart from student midwives all the respondents in maternity units held the midwifery qualification; of the 21 respondents who were employed in a teaching capacity 17 held a teaching qualification. As explained in Appendix 6, the classification of qualifications finally adopted did not retain all qualification details.*

The community nurses were asked whether or not they were attached to a general practice, and also whether they specialised in any particular aspect of the work.

A higher proportion of district nurses, 62 per cent, than of health visitors, 41 per cent, were attached to a general practice. This statement, however, masks a considerable difference between the pattern in the urban and the rural areas. Only a quarter of all designations of community nurses in urban areas were working as part of a general practice team, while three-quarters of rural community nurses were attached to a general medical practice. The difference was especially marked for the health visitors. In the urban areas only 5 out of 27 health visitors were attached, whereas 11 out of 12 health visitors in rural areas were working in such an association with a general practice. Nurses with 'combined' or 'triple' duties** were employed in the rural areas and were mostly associated with a general practice.

Respondents employed as school nurses or domiciliary midwives were mainly in urban areas. Apart from those nurses whose jobs were by definition specialised, such as the above, the majority of nurses working in the community had to deal with the whole range of problems and age groups in the area they covered. Only one district nurse had a specialised role, in geriatric care. One health visitor had responsibility for psychiatric patients, and 4 specialised in the care of mothers and young children. In view of this wide range of work, the importance of the number of qualifications often held by community nurses is apparent.

About half the district nurses had a midwifery qualification, but among the health visitors and other community nurses only 2, one health visitor and a school nurse, did not hold either the full midwifery qualification (SCM) or even Part I of it (CMB).† Apart from midwifery and qualifications in district nursing and/or health visiting, the most frequent qualification proved to be that of Registered Fever Nurse (RFN) held by 25 community nurses. Although the Register of Fever Nurses is now closed, the qualification gave some nurses their licence to practise and for others it provided an admission route to a shortened training for state registration. Four community nurses were qualified children's nurses (RSCN) and 3 were registered mental or mental deficiency nurses (RMN, RNMD). One triple duty nurse was qualified as RGN/RSCN/SCM/DN(R)/HV(cert) and another RGN/RMN/SCM/DN(R)/HV(cert).†† Such combinations of qualifications for people working in remote areas are clearly of great value.

---

* It is hoped to undertake further more detailed analyses relating individual qualifications to fields of work.

** Combined duties: combination of any *two* functions of district nursing, midwifery, health visiting, but mostly combining the first two of these.

Triple duties: combination of all three of the above functions.

† This qualification is no longer awarded.

†† The abbreviations are explained in Appendix 7.

TYPE OF HOSPITAL AND AREA

As hospitals differ considerably in size and in their position relating to urban or rural localities it was considered relevant to compare the staffing pictures on those two factors.

The four hospital groups in the study represented 56 hospitals and two schools of nursing; one specialist hospital had out-patients only. The bed numbers in the hospitals ranged from 12 to just over 1000.

Table 5/9 shows the distribution of respondents in the different types of hospitals. As can be seen from Table 5/9 more than twice as many respondents were working in urban hospitals than in rural hospitals. While there were hospitals of under 50 beds in the urban areas, the overwhelming majority of nurses in these areas were working in hospitals of more than 100 beds. With the exception of a large

TABLE 5/9
Distribution of respondents in different types of hospital

Type of district	Hospital Size by Number of Beds					
	Less than 20	20–99	100–499	500–999	1000+	Total
Urban	1	11	124	100	156	392
Rural	19	37	78	0	34	168
Total	20	48	202	100	190	560

psychiatric hospital which yielded 34 respondents, none of the rural hospitals had more than 250 beds. As indicated in Chapter 3, one of the rural areas in the study had 5 hospitals with fewer than 20 beds.

In a comparison between small hospitals of under 100 beds and larger ones some differences become apparent. Earlier discussion was focused on the length of time respondents remained in the same designation; this analysis suggests that there might be a fairly strong association between remaining static and working in a small hospital; respondents in rural hospitals were also more likely to remain in one designation for some time but this association was less marked.

In these small and predominantly rural hospitals the turnover in staff is clearly slower than in the larger hospitals. In the small hospitals, only one out of 15 staff nurses was newly qualified, compared with one-fifth of the staff nurses in the larger hospitals. One out of 10 enrolled nurses from the small hospitals had been an enrolled nurse for less than three years, compared with half the enrolled nurses in the larger hospitals. The data on length of employment in the respondent's present post showed a lower rate of turnover among qualified fieldworkers employed in small hospitals than among the much larger number employed in hospitals with at least 100 beds. Despite the small number of respondents who were working in small hospitals, this difference was highly significant.

In the small hospitals 22 per cent of the sisters, 33 per cent of staff nurses/midwives and 30 per cent of the enrolled nurses had come to their present post within the previous year, compared with 32 per cent of the sisters/teachers, 53 per cent of the staff nurses/midwives and 59 per cent of the enrolled nurses in the larger hospitals.

Nearly half the respondents working in small hospitals had been employed by their hospital group for ten years or more. In the small hospitals, 37 per cent of the staff were in their fifties, only 19 per cent in their twenties and none aged less than twenty. These figures are in marked contrast to those in the larger hospitals in which 46 per cent of respondents were under thirty years of age.

Community nursing staff did not differ in their length of service between those who worked in urban and those who worked in rural areas.

PART-TIME EMPLOYMENT AND MARITAL STATUS

Part-time employment in all types of work by women is assuming increasing importance in modern society. It is a crucial factor in nursing and, as such, is the concern of Chapter 9.

In the context of this chapter, which considers women as a work force in nursing, reference to their type of employment cannot, however, be omitted altogether.

TABLE 5/10
Full-/part-time work by designation

	Administrators	Sisters/ teachers	Staff nurses/ midwives	Enrolled nurses	District nurses	Health visitors	Other community nurses
Full-time	122	92	49	53	35	37	41
Part-time	1	14	70	36	13	2	9
Total	123	106	119	89	48	39	50

Table 5/10 shows that part-time work was practically non-existent for administrators and health visitors, whereas part-time staff nurses outnumbered those who were employed on a full-time basis.

Part-time working is, understandably, strongly associated with marriage and home responsibilities. The only part-time learner in the study, a pupil nurse in her late thirties, was also the only single part-time respondent; almost half the married nurses worked part time. Thus, although married nurses were not significantly more likely to work part time than full time, single nurses were highly significantly more likely to work full time than part time.

Clearly, the variables of marital status, designation, age and type of employment are closely inter-related and it would, therefore, be not only difficult but also dangerous to draw any causal inferences between them. For example, although the analysis showed that almost all the administrators and health visitors were full-time workers, the majority of this group was also single. Table 5/11 shows the marital status of the different designations. The high proportion of married staff nurses/ midwives, amounting to more than three-quarters, is particularly noteworthy. Almost twenty years ago a study of staff nurses[3] stated that 60 per cent of this group were single and working full time.

TABLE 5/11
Designation by marital status

	Marital Status								
	Single		Married		Widowed		Divorced/ separated		Total= 100%
	No.	%	No.	%	No.	%	No.	%	No.
Administrators	92	74.8	26	21.1	5	4.1	0	0.0	123
Sisters/ teachers	55	51.9	46	43.4	2	1.9	3	2.8	106
Staff nurses/ midwives	23	19.3	93	78.2	2	1.7	1	0.8	119
Enrolled nurses	26	29.2	54	60.7	4	4.5	5	5.6	89
Students	81	86.2	12	12.8	1	1.1	0	0.0	94
Pupils	37	72.5	12	23.5	0	0.0	2	3.9	51
District nurses	7	14.6	39	81.3	0	0.0	2	4.2	48
Health visitors	28	71.8	11	28.2	0	0.0	0	0.0	39
Other community nurses	19	38.0	27	54.0	2	4.0	2	4.0	50

The contrast in marital status between district nurses, most of whom were married, and health visitors is also worthy of mention.

Chapter 6 discusses the social characteristics of the respondents in much greater detail.

The intention of this chapter was to view the group of respondents as a work force and to highlight those aspects which have a relevance for manpower planning in nursing. The following trends suggest themselves from the findings.

The majority of recruits enter nursing between the minimum age of $17\frac{1}{2}$ and 25 years, as described in Chapter 7.

Of those who enter before they are twenty, few marry until after they have qualified. A high proportion of qualified nurses today marry during their early twenties and when they have children are likely to leave employment, at least for a period in excess of the maternity leave allowance. When they return to the National Health Service mothers of young children usually work part time. Thus, there is a relatively large labour force of young women who have not yet had children and work full time, but the amount of time which women in their late twenties and thirties can give to nursing is greatly reduced. There were fewer

---

[3] The Dan Mason Nursing Research Committee, (1960) *The Work, Responsibilities and the Status of the Staff Nurse*, The Dan Mason Nursing Research Committee of the National Florence Nightingale Memorial Committee of Great Britain and Northern Ireland, London.

respondents in their thirties than in their twenties and a greater proportion of them were working part time.

If, therefore, nurses in their twenties are not fully replaced and nurses in their thirties show a high propensity to work part time, staffing of the nursing service by female personnel* under forty years of age is likely to become increasingly difficult.

---

* Part-time employment of male staff is negligible.

CHAPTER SIX
Nurses as Women

Whilst the previous chapter looked at the sample of female nurses as a work force, attention in this chapter is directed to these nurses' social characteristics, their family background, their home life, their domestic commitments and the way they were able to combine a social life with their job as nurses.

In some categories we have deliberately presented small numbers of respondents and even single events in full awareness that they have no statistical significance. The purpose of this inclusion is partly the potential interest to a reader, and partly to show the complexity of survey data; clearly, one of the major factors in deciding on categorisation and classification is the purpose for which the data have been collected in the first instance. Small numbers in any one category can only be increased by merging two or more groups which results in a loss of detail. As some of this detail was deemed important in a descriptive base line study such as this, it was decided to present it in full.

FAMILY BACKGROUND

Although many public services in Britain have a considerable proportion of workers from overseas countries, the nursing services in the research areas did not follow this pattern.

Of the 719 nurses who were interviewed 83 per cent were born in Scotland and a further 10 per cent elsewhere in the United Kingdom, most of them in England. Eire contributed the highest percentage of nurses from outside the UK, though this amounted to no more than 2 per cent. Some of the respondents who were born abroad had fathers who had been born in the UK, leaving only 24 nurses who did not originate from the British Isles. Table 3, Appendix 4 gives details of the respondents' and their fathers' country of birth.

Occupational mobility between generations is of sociological as well as managerial interest. The respondents were therefore asked about their father's occupation, which was coded according to the classification in Appendix 2. Just over half the fathers had manual occupations, and of the eight occupational categories, skilled manual work was overwhelmingly the most frequently reported. Thirty-three per cent of the fathers were in the three higher non-manual grades, while 39 per cent were skilled manual workers. Figure 6/1 shows the picture and Appendix 2 should be consulted for the composition of the occupational groups.

Surprisingly only 20 per cent of the respondents had a father in medical, nursing or allied medical professions. Three nurses were doctor's daughters, 7 had a father in the nursing profession and 4 fathers were in allied medical occupations.

Mothers may, on the face of it, have had more influence in their daughter's career choice, 10 per cent being connected with nursing in some way, either before or after marriage. After marriage, 73 per cent of the mothers had not been employed.

Roughly 1 in 10 mothers had done routine non-manual work after marriage, the largest single group of working mothers. Half that number had been employed in semi-skilled manual work, followed closely by those in grade 3, the one which includes most qualified nurses. To say that marriage and child-rearing clearly tend to interrupt a woman's career would be to state a blinding glimpse of the obvious.

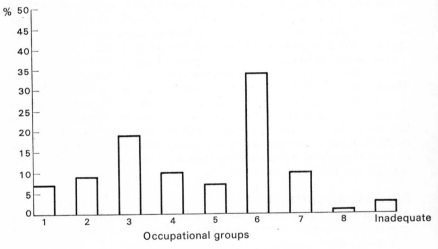

Figure 6/1 Fathers' occupational groups.

An attempt was made to discern if the nurse's family background was related in any way to her designation. A fairly clear cut pattern evolved which may be of relevance to career advisers and to research workers exploring professional mobility within nursing.

As seen in Figure 6/2, hospital nurses divide into three groups. In terms of father's occupation, administrators resembled sisters/teachers with 43 per cent of fathers in occupational grades 1, 2 and 3, and 41 per cent in manual occupations. The comparable proportions for pupil and enrolled nurses were 17 per cent and 73 per cent respectively. Staff nurses' and students' fathers occupied an intermediate position, 33 per cent being in higher non-manual and 58 per cent in manual grades.

Community nurses showed a curiously different pattern. It was considered appropriate to compare them with hospital administrators, the group in the hospital structure most like them in terms of age and qualifications; moreover, some community nurses had administrative responsibilities. The fathers of com-

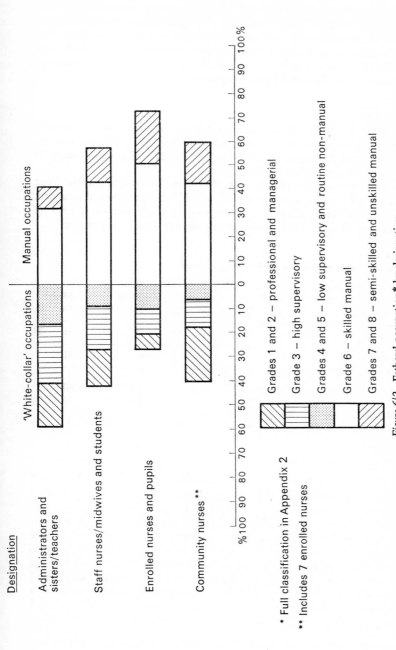

Figure 6/2 Fathers' occupation* by designation.
Respondents who gave inadequate answers and/or those to whom the question was inapplicable are excluded from the totals.

* Full classification in Appendix 2
** Includes 7 enrolled nurses

Grades 1 and 2 – professional and managerial

Grade 3 – high supervisory

Grades 4 and 5 – low supervisory and routine non-manual

Grade 6 – skilled manual

Grades 7 and 8 – semi-skilled and unskilled manual

Designation

Administrators and sisters/teachers

Staff nurses/midwives and students

Enrolled nurses and pupils

Community nurses **

'White-collar' occupations   Manual occupations

munity nurses polarised into grade 1 and 2 occupations at one end and into manual occupations at the other. They contributed the highest proportion of fathers in any group to the professional and managerial categories while the proportion of fathers in manual occupations was much higher than among the hospital administrators. The possibility of family background playing a part in the choice between hospital and community nursing merits consideration.

MARRIAGE

Female nurses have followed the trend of a rising marriage rate for women generally. This trend, and its implications for nursing, was a frequent topic in the early informal discussions which led to the decision to mount a study of women in nursing in the first instance.

Our sample was roughly equally divided into single and married, the latter including a small number, 4 per cent overall, of widowed and divorced/separated. It must be remembered, however, that the group of single nurses is inflated by the inclusion of all the hospital administrators, most of whom were unmarried.

TABLE 6/1
Percentage of single nurses in each 5 year age group

| | *Under 20* | | *20–24* | | *25–29* | | *30–34* | | *35–39* | |
	No.	%	No.	%	No.	%	No.	%	No.	%
Single nurses	58	100	83	70	32	42	20	29	31	34
Total=100%	58		118		77		68		91	

| | *40–44* | | *45–49* | | *50–54* | | *55–59* | | *60+* | |
	No.	%	No.	%	No.	%	No.	%	No.	%
Single nurses	30	39	35	41	32	51	40	57	4	44
Total=100%	76		86		63		70		9	

Table 6/1 shows the decrease of single nurses from 42 per cent of those aged 25–29, to 29 per cent in the 30–34 age group. However, beyond that age, right up to retirement age of sixty years, the proportion of single nurses increases again. It seems that the incidence of marriage diminishes from thirty-five years onward. As far as our sample is concerned, higher marriage rate is not reflected in lower marriage age. All the nurses under twenty years of age were single and so were 70 per cent of the 20–24 age group. This presents a striking contrast to the national statistics[1] on marriage, as in 1970 just under 60 per cent of spinsters had got married by the age of twenty-five, and in 1972 the average woman's age at marriage was twenty-two years and eight months. This discrepancy cannot be entirely explained by nurses postponing marriage until the completion of training, as most of them

[1] Central Statistical Office, (1972 and 1974) *Social Trends* Nos. 3 and 5, HMSO, London.

would be qualified by the age of twenty-two. Curiously enough 36 of the older nurses had married before they were twenty years old.

Differences in marital status between designations were alluded to in Chapter 5.

Most student and pupil nurses were unmarried, the exceptions being mainly post-basic students and those entering the profession late.

Administrators and health visitors were normally single whereas the majority of enrolled nurses and district nurses were married. In this study only 19 per cent of staff nurses were single, contrasting sharply with a survey undertaken twenty years ago when 60 per cent of staff nurses were single.[2] Relationships between marital status, designation and field of work are delicate and complex. One must consider for example, whether hospital administrators and health visitors are so career orientated that they do not seek marriage or whether they build up a career as an alternative. Our data show in Table 6/2 that the modal age of marriage for administrators was 26–29 years and for all other groups, including health visitors, it was 21–25 years. As administrative and health visiting careers do not often

TABLE 6/2
Age at marriage by designation

		Age Groups*						
	under 21	21–25	26–29	30–39	40–49	50–59	60 and over	**Total**
Administrators	0	8	11	9	3	0	0	31
Sisters/teachers	4	32	8	6	1	0	0	51
Staff nurses/ midwives	9	70	14	3	0	0	0	96
Enrolled nurses	29	26	4	3	1	0	0	63
Students	7	5	1	0	0	0	0	13
Pupils	10	4	0	0	0	0	0	14
District nurses	3	19	10	8	1	0	0	41
Health visitors	0	6	3	1	1	0	0	11
Other community nurses	0	13	12	5	0	1	0	31

* The age groups are deliberately chosen to emphasise the marriage pattern

become fully determined below these ages it may be that the second of the above alternatives apply, that is to say, women who remain single create a career for themselves.

In view of the possible influence of marriage on a woman's career, the timing of marriage and child-bearing in relation to that career is of importance. Of the married nurses in this study, just over three-quarters had married after completion of basic training and 15 per cent had commenced training as married women. It is relevant to note that 29 of the 53 respondents who had married before commencing

[2] The Dan Mason Nursing Research Committee, (1960) *The Work, Responsibilities and the Status of the Staff Nurse*, The Dan Mason Nursing Research Committee of the National Florence Nightingale Memorial Committee of Great Britain and Northern Ireland, London.

their basic training were either enrolled nurses or pupils, whereas only 1 in 10 of the nurses who had married after qualification were enrolled nurses. This significant difference suggests that married women are more likely to embark on training for the Roll than for the Register of Nurses. It may be that the shorter training period for the Roll is the attraction or that these women, though wanting to be nurses, are less concerned about career advancement. It is clear that for some of these women the course for enrolment was also more appropriate as its prerequisite qualifications were less demanding.

Marriage before training may mean early marriage, late entry into nursing, or both. Although the married entrants into nursing in this study were a minority group, it is worthy of note that they were not only more likely to work full time but also less likely to interrupt their service. They, therefore, form a stable potential work force; yet one still hears of reluctance to accept married women for nurse training in some areas.

It is appropriate here to draw attention to the intricate way in which a woman must make her career and her family commitments compatible. While married women in their fifties were likely to say that they had taken a major break from service simply because they had married, marriage alone is no longer so likely to lead to an interruption of service. The main family reason for young women ceasing employment nowadays is having children. However, it is possible that nurses who have married young will be deterred from taking further training, which is usually only possible on a full-time basis. Lack of further qualifications would then make it more difficult for them to enter community nursing or to ascend in the hospital hierarchy. Thus, a career can be thwarted even without a total break from service.

Compatibility between a woman's home commitments and career often involves compatibility between her job and that of her husband. It may be that there is a need for their working time to be opposite so that one of the partners can take responsibility for home commitments. Alternatively, it may be desirable for their working time to be similar so that husband and wife can have free time together. For these reasons each nurse was asked how her husband's job fitted in with her own and also what her husband felt about her employment in nursing.* Most replied that the jobs fitted together quite well or very well, but 12 per cent found it difficult. If the husband were a policeman, for instance, it could cause problems. One policeman's wife said:

> 'Well it doesn't fit. A policeman's work doesn't fit in with anything. He works shifts. Sometimes it fits, sometimes it doesn't.'

However, she emphasised that despite the inconvenience he gave her great support in her career pursuit.

Just over half the wives said that they thought their husbands were happy for them to be working and a further 8 per cent added comments to the effect that the husband was aware that the wife was happy working in nursing. However, 13 per

---

* Question 78. How does his job fit in with yours?
   Question 79. What does your husband feel about you nursing?

cent of the husbands were reported to have expressed objections; 5 per cent did not like the wife working at all, slightly fewer had objected at first but felt better about it now, and the same number were not pleased with the wife's current job. Maybe recruitment drives should be directed to husbands as well.

The importance of the husband's job to the wife's employment in nursing has already been mentioned. However, it is not only the compatibility of their jobs in terms of working hours which is of relevance. The husband's job determines to a large extent the social and economic circumstances of the family and therefore probably influences a decision about the wife working at all. The husband's occupation also largely determines the social class of the family. All the married nurses, including those widowed or divorced, were asked about their husband's occupation, which was again coded according to the classification in Appendix 2.

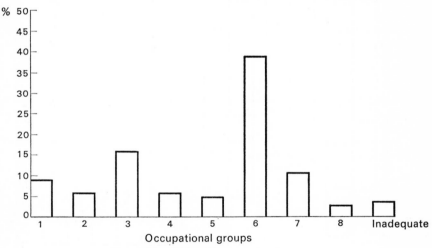

Figure 6/3   Husbands' occupational groups.

Figure 6/3 shows the distribution of husbands among occupational groups and Figure 6/4 the shift into 'white collar jobs' between the fathers and the husbands.

Staff nurses/midwives had the highest proportion of husbands representing the entire range of occupations. Relatively few administrators were married, but only a quarter of their husbands were in manual occupations against half who were in the 'middle class' occupations—grades 1, 2 and 3. While administrators did not differ from sisters/teachers in terms of their father's occupations, the occupations of their husbands did differ. A smaller proportion of the sisters'/teachers' husbands were in grades 1, 2 and 3, while nearly a half were in manual occupations. Thus the administrators' husbands had higher grade occupations than those of the sisters/teachers, the latter being similar to those of the staff nurses/midwives. Although there are differences between designations among community nurses, notably the very low marriage rate among health visitors, it is convenient to consider community nurses as a single group for this part of the analysis. Taking all the

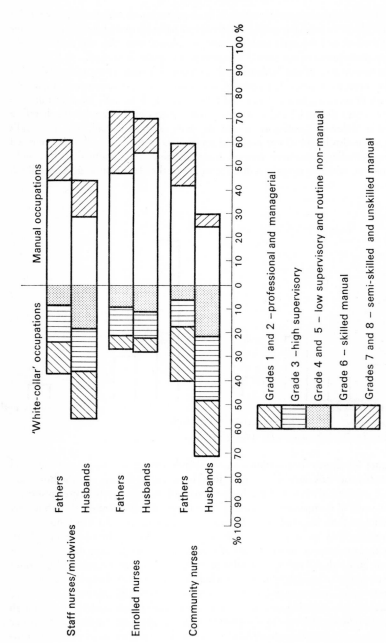

Figure 6/4   Occupational shift between generations.

husbands of non-administrative community workers together, half were in grade 1, 2 and 3 occupations—a distinctly higher proportion than the husbands of hospital staff other than administrators.

In any interpretation of these patterns, the age structure of the different designations must be borne in mind. As discussed in Chapter 5, the administrators and the community nurses were mostly over forty years old. Sisters and staff nurses are likely to be younger, and many of their husbands may move into higher grade posts in the future.

Upward occupational mobility seems unlikely among the husbands of enrolled nurses, many of whom are in middle life. There is little difference between the occupational patterns of the fathers and husbands of enrolled nurses. As shown in Figure 6/4 there is no shift from manual into non-manual occupations between the generations. The only shift is out of unskilled and semi-skilled work into skilled employment. In contrast, among all grades of registered nurses there is a substantial shift between the occupations of the fathers and of the husbands. This is especially striking among the community nurses, where 60 per cent of the fathers had manual occupations compared with only 30 per cent of the husbands.

Eighteen respondents were married to male nurses, 1 of the husbands had recently been appointed a Principal Nursing Officer. Several of these nurses had been encouraged to train by their husbands. Six husbands were doctors and 5 were in allied medical occupations.

HOUSEHOLDS AND FAMILY STRUCTURE

The type and size of a household can be expected to have a bearing on a woman's work outside the home. Both single and married women may have home commitments which play a part in the organisation of their lives. An attempt was made in this study to analyse nurses' households in some detail. However, the classification of household types presented a large number of problems because of the many different possible patterns. A scheme with 14 categories proved totally inadequate and even the 40 categories eventually coded, did not make provision for all possibilities. The coding frame was based on four main groups of households with sub-divisions within each of them. The groups were:

(i) respondents living in a nurses' home,
(ii) 'one generation' households, which were predominantly man and wife or all female,
(iii) 'two generation' households, in which the respondent could be either mother or daughter,
(iv) 'three generation' households, in which the respondent was usually the mother or far less frequently the grand-daughter: 1 respondent in the study was of the grandmother generation in such a household.

The sub-divisions within the above groups related to the age and sex composition of the household. Adults over the age of sixty years were distinguished from younger adults, and children were separated into two categories, those below the age of five years, and those between five and fifteen years. A major difficulty in the classification was presented by those households which departed from the basic patterns of the nuclear family. In only a few of these were the people in the household unrelated: the nurses did not have lodgers, but a small number were lodging and eating with the landlady and her family. There were many other households in which the relationships varied from the direct generations pattern. These included, for example, a married nurse in whose household her older sister was living and, alternatively, a single nurse living with her married sister and family. There were several households containing older generation aunts and uncles, and some containing nephews and nieces.

The purpose of collecting this type of information was not only to provide material for sociological comparisons but also, more importantly, to establish home commitments with which female nurses may have to cope. Such commitments may consist of children or of dependent adults.

Of the 320 married respondents, 121 lived with their husband, no children or other people sharing the household. These couples include those who were childless as well as those whose children were not living at home. Of the 169 respondents who had children under the age of fifteen living with them, 75 had one child, 58 had 2 children, 29 had 3 and 7 had 4 children who were not yet fifteen. Twenty-five of these two generation households consisted of a nurse, her husband and children of mixed ages, at least one being under fifteen, and at least one over that age. However, children below school age are bound to be more demanding of a mother's time than those in safe-keeping during school hours.

Fifty-seven respondents had at least 1 child under the age of five years but only 4 nurses had 2; understandably these 4 nurses worked part time. A small number of families included a seriously handicapped child.

Although the 'two generation' household was by far the most common type for all nurses who had young children, about a dozen married couples, whose children were all under fifteen years of age, also had one or more of their own parents sharing their home. Whilst this is a small minority, the proportion being about 1 in 10, it may be of great relevance to these individuals. An able-bodied grandmother may release a young mother so that she is able to work. Only 9 respondents had children less than two years old, and 3 of them had a grandmother in the household. Two households consisted of a grandmother, a married nurse with her husband and children of mixed ages.

SINGLE PARENT FAMILIES

The sample included 24 single parent families, but only in the case of some of the unmarried, separated and divorced were there children under the age of fifteen. This may be partially explained by the fact that the widows were generally older than the others.

Of the single parents with children under the age of fifteen, 8 mothers lived alone with the children, 6 were supported by being in a three-generation household, and 1 nurse had left the child with her mother and was temporarily living in a nurses' home. Some of the mothers had been obliged to return to full-time working, even though the children were under school age. One nurse with young children put it thus:

'The way things have happened I've literally been left with the baby to hold ... if I hadn't had my training I might have been in a sorry plight.'

The widows in the survey were in a more fortunate position than the others in the single parent group, in that none of them had children under fifteen, although 6 still had their children living with them.

TABLE 6/3
Household type of unmarried nurses

Age group	Total	Nurses' home	Women sharing	Two generations family home	Three generations family home	Living alone	Other
Under 20	58	27	4	22	3	0	2
20–29	115	42	21	36	3	10	3
30–39	51	5	6	24	2	12	2
40–49	65	3	5	30	0	26	1
50+	76	2	15	14	0	43	2
Total	365	79	51	126	8	91	10

LIVING WITH OLDER/DEPENDENT RELATIVES

A large number of the younger nurses were living at home with their parents and often their siblings and sometimes their grandparents or other relations. Nearly half the nurses under twenty, about a third of the single nurses in their twenties and half the single nurses in their thirties lived in the family home.

Although some nurses under forty had some relations over sixty years old, the problem of elderly dependants is likely to bear more frequently upon the over forties and more heavily upon the single nurse. Almost half of the 65 single nurses in their forties were living with older generation relations, 4 with both parents, 5 with their fathers, 2 with elderly aunts and the largest number, 17, with their mothers. The nurses aged fifty and over had fewer surviving parents, but these were likely to be increasingly dependent. Nine single nurses of this age lived with their mothers and 3 lived with both parents.* In several cases the elderly relatives were over eighty-five years of age.

Not all the respondents with responsibilities for adult relatives were single; a small number of married nurses had husbands who were, or had been, unwell for long periods. Some married nurses also had commitments to parents-in-law, as well as to their parents.

Unmarried nurses frequently mentioned responsibilities to the older generation. One nurse aptly expressed the rationale implied by others:

'To be single and a nurse makes one the obvious choice when one of the family needs nursing.'

---

* The problem of the single woman and her dependants has had some attention in recent years. An organisation was established in 1965 to look after the interests of such people: The National Council for the Single Woman and Her Dependants, 166, Victoria Street, London, S.W.1.

Thus, parents, grandparents, aunts and uncles were quoted as causing concern, whether they lived together with the respondent, in the same neighbourhood, or elsewhere. Some respondents had had to delay starting to train, others had been obliged to work part time or break their service. A district nurse in her fifties had been unable to start training until she was twenty-nine and later had to take a break of several years in order to look after her mother. She commented:

'I wish I hadn't had a break at all, but home commitments come before anything else, I think.'

She had returned to work after her mother's death, when she was in her early forties. Another older nurse said:

'I had a father-in-law to look after—that's what held me back.'

She had been working part time, and would have liked to work full time. Others found it necessary to change jobs in order to meet family needs. Some nurses had come back from abroad because of the increasing frailty of their parents. An administrator foresaw that she might have to leave her job. Reflecting on career plans, she said:

'This depends on my parents' health—they're on the west coast—I may have to go back.'

Another single respondent in her early forties had recently become a health visitor instead of combining health visiting and district nursing; she felt her new job was less satisfying but made it easier to meet her home ties, which she did not specify:

'All my free time is taken up with my family.'

In discussing the re-recruitment of qualified nurses* one respondent recognised the need for help with such problems, saying:

'Help at home for the old people they look after—there are one or two who can't come because of elderly mums and dads.'

Sometimes, the relation who needed help lived with the respondent. In response to a question about whether special arrangements had to be made to make work outside the home possible,** a married enrolled nurse in her forties said:

'Only if my mother is ill; I then make arrangements as they crop up. The hospital gave me special leave on one occasion, I've changed holidays and once I got a woman to come in.'

Another married enrolled nurse who had 2 young children said:

'Mother lives next door—she doesn't keep very well.'

A single nurse in her fifties took care of two old aunts who lived in an adjacent flat; one was in hospital at the time of the interview. A considerable number of

---

* *Question 61.* Are there any suggestions you would like to make other than those on the card? (See p. 81 for preceding question.)

** *Question 84.* Do you have to make any particular arrangements to enable you to go out to work or not?

respondents referred to relations whom they helped and who evidently lived in the neighbourhood. A few mentioned people who had recently died. It is apparent that many respondents gave a lot of time and care to older relations both inside and outside their own home. The financial relationships were not explored, but one unmarried sister said that while she had no one dependent on her for physical care, someone was financially dependent on her. A senior nursing officer lived with her invalid mother whom she probably supported financially as well as physically. She would have liked to receive overtime pay:

'As you go up on the scale you're not really as well off as you seem. The nurses get overtime for week-ends and for night duty. We don't get this.'

She commented also:

'I have very little social life. I find it difficult to get someone to look after my mother.'

She had to employ help to enable her to go out to work. Seven respondents reported that they arranged help for the care of relations other than children. Several foresaw that there would be difficulty sooner or later. Thus, a single district nurse of forty-two years of age living with her eighty year old mother and two brothers said:

'My mother took a stroke over a year ago. I had to arrange for a neighbour to come in. Recently she took another stroke and I have to arrange for someone to be there all the time.'

In a study of women in nursing the implications of female longevity are clearly relevant. Women tend to outlive their husbands and the nursing of these elderly women, much of it being personal intimate care, is most appropriately given by another woman. Obviously if that younger woman is a nurse, she will be, as a previous respondent commented, particularly in demand.

In society at large, when no daughter or other female relatives are available, institutional care of the elderly is resorted to. Paradoxically, it is possible that women may not be readily available to nurse in such institutions precisely because their own elderly relatives claim priority on them. A married Unit Nursing Officer said:

'My mother is a geriatric patient in the hospital. If she were not a patient in the hospital I could not work.'

Other households identified and analysed were single nurses' households, all women households, 'lone' nurse's households and nurses' homes. The data tend to suggest that the older a single nurse is, the less likely she is to be resident in a nurses' home, and the more likely she is to be living entirely alone. 'All women' households tend to be those of friends sharing a flat, or, less frequently, those of sisters.

ARRANGEMENTS FOR CHILDREN
Necessary arrangements for the care of children have implications for the choice of working hours, for family income, for social life and, in general, for the way in

which the family is organised. As alluded to earlier, some married couples choose opposite working times, thereby obviating the need for someone else to help with the care of young children. Others have relatives or friends, some have paid help and occasionally creches or nurseries are available.

This study showed that in households where there were dependent children, their care was frequently ensured by inter-locking the working hours of the mother and father. The obvious method is for the mother of young children to choose to nurse at night or at week-ends, knowing her husband is at home. For instance, a staff nurse married to a charge nurse, with a child of two years of age, worked three nights a week, although she said that she did not like night duty at all, but had to work when he was off duty. Another staff nurse who had 2 children under five years of age worked three nights a week and was luckier in that she, at least, liked night duty. A staff nurse with children under fifteen chose to work on Friday and Saturday nights although it was not financially necessary to do so.

While the children's needs are probably adequately met by such 'Cox and Box' arrangements, the companionship between man and wife must be affected. A full-time district nurse with children aged seven and four worked mostly mornings while her children were in school, but also evenings and week-ends when her husband was at home; she said:

'He sort of says sometimes "Oh, you're never in" and I say "Oh well—it's the job".'

Grandmothers, aunts and other relatives acted as child minders in a number of cases.

Twenty nurses reported that they had someone other than a relative to help look after the children; of these 5 stated that the help was paid.

A separated mother worked part-time, mornings only, as a district nurse; her two girls aged five and three years went to a paid baby-sitter's house. Another separated mother of two primary school children said she paid somebody to look after them when they came home from school and during the holidays. One family paid a woman to come in at 7.30 a.m. before the husband left home and to stay until the wife arrived home after night duty at about 9.00 a.m. In another instance the help was probably paid but this was not explicitly stated. A night sister married to a police constable, both in their late thirties, had 4 children aged nine to fourteen; her work and his shifts did not fit well; but she coped:

'I have a baby-sitter who stays each night I am working—she's an O.A.P.'

Friends or neighbours who helped out were probably not paid. An unmarried mother said she had a neighbour who minded the child during school holidays and the grandmother, who lived with her, helped usually after school hours. A full-time district nurse said:

'I have to have an emergency stand-by, my girl friend helps out.'

Five out of the 20 nurses who reported having help were women without husbands (2 unmarried, 3 separated/divorced). Two of the 5 mothers whose children went to a day nursery were also unmarried. Single-parent families may have to find non-family help relatively more often, even though some had obtained support and help from relatives.

Thirty-one respondents described how their children were looked after by relations—usually relations who were not living in the household. Relations, other than the husband, who were resident, could allow a mother to return to work. This, for example, was clearly the case in one family where a deliberate decision to include an aunt in the household had been taken:

'My husband's aunt stays—it was an arrangement we came to.'

Most frequently a grandmother in the district helped to mind children out of school hours. Often she lived with them or conveniently near, but a few lived at some distance and complicated travel arrangements were necessary. Daytime care was the more usual arrangement, but some families had help to cover night duty. An enrolled nurse of twenty-two whose husband was an unskilled labourer had a son of twenty months—she had returned to work three nights a week when he was six months old by arranging for the baby to stay with relatives on the nights when she was working, as her husband started work early. The widowed mother of a girl of seventeen said:

'When I'm on night duty my daughter stays with my mother.'

Many of the relations probably helped out without needing any recompense whether in services or money, but sometimes there was a complicated mutual help relationship. One community nurse said she 'looked after' her mother and uncle and paid for help in their house, while they took charge of her eight year old child after school and during holidays.

Many community nurses fitted in their work round their family commitments. School nursing is an easy solution, as working hours coincide with school hours. A district nurse working near her home can often fit in the needs of growing children fairly easily, especially if she works part time. For instance, a district nurse said she had sometimes taken her children on her rounds, in the car, when they were younger—now that they were older she worked full time:

'This suits me so well—having a family. Popping in in the passing to see that everything is all right.'

Another respondent, who had teenage children, had recently decided to leave a maternity hospital for a full-time triple duty job:

'Well, you see I really changed because the hours suit my family commitments. My great love is midwifery and on district there's virtually no midwifery.'

None-the-less one full-time district nurse with boys ten and nine years of age was planning to give up work:

'I feel my children need a bit more time.'

A full-time domiciliary midwife who said she didn't mind going out at night because:

'I have school children and they don't know I'm away.'

also said:

'My one strong point is against working with children under school age. I think the child is deprived. I've seen it often.'

Several others echoed this sentiment.

This attitude accords with the reluctance of community nursing management (for other reasons) to employ nurses with young children. It is probably not too surprising that community nurses, particularly health visitors, seemed more aware of a danger of deprivation, although this study does not pretend to have explored it. However, the health visitors in the national study 'Use or Abuse'[3] were also found to have significantly longer breaks than other nurses, which suggests that they may wish to devote more time to their young children. The apparent reluctance of employing authorities to employ health visitors on a part-time basis may have been a contributory cause as it meant 'all or nothing'. Of the 57 respondents in this study who had a child under five years of age, two-thirds worked part time and the remainder represented several examples of financial pressure. The examples above are presented to show some of the complexity of arrangements, many of them financially costly, which some nurses with young children have to make. It is understandable, therefore, as Chapter 7 shows, that flexible working hours and facilities for children were the major incentives which nurses considered important in bringing inactive nurses back to the profession.

INCOME

A consideration of income and other conditions of service is particularly relevant to a study of women in nursing.

If a woman is single she has to support herself and possibly also dependent relatives. Married nurses who have earning husbands might work in nursing for interest only or in order to supplement the family income. For those who nurse for interest alone, hours and conditions of service can be expected to be of great importance. For example, a married woman whose husband's income is adqeuate for the needs of the family is likely to be dissatisfied with a job which prevents her from having free time with him and the family. For those who nurse for financial reasons it is important that the income is acceptable, even though interest in the work may also play a major part. As one nurse put it:

'Let's face it, I have to work and obviously I want to use my training. It would be a shame if I had to do something quite different simply because it is better paid, but we need as much money as we can get.'

Even nurses can, of course, become dissatisfied when they see other people's earning power exceeding their own. A health visitor in her forties said:

'I really think that as salaries are, you don't get very much for an awful lot of work and study. A girl in a factory with no qualifications can earn more than

[3] Hockey, L., (1972) *Use or Abuse? A Study of the state enrolled nurse in the local authority nursing services*, Queen's Institute of District Nursing, London.

me with 22 years experience and all my certificates. We are not paid for our certificates and with all our study we can end up lower paid than people with fewer certificates.'

Although such explicit dissatisfaction was rare and sometimes associated with special personal circumstances, income is an important consideration for most people, whether they are nurses or not.

In the past, nurses were made to feel that their vocational incentive should out-weigh the financial consideration. This was one of the reasons why the respondents were given the opportunity to give their views without themselves appearing to be primarily occupied with money.

They were asked to select from a list three incentives which would encourage qualified nurses to return to nursing*. Higher salaries were chosen by 28 per cent, a sizeable, but not the largest, group. It was exceeded significantly by the group of 80 per cent who considered flexible working hours and that of 66 per cent who felt that the provision of child care facilities were the most important issues. In fact, the answer to this multiple choice question appeared to provide a good indicator of respondents' own feelings on the topic under discussion, although they answered it in relation to inactive nurses. The more direct questions, however, elicited enough information to show that income was an important, though not the only, factor of concern to nurses. Some respondents expressed total satisfaction with their pay and conditions of service:

'. . . the salary is right, the hours are right and you meet a cross section of the community as well.'

Others thought that, although professional life had been difficult for them, it looked more hopeful for the new generation of nurses. A district nurse in her forties said:

'I find that the student nurse of today has a great many opportunities open for her—salaries are good, holidays are good, everything looks good for her.'

Several respondents expressed similar sentiments and talked about the 'lucky young things of today to get so much.'

---

* *Question 60.* As you know there are thousands of qualified nurses in the country who are no longer nursing for various reasons. What do you think would encourage them to return to nursing?

Perhaps you could tell me which three on this list you consider to be the most important?

Back to nursing courses	01	01
Help with transport	02	02
Higher salaries	03	03
Proper changing and rest rooms	04	04
Opportunities for promotion	05	05
Facilities for further qualification	06	06
Extra payment for night and/or weekend work	07	07
Creches or nurseries	08	08
Flexibility of working hours to meet family commitments	09	09
Opportunities to specialise	10	10
None of these	00	00

Code three most important in left hand column and single most important in right hand column

W.N.—6

Comparison between the generations possibly make such statements justifiable. Some of the older nurses in the study trained 25 years ago and the newspaper extract* below makes their point abundantly clear:

'PAYMENT OF NURSES
In England and Wales some 51,000 hospital beds are unoccupied through lack of nurses. To bring these beds back into use about 40,000 more nurses are needed. The dearth of nurses, though it was serious before the war, has become acute in the past ten years.

Nurses have always been ill-paid, but in the last eighteen months an attempt has been made to set their salaries at last on a realistic basis. Ward sisters, who previously received a maximum of about £260 a year, including board, now get a maximum of £500, from which £120 is deducted for those who are resident. At the other end of the scale the first-year student nurse, who from July 5th, 1948, received £70 and free board (then valued at £75), is now given £200, from which £100 is deducted for board. At first sight this would seem to represent an increase, but as a correspondent today points out, the net sum after deduction of income-tax on the whole £200, and other unavoidable expenses . . . is less than before.

From *The Times* of Tuesday, September 6, 1949.'

As is apparent from Chapter 7, a considerable number of nurses returned to work after a break because of the need for extra income. A small number of interviews gave a sense of deep financial anxiety. For instance, a nurse with an invalid husband had returned to work full time after the birth of her daughter, although she did not particularly wish to return. A few married respondents appeared to be the principal wage earner in the family. Their husbands were students, invalids, retired on a small pension or had lost their jobs. A nurse may earn more than her husband if he is in a low income occupation. A staff nurse working 30 hours a week said that her husband was bitter because she made more money than he did. Throughout the interview respondents were given direct and indirect opportunities to express financial concern. For example, the nurses were asked if they worked overtime and if they were paid for it. The topic was further explored by asking if they would prefer to be paid for overtime or be given free time in lieu. Those who did not already work more than their official hours were asked if they would like the opportunity to work overtime for pay or not.** Most respondents said that they worked more hours than they needed to but this was usually irregular and unofficial. Overtime pay for such time did not seem as popular as an atmosphere of flexibility with 'give and take' on both sides. A young staff nurse said:

'I don't think anyone minds staying a bit longer when we are busy. It balances out and this is a better system than clocking in and out.'

Thus, in a way, nurses wanted time in lieu but they did not want it made formal and official. The general 'cri de coeur' seemed to be for more flexibility and less officialdom.

Forty-seven respondents said that they would like to work overtime for more pay, more than half of them being single. It was this unmarried group who gave the need for extra money as their reason for wanting to work paid overtime.

---

* '25 years ago', (1974) *Times*, 6th September, London.
** *Question 31.* Would you like the opportunity to work overtime for pay or not?

Clearly, need for money is subjective. For some people, modern gadgets and holidays are needs, others consider them luxuries; of the married nurses who wanted to earn more money some said that they wanted it for 'extras'. Ironically, those married women who would have liked to work overtime for pay because they really needed the money for the support of dependants, would have had little time to spare to work extra hours as their dependants kept them busy.

Apart from money for necessities and for luxuries, a small number of respondents mentioned the need for money to provide help with the household whether for cleaning or for the care of children and other dependants. A small number of nurses said that they earned very little more than they paid out for such help in the house, but they preferred to go out to work. One community nurse had carefully worked out her optimum hours to 'break even'. Travelling expenses was another item which had to be set against income. If relatives and friends had not been available, more paid help would have been needed. Only 5 nurses said that they used creches or nurseries. Taken in conjunction with the high proportion of nurses who considered that creches and nurseries would be an important inducement in bringing back inactive nurses to the service, there seems to be a case for more such facilities. The interviews for this study were undertaken a year before the new salary structure for nurses was announced;[4] this must, undoubtedly, help the many respondents who expressed financial problems and for whom the need for an income from their work was paramount.

HOUSING

Where people live is of great importance to them and their families. Nursing is one of the types of employment where housing provisions may sometimes be made. Such provision may be in the form of a nurses' home, tied housing which goes with the job, or possibly priority consideration for a council house, or occasionally for a mortgage. Table 6/4 shows the type of accommodation occupied by the various groups of respondents.

As can be seen from Table 6/4 the sisters/teachers had the largest proportion of respondents, 61 per cent, in privately owned houses; they were followed by administrators and community nurses. Smaller proportions of staff nurses/midwives and enrolled nurses had privately owned accommodation. However, especially among single nurses, the houses often belonged to parents or other relations and not to the respondent. Whilst 28 per cent of the total sample of respondents lived in council housing, 48 per cent of enrolled nurses did so. The latter was the only group of qualified nurses who were more likely to live in council houses than in private housing. Fourteen per cent of the respondents lived in rented property, including houses tied to the husband's job. Houses provided by the employing authority as tied housing were used by only 7 per cent of respondents who were mainly administrators and community nurses, mostly single and who tended to be forty years of age or older.

---

[4] Department of Health and Social Security, (1974) *Report of the Committee of Inquiry into the Pay and Related Conditions of Service of Nurses and Midwives* (Chairman: The Rt. Hon. The Earl of Halsbury, FRS), HMSO, London.

The other form of accommodation provision for nurses is nurses' homes. This was taken advantage of by 11 per cent of our respondents, of whom just over half were students and roughly 1-in-7 were pupils. Although there was no compulsion in any of the hospital groups for either students or pupils to be resident, unmarried nurses are usually encouraged to 'live in' at least during the first year of training. No doubt the provision of residential accommodation during the training period

TABLE 6/4
Type of accommodation by designation

Designation	Privately owned flat/ house	Council flat/ house	Rented* flat/ house	Tied home	Nurses' home	Other	Total
Administrators	55	25	12	23	7	1	123
Sisters/teachers	64	16	20	1	3	1	105
Staff nurses/ midwives	46	36	27	2	6	2	119
Enrolled nurses	24	43	11	3	7	1	89
Students	8	21	16	C	46	3	94
Pupils	7	26	6	0	12	0	51
District nurses	22	17	5	4	0	0	48
Health visitors	19	9	4	4	0	3	39
Other community nurses	25	10	1	14	0	0	50
Total	270	203	102	51	81	11	718

* Includes houses tied to husband's job—e.g. police house, manse.

is of value particularly for young women who have no family home nearby. Some students enjoyed it, others 'suffered it' and several complained. For example, one student in her third year remarked:

'It's fun living in although we often grumble, we really have everything we need and it's a lot cheaper than living out.'

One of the more recent entrants into nursing did not share that view, she said:

'Well, I suppose it's good to have a place to live in but it would be a lot nicer to have a flat outside.'

A qualified resident nurse voiced the opinion of quite a number when she said:

'It could be a lot better, so many things are shabby, kettles and things don't work, there are lots of rules and really it isn't all that cheap for what one gets.'

Eight nurses lived in lodgings, two in convents and one young married staff nurse lived in a caravan on the family farm.

The frequent use of rented accommodation by nurses in their twenties living in groups or when newly married, is clearly important.

Half the nurses aged thirty years and over lived in privately owned housing and 28 per cent in council housing; in one area at least, it was policy to make council housing available for nurses; such policies are discussed in Chapter 4. The remaining nurses aged thirty and over lived mostly in rented houses, in houses tied to their husband's work and in houses tied to the respondent's job. Whereas 52 per cent of the married nurses lived in privately owned homes, only 20 per cent of single nurses aged twenty and over did so; a proportion of these were living in their parents' home or in the home of other relations.

The single nurse is significantly less likely to own her home than a married nurse of similar age; 56 per cent of married nurses aged thirty years and over lived in privately owned houses as against 41 per cent of single nurses of the same age group. Many factors must account for this. First, it must be remembered that Building Societies were, until recently, reluctant to provide mortgages for single women. It is, therefore, relevant to note that among the older single nurses there was a strong likelihood of living in a tied house, as shown in Table 6/3. In this context it should be remembered that administrators, many of whom are single, are over-represented in the sample. The provision of tied housing for nurses is briefly discussed from the management point of view in Chapter 4. As in the wider sense tied housing is a topical political issue, especially in relation to farm workers, some of the comments of nurses living in tied houses are of interest. Tied housing did seem to be very much of a 'mixed blessing'. A senior nursing officer said of the flats in one of the largest hospitals:

'I think they're very substandard. The lavatory opens immediately off from the kitchenette . . . the plumbing is archaic. When new curtains were required I was given no choice. There's no carpet on the stairs or main hall—nothing to reduce noise at all.'

but she also said:

'If I lived out I'd be moaning about my hours a darn sight more.'

The provision of housing for rural community nurses was useful in attracting younger staff:

'This is one of the reasons I came here—the housing was a great incentive.'

and:

'Accommodation is another reason for working here—few places offer accommodation for health visitors.'

But tying the job and the house too rigidly could be unfortunate—one respondent was told she could only have the job if she took the house, and had to sell her own house. Since both she and her husband were unwell this was a cause of anxiety and she said it made them feel insecure. It is widely recognised that coping with illness and approaching retirement is made more difficult when people live in tied houses, and several respondents touched on this anxiety.

There is currently an increasing shortage of rented accommodation, and the age group that this will particularly affect is that very important group of nurses who are in their twenties and working full time. In these circumstances there may be a growing demand from this age group for National Health Service accommodation.

However, if living in a nurses' home is a necessity rather than an option it is essential for its facilities to be acceptable. The degree of dissatisfaction voiced by the 132 respondents who were living in nurses' homes and tied housing and also by others who had recently moved out of such accommodation, must cause concern. Nurses' homes held 81 respondents of whom 80 per cent were under thirty years of age; these residents were the least satisfied with their housing. Their main complaints were social restrictions, inadequate facilities, noise and lack of privacy. Yet, the top managers whose views are presented in Chapter 4, considered the rules in nurses' homes to be minimal. It is possible that their idea of minimal rules is still too rigid for the younger generation. It is equally feasible that the residents in nurses' homes would always find some cause for complaint whereas they would not readily express dissatisfaction with low grade accommodation privately rented or owned. Tied houses and flats also came under criticism, usually for reasons of limited space and lack of facilities. Nurses' homes were considered to be 'redundant' by some respondents but used as an optional facility by others. Dissatisfaction decreased with age but so did the tendency to be resident. It is clearly desirable to provide the best possible accommodation for staff and to impose minimum restrictions so that legitimate causes for complaint are reduced. At the same time, it is worth noting that half the resident respondents expressed no dissatisfaction with the nurses' home.

TRAVEL TO WORK

There is an obvious relationship between housing and travelling. On the whole, people can be expected to consider the distance from their work in the choice of their home, a long journey to work being not only time consuming but also expensive.

In view of the general shortage of nurses it is usually possible for a nurse to find work almost anywhere; moreover, qualified nurses can normally remain at the same level in their professional career wherever they work. A single woman in nursing may seek accommodation near her preferred place of employment. If a privately owned home is not possible for one reason or another, she will attempt to rent or decide to be resident in a nurses' home or hostel. A married woman in nursing is likely to seek employment near her home, probably selected to suit her husband's place of work, and so tends to have less option. If she cannot find a nursing post near home she may decide not to work at all or to leave nursing for other work. In all cases, travelling time to work is an important factor. It reduces time available for other purposes and it does not attract payment, thus it is unproductive and unpopular.

The study, therefore, included a number of questions on travelling time, mode of transport and respondents' views on this topic. Tables 6/5a, b and c show details of travelling methods and times.

Fifteen per cent of staff nurses/midwives reported a journey of 31–45 minutes but very few staff nurses/midwives or sisters/teachers took longer than that. In contrast, 13 per cent of enrolled nurses and 14 per cent of pupils reported a journey of over 45 minutes. A relatively low proportion of enrolled nurses used cars and a relatively high proportion depended on buses. By all criteria pupil nurses had the most trouble with travel, faring distinctly worse than students. Thirty per cent of pupils took more than 30 minutes to get to work, 53 per cent used buses against 23 per cent of students. It was the enrolled nurses and pupils who suffered particularly from Sunday travel problems. Buses were the main cause for complaints about travelling. Eighty-six nurses, 12 per cent, considered that it took them too long to get to work and over a hundred, 15 per cent, had other more specific complaints about transport. Six per cent found the bus service generally poor and 7 per cent complained particularly of difficulty on Sundays when several respondents had to take taxis to get to work. Smaller numbers found problems with travel

TABLE 6/5a
Time for travel to work by designation

	15 mins or less No. %		16–30 mins No. %		31–45 mins No. %		46 mins or more No. %		Total =100% No.
Administrators	78	64	30	25	4	3	10	8	122
Sisters/teachers	59	56	28	26	13	12	6	6	106
Staff nurses/midwives	60	51	34	29	18	15	5	4	117
Enrolled nurses	40	45	28	31	9	10	12	13	89
Students	59	63	22	23	5	5	8	9	94
Pupils	25	49	11	22	8	16	7	14	51
District nurses*	39	81	7	15	2	4	0	0	48
Health visitors	25	64	10	26	3	8	1	3	39
Other community nurses*	43	86	5	10	1	2	1	2	50

* Many community fieldworkers worked from their homes.
Respondents who gave inadequate answers and/or those to whom the question was inapplicable are excluded from the totals.

at rush hours, evening or night-time. Slightly older nurses, those in their late thirties and forties, made less use of buses for getting to work and had a significantly shorter travel time. A substantial proportion of that age group lived at, or within walking distance of, their place of work. Nurses in their twenties were most likely to consider their journeys too long or to report transport problems. Twelve per cent of nurses in their twenties reported difficulty in getting to work on Sundays compared with 1 per cent of nurses in their forties. Ease or difficulty of travel will depend not only on the distance between the respondent's home and her place of work, but also on her financial situation. Since this survey was undertaken the cost of running a car has increased dramatically. Thus, transport is an additional problem, in particular for people in the younger age groups and lower grades, and, together with the housing shortage, may well add to the general unrest amongst nurses which became apparent as this report was being written.

More than a third of the community nurses worked from their homes. Most of these were district nurses or combined duty nurses; only 5 of the health visitors were home-based. Of the 92 community nurses who did not work directly from their home, 83 per cent were at their place of work within half an hour and none took longer than an hour. Sixteen community nurses went by bus to their base, and six walked there; none reported using a bicycle. A car was the mode of transport to work for 73 per cent, but sometimes this was a lift and the nurse did not herself drive a car. A few respondents did not go by car to their base, but then used a car on their rounds. The interview did not set out to explore what methods

TABLE 6/5b
Method of travel to work by designation

	No need to travel		Walk		Car		Bus		Hospital transport		Other		Total =100%
	No.	%	No.	%	No.	%	No.	%	No.	%	No.	%	No.
Administrators	25	20	15	12	59	48	17	14	1	1	5	4	122
Sisters/teachers	3	3	10	9	58	55	22	21	6	6	7	7	106
Staff nurses/ midwives	5	4	22	19	52	44	33	28	2	2	3	3	117
Enrolled nurses	4	4	20	22	26	29	31	35	4	4	4	4	89
Students	29	31	21	22	13	14	22	23	6	6	3	3	94
Pupils	10	20	6	12	5	10	27	53	3	6	0	0	51
District nurses	20	42	1	2	18	37	8	17	0	0	1	2	48
Health visitors	5	13	2	5	26	67	5	13	0	0	1	3	39
Other community nurses	28	56	3	6	16	32	3	6	0	0	0	0	50

Respondents who gave inadequate answers and/or those to whom the question was inapplicable are excluded from the totals.

of transport were used by community nurses for their work, but strong feelings about transport were spontaneously expressed at various points in the interview, especially by nurses who clearly did not use cars on their rounds.

All the interviewing schedules from one urban area in which few district nurses and health visitors worked from home were scrutinised for information on this point. In this area, 21 district nurses were interviewed; 3 of them were enrolled nurses. Two were working from home, 1 walked to base but used a car on her round, 7 went by bus and 11 went to work by car. Thus, about half seemed to use a car for their work; the 3 enrolled nurses used buses.

In response to a general question about working conditions,★ 1 registered nurse and 2 enrolled nurses made specific comments about travelling. The registered nurse in her twenties said:

★ *Question 67.* Is there anything at all that would make work easier or more enjoyable for you?

'I find that getting buses and walking for miles is a terrific waste of time—we could be helped greatly with more transport.'

while an enrolled nurse said:

'With all these group attachments you now don't have patients in areas—they're scattered all over and so you spend so much time travelling.'

All except 4 of the 19 health visitors in this area used cars. Two of these would have liked to use a car but one had not yet passed her driving test and the other could not afford to buy her own car because of difficult personal circumstances:

'With group attachments, those of us not attached get bigger districts as our numbers go down. No help is given to buy a car.'

Also, a health visitor in her late fifties saw a car as a necessity but did not wish to drive.

'It's becoming more difficult with bigger areas—that's more to do with group attachment—it's an excellent thing but I can't see the good of having to travel so much. Three or four health visitors visiting in one street is a fearful waste of time.'

Five out of the 11 domiciliary midwives in the survey worked in this district. All five worked from their homes but one said when asked if she had to make any special arrangements in order to go out to work:

'I bought a car.'

Similar comments were made by community staff working in the other urban area, but the transport situation appeared to be better in the rural areas where it was probably impossible to work without a car. A driving licence seemed to be an essential qualification for rural community nurses—certainly a few hospital

TABLE 6/5c
Method of travel to work by age groups

| Method of travel | Age Groups | | | | | | | | | | | |
| | Under 20 | | 20–29 | | 30–39 | | 40–49 | | 50+ | | Total | |
	No.	%	No.	%	No.	%	No.	%	No.	%	No.	%
No need to travel	19	33	30	16	23	14	30	19	27	19	129	18
Walk	11	19	42	22	11	7	21	13	14	10	99	14
Car	3	5	47	24	81	51	82	51	59	42	272	38
Bus	18	31	61	32	32	20	22	14	34	24	167	23
Hospital transport	6	10	2	1	8	5	3	2	3	2	22	3
Other	1	2	11	6	4	3	3	2	5	4	24	3
Total=100%	58		193		159		161		142		713	

Respondents who gave inadequate answers and/or those to whom the question was inapplicable are excluded from the totals.

nurses thought they were not qualified to work in the community because they could not drive.

Some of the community nurses who had cars referred to parking difficulties. In discussing what would encourage inactive qualified nurses to return to nursing, 10 per cent of the respondents, mostly enrolled nurses and district nurses, thought that help with transport would be useful.

Nine per cent of all the administrators considered that such help would be useful in this context but this group included none of the 7 community administrators. It may be that they felt less concerned than their hospital peers about transport as an incentive to recruitment in general: they experienced little difficulty in recruiting district nurses, the only group of community staff who might include enrolled nurses whose transport problems seemed the most serious.

SOCIAL LIFE

In 'round the clock' occupations some people have at times to work at what are conventionally called 'unsocial hours'. Nursing, being one of these occupations, imposes some constraints on the free time of some nurses.

Many female nurses who have home commitments in terms of husband, children or elderly relations, have already been shown to have their 'hands full'. Single nurses without domestic responsibilities may be particularly anxious to have a reasonable social life; in any event, it was considered pertinent to find out how the nurses felt about their ability to combine nursing with an acceptable social life. The question* was clearly understood to mean social activities outside the family circle, to which some people are, naturally, more inclined than others. The overwhelming majority, 86 per cent, said that they did have an acceptable social life; however, some found it difficult to engage in social activities. A student nurse aged twenty said:

'You don't get enough time for social life. You realise this before you come into nursing. You don't complain about it—it's a fact.'

Others echoed this sentiment, accepting a restriction of social life as part of the job. The irregularity of hours which a student experiences is not characteristic of all nursing jobs, and after qualification it is possible to choose a different type of job if this restriction is too irksome. Thus, while a full time triple duty nurse said:

'When you're on call 24 hours, apart from 8 days out of 28, you couldn't make definite social arrangements';

another respondent found she could have a better social life as a health visitor than when she was a district nurse. Therefore, a restricted social life might be characteristic of the job, but in many cases the respondent's personal circumstances might be the limiting factor. Family commitments often took up all the available time and energy.

Few student nurses reported heavy family responsibilities, yet 16 per cent said they were not able to have an acceptable social life. It was worse for pupil nurses

---

* *Question 85.* Are you able to combine nursing with an acceptable social life or not?

with 20 per cent finding social life inadequate. Pupil nurses were more likely to 'live out' and spend more time travelling than students, and a higher proportion were mature and had family commitments.

Whereas only 6 per cent of district nurses found their social activities restricted, a relatively high proportion of health visitors and other community nurses considered their social life unacceptable. As the number of health visitors is small, the influences of their individual circumstances on the total picture is marked. Five health visitors stated that they were unable to have an adequate social life; one was an unmarried mother living alone with her child. Another was using her spare time to do an Open University course. One single nurse with demanding family responsibilities had left district nursing for health visiting and, although she found her private life was better in consequence, she remarked that her free time was taken up with her family.

There remains a significant difference between the replies of the district nurses and of the other community nurses, although both groups contained many married nurses and had other similar characteristics. This difference may be attributable to the 'on call' responsibilities of some of the rural nurses and the domiciliary midwives. For example, one triple duty nurse described her social life as 'limited' because:

> 'If you're on call you can't go far away . . . it's very tying. If we want to go out during the week, it must be someone with a telephone.'

She was also on call at week-ends. All the same, many did not find this unduly restrictive. Studies of community nurses, undertaken nearly ten years ago, have drawn attention to their dissatisfaction with 'on call' arrangements.[5, 6]

Understandably, the combination of full-time work with substantial family responsibility leaves little opportunity for social life outside the family. The mother of 2 children aged nine and ten who was a full-time district nurse with no domestic help said:

> 'I think when you have finished work you're too tired.'

Another mother of 3 young children, twelve, six and four, who worked full time considered her social life inadequate because:

> 'I've got a family and they need my attention after I come in.'

However, a pupil nurse, whose household included 6 children from eleven to sixteen and whose journey to work took more than an hour, said she was able to have an acceptable social life because they were well organised; her comment was:

> 'We have a good routine, having automatic appliances helps a lot—we all pitch in together. We're all very busy studying just now. It all combines, if we want to go somewhere, that's it.'

---

[5] Carstairs, V., (1966) *Home Nursing in Scotland*, Scottish Health Service Study No. 2, Scottish Home and Health Department, Edinburgh.

[6] Hockey, L., (1966) *Feeling the Pulse—A Survey of District Nursing in Six Areas*, Queen's Institute of District Nursing, London.

About a tenth of nurses aged thirty and over said that they could not have an acceptable social life, whilst 14 per cent of those under twenty held that view, all of whom being learners. Learners cannot normally opt for part-time work if they find the combination of work and home duties too heavy and older learners were especially likely to have little time left for social activity. However, some nurses in all groups found the combination of job and home life worked well and did not appear to regret that their social life outside the home was limited or non-existent.

CHAPTER SEVEN
Career Patterns

There is no dearth of theories on career development[1] but it is generally agreed that careers have stages which provide a sequence of roles for the individual from the novice to the retired person. It is the sequence reflecting purposeful and predetermined development which distinguishes careers from occupations, although this distinctive feature may only be identified retrospectively.[2] Nursing provides a career structure with beginners entering as learners and purposefully working their way up a predetermined ladder; only a few nurses, however, reach the apex of the hierarchical pyramid.

Although the stages in the nursing career are fairly rigidly structured, entry into the profession, as well as method and speed of progression between stages, follow different patterns. Some nurses enter the profession straight from school and continue to nurse throughout their working lives, while others may have breaks from nursing for various reasons or enter the profession after a period of time working in other occupations.

OCCUPATIONAL CHOICE

Occupational choice may be the result of a process happening over a period of time, perhaps several years, during which a number of factors predispose the individual towards certain kinds of occupation or careers while limiting or prohibiting others.[3] The choice of an occupation is not free but tends to be determined by a number of factors outside the individual's control. Different types of personality are attracted by and suited to different kinds of occupation.[4] Values also have an important role to play in the choice of an occupation.[5, 6] They develop through the socialisation process which is influenced by social and economic factors. It has been argued that the choice of occupation does not always develop in this

[1] Osipow, S. H., (1968) *Theories of Career Development*, Appleton, New York.

[2] Fogarty, M. P., Rapoport, R. and Rapoport, R. N., (1971) *Sex, Career and Family*, PEP, George Allen and Unwin Ltd., London.

[3] Butler, J. R., (1968) *Occupational Choice*, Science Policy Studies, No. 2, HMSO, London.

[4] Roe, A., (1956) *The Psychology of Occupations*, John Wiley, New York.

[5] Rosenberg, M., (1957) *Occupations and Values*, Free Press, Glencoe.

[6] Ginsburg, E., et al., (1951) *Occupational Choice: an approach to a General Theory*, Columbia Press, New York.

way,[7], [8], [9], [10] but that it may be the result of sudden fortuitous events at crucial times, which lead to unplanned occupational choice. This type of explanation fails to take into account the fact that over a long period of time a number of choices are made, which as Katz and Martin[11] argue, may not be directly related to occupation but which may, nevertheless, determine the final decision as to the choice of occupation.

CHOICE OF NURSING CAREER

In this study each respondent was asked to give her reason for having chosen a nursing career.* Individuals cannot always recollect and identify past decisions and may find it difficult to recall how views and conditions were modified with time.[12] For these reasons responses to such retrospective enquiry may not be reliable and must be viewed in this awareness; a greater level of accuracy would have been achieved by a longitudinal prospective study of the period leading up to actual entry into nursing, which was not possible. The fact that 40 per cent of respondents had been nursing for at least twenty years accentuates the need for cautious interpretation of the data, retrospectively recalled.

Table 7/1 relates the respondents' present age to their reasons for choosing nursing. Responses have been grouped into the three main categories:

1 Those who said that they had always wanted to nurse—inherent interest.
2 Those who said that they had been influenced by some contact with nursing or stimulated by other people—developed interest.
3 Those who had chosen nursing as the best alternative at the time—best alternative.

The remainder included those who gave other diverse reasons or did not know.

In spite of the known difficulty of recall, only 6 per cent of respondents said that they did not know why they chose nursing. The largest group, 46 per cent, stated that they had always wanted to be a nurse, while 13 per cent said that they entered nursing because of a desire to meet and help people or because it was a vocation and satisfying.

'It's a thing I've always wanted to do, I liked looking after children and old folks.'

'From the time I was a child I've always wanted to be a nurse—it was my one aim in life.'

[7] McGuffin, S. J., (1958) Factors influencing the choice of careers by boys in two Belfast grammar schools, a summary in *British Journal of Educational Psychology*, Vol. 28, No. 2.

[8] Chown, S. H., (1958) The formation of occupational choice among grammar school pupils, *Occupational Psychology*, Vol. 32, No. 3, pp. 171–182.

[9] Roe, A., (1956) ibid.

[10] Rogoff, N., in Merton, R. K., et al., (1957) *The Student Physician*, Harvard University Press, Cambridge, Mass.

[11] Katz, F. E., and Martin, H. W., (1962) Career Choice Processes, *Social Forces*, Vol. 41, No. 2, pp. 149–154.

* *Question 52.* Why did you choose to become a nurse?

[12] Butler, J. R., (1968) *Occupational Choice*, Science Policy Studies, No. 2, HMSO, London.

Experience as a patient, experience as a nursing auxiliary, experience obtained in the war in direct contact with nursing and, alternatively, the influence of family and friends many of whom were in nursing or medical occupations, were given as reasons for entering nursing by 21 per cent of respondents.

'Firstly because I had an illness myself and had been a patient in hospital. It gave me an insight into hospital life and I chose to work in hospital after that.'

'I really wanted a job for my summer holidays before going back to do my Highers. Someone got me a job as an auxiliary—I liked it, so I thought I'd stay on and do my training. I didn't see how my Highers would benefit me.'

TABLE 7/1
Reasons by age for choosing nursing

	Field of Employment		Age					All Nurses
	Hospital %*	Community %*	Under 20 %*	20–29 %*	30–39 %*	40–49 %*	50+ %*	%*
Always wanted to be a nurse	45	49	49	48	50	45	38	46
Interested in people	14	10	14	17	11	11	12	13
Best alternative	33	27	39	33	32	29	33	32
Consumer, war or nursing experience and outside influence	19	27	14	13	19	27	31	21
Other or combined answer	7	5	0	4	6	11	6	6
Don't know	6	5	7	11	5	3	3	6
Number of nurses	567	144	57	191	155	161	141	705

* Total percentage greater than 100 is due to multiple answers.

For 13 per cent nursing was the best occupation available, or it was an alternative to an occupation such as teaching which the respondent would have preferred.*

'I don't know. I never had any life-long ambition to be a nurse. I took a job as a shorthand typist and got no satisfaction out of it. The nurses were coming in and out of this office and I decided nursing must be a worthwhile job and I'd have a go.'

and:

'I suppose—when I left school I was the eldest of four so I had to go where the money was. I saw an advert for part-time training so I thought I'd have a go at it.'

* Those who chose nursing as an alternative to medicine are not included in this number.

Six nurses said that they would have liked to study medicine and had chosen nursing as an acceptable alternative. The remainder, about 5 per cent, gave a variety of reasons for entering the profession including a desire to get away from home or to travel abroad. Analysis of the main reason for choosing nursing given by respondents showed that 80 per cent had made a positive choice of their desired career, 10 per cent had seen nursing as the best occupation for them; the remainder either gave other diverse reasons or did not know why they had entered nursing.

The frequently voiced view that a positive inclination towards nursing as a vocational career used to be stronger than it is now, would have been supported if a significantly higher proportion of older than younger nurses had made nursing the first career choice. The data tended to support the opposite view; of the nurses under fifty years, 48 per cent had chosen nursing as first preference against 38 per cent of their older colleagues. There was, however, a significantly greater tendency for older nurses to say that they had been positively influenced by direct contact with nursing or by friends or relations in the nursing or medical profession. In making any inference about the age factor in career choice, the fact that older age-groups included late entrants to the profession must not be overlooked.

The only difference of any significance between hospital and community nurses was that a larger proportion of the latter, 27 per cent, than of the former, 19 per cent, gave direct contact with nursing or influence of friends as the main reason for starting nursing. This difference might be accounted for by the fact that 90 per cent of the community nurses were at least thirty years old. The significance of the age factor may lie in the exposure of older nurses to the war and its aftermath; it could also be possible that the tendency for friends or relatives to follow each others' professions was, as with teaching,[13] greater than it is now.

As mentioned earlier, there are difficulties when asking people about their choice of career and the reasons for it, one of the pitfalls being that those who are unhappy with their jobs tend to gloss over or conceal that they regret their choice or think it a mistake. With this in mind the respondents were asked about their 'ideal' occupation in which success was guaranteed.* The majority, 62 per cent, still opted for nursing, suggesting a relatively high degree of consonance between actual and projected choice.

PRE-NURSING EXPERIENCE

As is shown in Table 7/2, the majority of respondents, 72 per cent, had started nursing training before they were twenty, and altogether 88 per cent had commenced before their twenty-fifth birthday. Only 21 nurses had begun to train after the age of forty and only three of these had made a late decision and started at fifty.

The majority of each single age group, cumulatively 61 per cent, had started nursing at eighteen or under; 51 per cent of this group had 'always wanted to nurse', and 44 per cent were doing it for positive reasons such as the desire to work

---

[13] Ministry of Education (Kelsall, R. K.), (1963) *Women and Teaching*, HMSO, London.

* *Question 53.* If you were able to choose absolutely any occuaption or job in the world, with a guarantee of success in this occupation, what occupation would you choose?

with and help people, interest, or because they had personal experience of nursing, or had been influenced by friends already in the profession. Only 2 per cent had chosen nursing as a result of boredom with a previous job and a further 4 per cent said that they just drifted into nursing. These reasons for choosing nursing, in conjunction with the fact that the minimum age for training is $17\frac{1}{2}$ years,[*] suggest that the majority of these girls were waiting to start nursing and where they had had interim occupations, these were 'fillers' before the next intake of students. This hypothesis receives confirmation from analysis of the number and type of

TABLE 7/2
Age of entry into nursing by present age

Age of entry into nursing	Present Age						Total	%
	Under 20	20–29	30–39	40–49	50–59	60 and over		
Under 18	7	27	29	31	13	0	107	15
18	49	109	71	54	38	4	325	46
19	2	24	15	22	16	2	81	11
20–24	0	30	19	28	34	3	114	16
25–29	0	4	12	7	13	0	36	5
30–39	0	0	12	12	3	0	27	4
40 and over	0	0	0	8	13	0	21	3
Total	58	194	158	162	130	9	711	100

Respondents who gave inadequate answers and/or those to whom the question was inapplicable are excluded from the totals.

interim occupations. In fact, 87 per cent of the early entrants had only one job, or no job at all before training, 22 per cent having done 'nothing', 6 per cent having been at home helping with the family, while a further 35 per cent within this group had done something allied to nursing such as pre-nursing school, nursing auxiliary work or nursery nursing. Most of the remaining early entrants had done service work in offices or shops.

The picture is different for the group who started training between their nineteenth and twenty-fifth birthdays. Again the majority had had only one job between school and nursing but their reasons for choosing nursing and their pre-nursing jobs were slightly different. A smaller group had specifically 'always wanted to nurse', a slightly larger proportion than in the group of early entrants wanted a job in which they could meet, work with and help people. It appears that the latter group, in spite of their orientation toward 'caring' work, had not initially singled out nursing and so had not gone into it straight from school. The suggestion that nursing was not their first choice of career is supported by the fact that 58 per cent had done service work and 9 per cent specifically mentioned turning to nursing from boredom with a previous job. Twenty-two per cent had been led to nursing

[*] In Scotland.

by an interest that had been aroused in their first job, or through 'consumer' experience or through the influence of someone in nursing.

The group of late entrants—those who entered nursing after their twenty-fifth birthday—represents only 12 per cent of the respondents, but their pattern of pre-nursing experience, intentions, as well as the number and type of jobs, seems to divide the group along the lines of the other two groups of entrants.

Just over half of this group had 'always wanted to nurse' or had always had the interest. Their late entry may be explained by the fact that 47 per cent had been detained at home at some point, suggesting that for some an initial intention of

TABLE 7/3a
Types of occupations between school and nursing by time interval since training

| | Time Interval Since Training | | | | | Total |
	Under 3 years %	*3–9 years* %	*10–19 years* %	*20–29 years* %	*30+ years* %	%
None	9	11	14	15	22	14
Home occupations	11	12	14	17	25	16
Nursing allied	43	39	28	23	12	29
Service work	58	54	46	47	45	50
Teaching or learning	4	6	7	3	5	5
Other occupations	14	15	16	1	8	13
Number of respondents	114	157	153	40	144	708

Respondents may have given more than one occupation.
Respondents who gave inadequate answers and/or those to whom the question was inapplicable are excluded from the totals.

TABLE 7/3b
Types of occupations between school and nursing by age at time of interview

| | Age | | | | | Total |
	Under 20 %	*20–29* %	*30–39* %	*40–49* %	*50+* %	%
None	9	14	14	15	16	14
Home occupations	0	4	12	23	36	16
Nursing allied	55	41	24	23	16	29
Service work	48	50	54	49	46	53
Teaching or learning	3	5	6	4	5	5
Other occupations	7	10	16	16	13	13
Number of respondents	58	194	157	162	140	711

Respondents may have given more than one occupation.
Respondents who gave inadequate answers and/or those to whom the question was inapplicable are excluded from the totals.

nursing was frustrated by family commitments. An example of this was supplied by a student aged thirty-nine, who had left school at fourteen and married at nineteen, and whose youngest child was now fifteen.

'It's the only thing I ever wanted to do. I didn't have the opportunity before. My mother died when I was sixteen, I had to look after my dad . . .'

None of this group had done 'nothing' before training; 45 per cent had had one job, 35 per cent two and the rest three or more. Although 68 per cent had done service work, mainly in shops or offices, it is worthy of note that 26 per cent had experience of an occupation allied to nursing, a higher proportion than in the middle group. It would be helpful to know if some of those who were orientated to nursing, but had home commitments, took occupations allied to nursing as well as non-nursing jobs because of the much greater flexibility of the working hours compared with those of a student or pupil nurse. However, 10 per cent specifically mentioned coming to nursing as a result of experience as a nursing auxiliary or during the war, while 15 per cent cited their experience as consumers, influence of a friend in nursing, or an interest that had been fostered by a previous job. Ten per cent had turned to nursing from boredom with a previous job while 17 per cent mentioned the positive desire to work with and help people.

Tables 7/3a and b show the historical changes in pre-nursing experience. It is evident that the recent groups of entrants were progressively more likely than earlier groups to have experience of work allied to nursing. They were also progressively less likely to have done 'nothing' before training, or to have been detained at home.

BREAKS IN SERVICE

As can be seen from Table 7/4 just under half the respondents had had a break of three months or more from the National Health Service (NHS).* More married than single women had had a break, more part-timers than full-timers and more women in their thirties than any other age group. Further, these same groups were more likely to have had two or more breaks than the other groups. It must be remembered, however, that these figures relate only to nurses who had returned to nursing, as no provision was made in our sampling for nurses who were in the course of a break. Thus, the table does not show which groups are most likely to take a break; it only describes the experience of our respondents. Similarly, it should not be thought that part-timers are more likely to take breaks from nursing; the table shows that women who had already taken breaks were more likely to work part time afterwards. In fact, of those nurses who had taken a break only 19 per cent had worked part time previously, but the numbers soar to 51 per cent after the break.

Long breaks of five years or more from the NHS were more often reported by married women and those people over the age of thirty. It is notable that 42 per

* *Question 14.* Since you first started have you had any breaks of three months or more from nursing in the National Health Service? By this I mean either leaving nursing altogether or nursing outside the National Health Service.

cent of those over the age of fifty reported a break of ten years or more, whereas the thirties and forties groups both peaked in the one-to-five year category.

TABLE 7/4
Number and length of breaks by age and marital status

	Age					Marital Status	
	Under 20	20–29	30–39	40–49	50+	Married	Single
Number of breaks	%	%	%	%	%	%	%
None	98	74	34	40	40	34	70
One	2	20	36	39	48	41	23
Two	0	6	18	15	10	17	5
Three or more	0	0	12	6	2	8	2
Number of respondents	58	195	158	161	141	348	368
Length of break	%	%	%	%	%	%	%
Less than 1 year	0	49	19	12	17	16	33
1 year, less than 5 years	100★	45	54	46	24	41	47
5 years, less than 10 years	0	6	20	24	17	23	8
10 years or more	0	0	7	19	42	21	12
Number of respondents	1	51	104	96	83	228	109

★ Only one nurse under 20 had a break.
Respondents who gave inadequate answers and/or those to whom the question was inapplicable are excluded from the totals.

REASONS FOR A BREAK IN NURSING CAREER
The respondents were asked about their reasons for a break in their career and about the activities which they pursued during the period away from nursing. The focus was on the longest break, and breaks of less than three months were ignored.

Not surprisingly, the most important factor that discriminated amongst the various reasons and activities was marital status, as can be seen from Table 7/5.

The two main reasons married women gave for their break were either to get married, 30 per cent, or to have children, 47 per cent. Fifteen per cent of the married women left because of family commitments such as looking after relatives, and within this group are located the 6 per cent who had to move house because of the husband's job.

When the other activities during the break are taken into account, it can be seen that 89 per cent of married women were occupied with having a family. Comparatively few married women left initially to travel or work outside the NHS, whereas these were precisely the categories into which the largest numbers of single women fell. The greatest single cause for unmarried nurses to take a break was to go abroad, 33 per cent. They went mainly to nurse, though some went to

TABLE 7/5
Main reason for and all activities during break by age, marital status and employment status after break

| | Age* | | | | | | | | Marital Status | | | | Employment Status after Break | | | | Total | |
| | 20-29 | | 30-39 | | 40-49 | | 50+ | | Married | | Single | | Full-time | | Part-time | | | |
	Main reason %	All activities %	Main reason %	All activities %	Main reason %	All activities %	Main reason %	All activities %	Main reason %	All activities %	Main reason %	All activities %	Main reason %	All activities %	Main reason %	All activities %	Main reason %	All activities %
Marriage	14	14	20	21	24	27	20	24	30	33	0	0	14	17	26	28	20	22
Children	29	41	43	79	38	72	18	42	47	89	4	4	5	17	59	99	33	61
Family commitments	8	18	7	12	10	13	18	27	10	15	12	19	15	23	7	12	11	17
Other work (non-nursing)	2	20	0	6	2	9	0	6	0	8	2	12	1	13	1	5	1	9
Nursed outside NHS	10	24	2	12	4	11	12	24	1	8	16	35	13	30	0	4	6	17
Travelled and nursed abroad	6	12	18	24	9	14	15	29	3	7	33	47	25	37	2	4	13	20
Other answers	31	33	10	10	13	13	17	17	7	11	34	37	27	31	5	10	16	16
Total=100%	51		104		96		84		229		110		163		170		339	

Total percentage greater than 100 is due to multiple answers.
* Only one nurse under the age of 20 had had a break.
Respondents who gave inadequate answers and/or those to whom the question was inapplicable are excluded from the totals.

visit relatives or to take a long holiday. The other major reasons put forward were to nurse outside the NHS, 16 per cent, or because of family commitments, 12 per cent.

Other reasons for taking a break, given by 16 per cent of the combined group of married and single nurses included the respondent's own ill-health, 6 per cent. Dissatisfaction with the work or conditions of service, desire for a change or failing nursing exams were among the reasons given by the remaining 10 per cent.

Having left for a particular reason, just under half the nurses did not become involved in other activities before returning to the NHS and only 13 per cent of them had been engaged in more than one extra activity. As can be seen from Table 7/5 most of the married women were busy with children and for those who returned to nursing as part-timers, there was an overwhelming likelihood that their break had also been taken up with children. It is also clear from the table that compared with the married women a substantial number of the single women were nursing during their break, either abroad, outside the NHS, or within their families. This has obvious relevance to the question of the effect of the break upon subsequent career and promotion prospects, and so will be discussed later in this chapter.

REASONS FOR RETURN

Respondents were asked why they had returned to nursing in the NHS, and the main response categories are set out in Table 7/6a.

As can be seen, just under a third of all nurses said that they were specifically motivated to return; 27 per cent were able to return because of a change in their circumstances—such as returning from abroad, or the family growing up. The other major reasons for return were that NHS nursing was the best alternative to boredom at home, dissatisfaction with a particular job, that the income was needed or that there were career reasons such as the desire for further training.

Yet again, there are obvious differences between the married and single nurses, and these become even clearer if the reason for return is considered in relation to the cause of the break and the activities pursued during it. Most of the married women had had their breaks because of marriage and children, and very few, compared with the single women, had been nursing either abroad or outside the NHS.

As can be seen from Table 7/6b, those women who had left to get married or produce a family, gave as their main reasons for return that they had missed nursing or that they needed the income. When all additional reasons for return are taken into account, the need for income emerges as the single most important factor. As most of the nurses who left for reasons other than getting married or producing a family had been employed during their break, and many had been nursing, it is not surprising that they did not give income or missing nursing as major reasons for return.

One important fact which emerges from Table 7/6b is that 10 per cent of married nurses gave as the main reason for return that they had been asked to return. Given this group's high score on boredom and the need for income, together with the fact that 22 per cent had missed nursing while they were away

TABLE 7/6a
Main reason and all reasons for returning to NHS after break by age, marital status and employment status after the break

| | Age | | | | | | | | Marital Status | | | | Employment Status | | | | Total | |
| | 20-29 | | 30-39 | | 40-49 | | 50+ | | Married | | Single | | Full-time | | Part-time | | | |
	Main reason %	All reasons %	Main reason %	All reasons %	Main reason %	All reasons %	Main reason %	All reasons %	Main reason %	All reasons %	Main reason %	All reasons %	Main reason %	All reasons %	Main reason %	All reasons %	Main reason %	All reasons %
Best alternative	18	22	16	20	17	33	12	13	19	24	7	10	10	14	20	26	21	26
Motivated	30	32	36	39	24	33	33	35	36	41	20	24	26	30	36	43	31	37
Changed circumstances	12	12	21	27	35	38	32	40	16	20	49	55	37	46	16	20	27	33
Career reasons	10	14	9	16	7	11	11	16	6	11	15	22	15	22	4	8	9	15
Need for income	22	22	17	24	16	23	11	12	20	26	7	9	10	11	21	29	16	20
Other answers	8	10	2	3	1	1	1	1	3	3.5	2	2	2	2	3	5	2	3
Total=100%	50		103		95		82		224		109		163		168		333	

Respondents who gave inadequate answers and/or those to whom the question was inapplicable are excluded from the totals.

Total percentage greater than 100 is due to multiple answers.

from it, it seems that asking married women to return might be an effective way of getting them back.

For the women who had not left to get married or to have a family some of the reasons for return corresponded with the reasons for leaving. Thus, of those who left due to ill-health, the majority returned when they were better, others saying that they had always intended to come back. Similarly, a substantial number of nurses left to travel or nurse abroad and returned to the NHS when they came back to Britain.

It is notable that a good proportion of single women had always planned to return. Indeed, if some of the answer categories are grouped together according to whether they show positive or negative motivation, the single women emerge in

TABLE 7/6b
Reasons given for returning to nursing

Main reason	Married nurses* N=175 %	Other nurses N=158 %
Need for income	23	6
Missed nursing	22	8
Bored	17	4
Family circumstances permitted	11	9
Asked to return	10	2
Career	8	9
Planned to return	4	13
Returned from abroad	1	27
Unhappy in other job	1	6
Health improved	0	10
Attracted by NHS	0	4

* Women whose main reason for leaving was to get married or produce a family; this does not imply that none of the other group was married.

a more favourable light. Both groups, single and married, showed approximately equal positive impetus if missing nursing, having career intentions, and planning to return, are considered as one category. However, the single nurses showed substantially less negative motivation when boredom, dissatisfaction with previous occupation, and the need for income, are grouped together.

Differences between the married and single nurses again became apparent in relation to the length of the break taken. Of those whose main reason for leaving was marriage and family responsibility, 40 per cent had a break of between one and five years, while 45 per cent had a break of five years or more. In all, marriage and family accounted for 80 per cent of breaks over five years in duration. Where nurses left in order to work outside the NHS or to go abroad, a quarter returned within the year, half had a break of between one and five years and only 22 per cent were away for longer than that. For those people who left for other reasons such as ill-health, there was yet greater chance of early returning, 30 per cent returning within the year.

The hours worked by nurses returning from a break showed yet again a clear differentiation according to whether the respondent had children or not. Table 7/5 shows that the association between part-time working on return to nursing and previously having left to get married or produce a family could, at 98.8 per cent, hardly be more marked. Only 17 per cent of those returning full time had been occupied with children. It was much more likely that the full-timers had left for other reasons such as travelling, nursing abroad or outside the NHS.

Table 7/6a shows that those who returned part time were significantly less likely to have career motivation than the full-timers, were more likely to see nursing as the best alternative to their previous position and also to have greater need for the income.

EFFECTS OF A BREAK

Respondents who had had a break were asked to say how they felt about their longest break. First they were asked whether they felt it had been too long or too short, and why they felt as they did, and secondly whether their break had influenced their career or not, and if so, how.

The majority of nurses, 60 per cent, felt that the length of the break had been about right, exactly a third of the respondents that it had been too long, and just three per cent that it had been too short. Just over half of those who thought the break had been too long gave as their reason new trends in nursing—changes in hospital nursing techniques, and in drugs and treatments. As one nurse put it:

'. . . there was so much new in the way of drugs and it took a wee while to feel myself confident in my work.'

Some of the respondents who thought their break had been too long had been unsure about returning and had been apprehensive or nervous in case they had forgotten their skills. It is notable that in most cases the reasons given for feeling that a break had been too long expressed worries about the ability to cope after a break; only 21 per cent of the respondents gave other reasons connected with family or finance and so on. In fact, all the respondents were asked about the problem of attracting back qualified staff to nursing and which sort of encouragements they thought would be the most successful. Although flexible hours emerged as the one most important inducement, 'back to nursing' courses came out as almost equal, second to creches and nurseries. However, these issues are discussed in greater detail below.

About three-quarters of the respondents who had left the NHS to nurse elsewhere were more likely to consider their break had been 'just about right' as against just over half of those who had left for marriage or family reasons. Married nurses generally were very aware of the conflicts of interest between professional life and home needs. Some had returned earlier than they would have wished because of pressing financial need, but many felt quite strongly that their first duty was to their children, and a high proportion that it was undesirable for mothers of children who were under school age to go out to work.

Less than half the respondents, 43 per cent, who had had breaks felt that the break had influenced their career. One in five of this group thought they had gained in maturity and understanding, and half that number that the experience of having a family was valuable to their career. For instance a midwifery sister said:

'I felt that having had a baby, my attitude to the patients in labour was different. You understand more when you've had to experience it yourself.'

Ten per cent of the respondents considered that they had widened their nursing experience during their break and 19 per cent that their careers had changed direction as a result of the break. A further 12 per cent considered that the break had affected their career but in the sense that family commitments restricted potential development. However, probably the most important claim, and one which deserves extended consideration, is the one put forward by 22 per cent of the group who thought the break had affected their careers; they claimed that the break in service had delayed or prevented promotion, or had meant demotion.

The fact that this claim was made by only thirty women should not cause it to be lightly dismissed. It may be the case that this group voiced the feelings of many married women, but that such feelings are not normally expressed because people in this group tend to lower their expectations in accordance with their view of an acceptable career pattern for a woman with family commitments. A few respondents freely admitted that they had become less ambitious than they might have been if they had not married. Thus, a respondent who was an administrator could say:

'Marriage has made it different, not just the break. I don't think you're quite so ambitious when you're married.'

The respondents were asked what post they held before, and then after, their break. Table 7/7 presents these results and shows the differences, if any, in status that the respondents experienced on their return.

As can be seen a substantial number, 64 per cent, of those who had had a break returned to a similar post. Some administrators, sisters, teachers, staff nurses and midwives returned to a grade below the one they had left, while a few others advanced up the ladder. However, changes in status can be of two sorts, vertical or horizontal. The former would encompass promotion or demotion but the latter is more complex. Horizontal mobility would include either a shift sideways into another employment group or a period of further training. Training in this context might be an extended refresher course, training for a different specialty of comparable status, or training as a springboard to promotion.

If this is taken into account, it can be gleaned from Table 7/7 that overall a larger number of nurses moved horizontally, 14 per cent, on their return from a break than were immediately promoted, 12 per cent, while the demotions formed the smallest group, 9 per cent, of those who experienced a change in status.

As can be seen, the same number of community nurses moved into hospital as the number of hospital nurses who moved the other way. This move on the part of community nurses was mainly because of the decreasing number of home confinements so that it was the domiciliary midwives who moved back to hospital. The move from hospital to community may be the result of a number of factors

TABLE 7/7
Designation after break and effect of break on status

Designation before Break	No.	Designation after Break						Effect of Break on Status			
		Administrators	Sisters/teachers	Staff nurses/midwives	Enrolled nurses	Learners	Community nurses	No change	Promoted	Demoted	Horizontal movement
Administrators	9	5	2	1	0	0	1	5	0	3	1
Sisters/teachers	64	4	28	24	0	1	7	28	4	24	8
Staff nurses/midwives	149	1	21	108	4	5	10	108	22	4	15
Enrolled nurses	19	0	0	1	17	0	1	17	1	0	1
Learners	46	0	2	5	6	32	1	32	13	0	1
Community nurses	41	0	5	14	0	1	21	21	0	0	20
Total	328	10	58	153	27	39	41	211	40	31	46
								64%	12%	9%	14%

Respondents who gave inadequate answers and/or those to whom the question was inapplicable are excluded from the totals.

including the greater flexibility and autonomy experienced by the individual nurse in community work. Other attractions might include pay scales on a par with ward sisters and the greater possibility of a training course to provide up-to-date knowledge which would, at the same time, increase the nurses' confidence. As mentioned earlier in this chapter, a substantial number of nurses felt that 'back to nursing' courses would be a powerful inducement in persuading qualified staff to return to the NHS.

In fact, only a small number of nurses suffered demotion when they returned after their break, though horizontal movement to community nursing might be construed in some cases as an avoiding action on the part of those who otherwise saw the prospect of loss of status ahead of them. However, when factors such as length of break, reason for break, and full- or part-time working are considered, the pattern of demotion becomes much clearer.

TABLE 7/8
Current designation by reason for a break

| Designation now | Marriage and/or children | | Reason for a Break | | | | | |
| | | | Travel/non-NHS nursing | | Other* | | Total= |
	%	No.	%	No.	%	No.	100%
Administrators	21	14	45	30	33	22	66
Sisters/teachers	49	26	30	16	21	11	53
Staff nurses/midwives	73	56	3	2	24	19	77
Total		96		48		52	196

* Other includes nursing sick relatives, own ill-health, non-nursing work and other combined answers.

Nurses who left to travel and nurse either abroad or outside the NHS were likely to maintain or improve grade. Thus, whereas 20 had been sisters or teachers beforehand, there were 31 in this designation after the break. However, women who left to get married or have a family experienced a different outcome—here the number of sisters and teachers dropped from 36 before the break to 21 after it. These findings are further supported by the evidence in Table 7/8 which shows the designation at the time of interview related to the reason for the break in service. It is apparent that women now in the administrative grade had a significantly different pattern of reasons for a break compared with those given by both the staff nurses and the sisters and teachers, with the latter two groups also showing significant differences.

Much is explained when it is remembered that the married women were more likely to have longer breaks than their single colleagues. Moreover, married women were significantly more likely to return on a part-time basis than were the single women, 74 per cent against 4 per cent.

Analysis of the employment status of those who had had breaks in relationship to full- or part-time working showed that only one administrator worked part time on return, compared with 20 per cent of sisters and teachers, and with 74 per cent of staff nurses. This finding suggests that the greater the degree of administrative responsibility of a post, the greater the preference of the employing authority for a full-time worker; but the possibility that it may be a result of diminished career ambition in part-time workers cannot be discounted.

FUTURE PLANS

The respondents were asked what they hoped to do in the future. The largest single response to this, 37 per cent, was 'to carry on here', while 14 per cent either had no plans or did not know what they would do. Sixteen per cent intended to take further training or go into other fields of nursing. Three per cent envisaged marrying or having a family, while 4 per cent planned to travel, nurse abroad or even emigrate. Eight per cent were approaching retirement and so had no plans as far as nursing was concerned, and a surprisingly small proportion, 5 per cent, hoped for, or expected, promotion.

Not surprisingly, these answers obtained differing degrees of support from the various age groups and designations. Thus, all but one of the nurses planning to go abroad were under the age of thirty, and two-thirds of those planning to take further qualifications were also in that age group. The learners were in the main looking forward to passing their exams and a good number were not looking beyond that; however, the learners group did provide 52 per cent of those who wished to do some further training. The group who thought they would 'carry on here' included many part-timers with family responsibilities, nurses in their forties and fifties, and those who were obliged, because of limited qualifications, to stay in their current grade. The community nurses were the group most likely to plan to carry on where they were, with 60 per cent of the district nurses voicing this intention.

Both the hospital and community nurses were asked if they planned to work in the other sector, but in each case the majority, 79 per cent and 90 per cent respectively, said they did not. The reasons given in answer to this question, however, do throw more light on how these nurses saw their own future and how they regarded the two branches of nursing.

A similar percentage of each group, 46 per cent of hospital nurses and 44 per cent of community nurses, said they were happy in their current post and would not change. A further group in each category, 10 and 17 per cent respectively, were not considering any move as they were coming up for retirement. Fifteen per cent of hospital nurses had never considered community work. Eight per cent said they were unqualified for it and a further 8 per cent, mainly single women, considered it unattractive.

Ten per cent of the hospital nurses were planning to work in the community, whereas only 2 per cent of community nurses thought to return to hospital. In view of the number of people who thought community work unattractive, it is pertinent to compare the degree of congruence between the hospital group who wanted to shift and the community nurses who intended to remain.

Forty-four per cent of community nurses preferred their work to that in hospital, while 19 per cent of nurses planning to change to the community said they too would prefer it. The gap is more than made up by the hospital nurses who wanted to change for one reason or another. The independence of community work was valued by 13 per cent of the group already working there and by 8 per cent of the hospital nurses planning to change.

A further 8 per cent of each group mentioned that community work would fit in with their home arrangements.

CAREER PATTERN

It is clear from the previous description that respondents in this study followed a variety of nursing careers which may be broadly divided into categories of career pattern. The concept of career pattern stems from work by Miller and Form[14] and by Super.[15] It usually means the *continuity* of jobs or occupations and the general *progression*, *stagnation* or *retrogression* inferred from the inter-relations among successive jobs. These aspects of the career are limited abstractions of an individual's work history and serve as a useful indicator of the type of activities pursued by respondents during their working lives. In accordance with Mulvey[16] the concept has been extended here to include non-occupational activities, particularly home-making. However, the categories employed in this analysis have not been concerned solely with career in terms of its meaning for the individual, but also have regard to the NHS and its perspective on employment and such issues as man-power planning. Thus, in purely personal terms, women who nursed abroad or outside the NHS were pursuing a coherent and uninterrupted nursing career. However, in terms of the NHS they can be regarded as having an interrupted record of service. Similarly, this categorisation would apply to those who have had a long period of illness and so interrupted their nursing service.

Because of the obvious difficulties of categorisation, it was decided to employ strict criteria about inclusion in the category of 'uninterrupted career'. As a result, those women who were not in nursing for their entire potential employment span —that is those who embarked on nursing after the age of twenty—were excluded. Again, in personal terms they may have had uninterrupted careers, but to the employing authorities the late entrants are a minority who, by definition, do not follow the standard career pattern.

In the following analysis all respondents under the age of twenty-five have been excluded on the ground that few would have developed career patterns at that early stage.

From the analysis of the respondents' work histories, three broad career patterns emerged, 'stable', 'dual' and 'interrupted'. The stable career is largely self-explanatory, showing no breaks of longer than three months, in fact the type of career that would be expected of a man. The 'dual' pattern describes the respondents who had had a moderately stable career but interrupted by breaks of more than three

---

[14] Miller, D. and Form, W. H., (1956) *Industrial Sociology*, Harper, New York.

[15] Super, D. E., (1957) *The Psychology of Careers*, Harper, New York.

[16] Mulvey, M. C. (1963) Psychological and sociological factors in prediction of career patterns of women, *Genetic Psychology Monographs*, 68.

months though less than three years, because of marriage, child-rearing, or other family commitments such as the care of an infirm relative. This group shows women taking on two roles—that of employed nurse and that of homemaker. Finally, there is the 'interrupted' career pattern, comprising those nurses who began training after the age of twenty and/or reported a break of three years or more from service in the NHS.

Each of these three groups was subdivided, giving a total of six categories. The subdivisions are between respondents who have been exclusively employed in the NHS, and those who have worked either as nurses elsewhere, or in non-nursing occupations during their breaks.

Table 7/9 summarises the characteristics of the individuals in the six groups, while Table 7/10 shows the age distributions.

More than half the nurses aged over twenty-five showed a stable career pattern and in fact 70 per cent of this group were single. The rest were married, though few

TABLE 7/9
Career patterns by marital status, children and part-time work

Career pattern	No.	Single	Married	With children under 15	Work part-time now	Explanation of definitions
Stable						
NHS nursing only	120	80	40	4	3	no breaks for home commitments and no breaks for other work
Nursing and other work	165	119	46	11	12	no breaks for home commitments
Dual						
NHS nursing only	68	5	63	49	35	have breaks of up to three years for home commitments
Nursing and other work	16	6	10	6	6	have breaks of up to three years for home commitments and other employment
Interrupted						
NHS nursing only	105	5	100	64	59	these respondents began training after they were twenty years old and/or had breaks in service of more than three years
Nursing and other work	64	10	54	22	22	
Total	538	225	313	156	137	

Respondents who gave inadequate answers and/or those to whom the question was inapplicable are excluded from the totals.

of them had children. Seventy-one per cent of nurses between the ages of twenty-five and twenty-nine were in this group, but many of them can be expected to move into other categories.

The dual career group is relatively small, including only 16 per cent of the respondents. In the main, they are married, 85 per cent, likely to have children under the age of fifteen, 65 per cent, and half of them, 49 per cent, work part time. The dual career pattern is more frequent amongst the younger nurses, an observation consistent with the trend of an increasing number of mothers working while their children are young.

The interrupted pattern is also characteristic of married women with children

TABLE 7/10
Career patterns by age

Career pattern	No.	25–29	30–34	35–39	40–44	45–49	50–55	55+
Stable								
NHS nursing only	120	31	15	9	16	25	10	14
Nursing and other work	164	24	17	29	19	20	21	34
Dual								
NHS nursing only	68	13	12	17	9	10	3	4
Nursing and other work	16	6	2	3	2	2	1	0
Interrupted								
NHS nursing only	105	2	12	24	18	17	17	15
Nursing and other work	62	1	9	8	11	12	10	11
Total	535	77	67	90	75	86	62	78

Respondents who gave inadequate answers and/or those to whom the question was inapplicable are excluded from the totals.

and was shown by more nurses, 31 per cent, than was the dual career pattern. Of those with the interrupted pattern, typically breaks in service of more than three years, 81 per cent were married, 51 per cent had children under the age of fifteen, and 48 per cent were working part time. One-third of nurses over the age of fifty-five reported this pattern as against the 5 per cent reporting the dual pattern. Among the younger nurses aged twenty-five to thirty-nine, equal numbers come from the interrupted and dual patterns, but obviously no final conclusions can be drawn at this stage as many nurses in this age group will not yet have returned to the NHS after a break.

Table 7/11 shows the number of nurses of each designation in the six different career categories. It is noticeable that a higher proportion of administrators, sisters and teachers had stable careers than other designations, and in the case of the administrators there was a close correspondence between career pattern and marital status; 78 per cent had a stable career and 75 per cent were single. The correspondence was not so close in the case of sisters and teachers; 66 per cent of them had stable careers and 52 per cent were unmarried.

The pattern is entirely different for staff nurses and staff midwives, as 52 per cent fall into the interrupted career group, with the stable and dual career patterns comprising a quarter each. There was a clear difference between them and the higher grades in terms of marital status, as only 19 per cent of all staff nurses and midwives were single. They were, moreover, younger than the administrators, sisters and teachers.

Forty-three per cent of the enrolled nurses aged twenty-five or over had a stable career pattern, a higher proportion than the staff nurses and midwives, and

TABLE 7/11
Career pattern by designation

Designation	No.	Stable Career		Dual Career		Interrupted Career	
		NHS nursing only	Nursing and other work	NHS nursing only	Nursing and other work	NHS nursing only	Nursing and other work
Administrators	120	42	51	9	1	9	8
Sisters/teachers	100	33	33	13	4	11	6
Staff nurses/ midwives	90	9	13	17	4	38	9
Enrolled nurses	63	6	21	10	1	7	18
Learners	32	4	11	1	1	4	11
District nurses	45	7	7	6	1	18	6
Health visitors	39	11	17	3	3	3	2
Other community nurses	49	8	12	9	1	15	4
Hospital nurses	396	92 23%	127 32%	48 12%	11 3%	67 17%	51 13%
Community nurses	141	27 19%	38 27%	20 14%	5 3%	38 27%	13 9%

Respondents who gave inadequate answers and/or those to whom the question was inapplicable are excluded from the totals.

again corresponding with the marital status pattern and age distribution, as 29 per cent were single and 64 per cent were aged forty or over.

The highest proportion of stable careers amongst the community nurses was found in the health visitors, with 72 per cent, whereas the district nurses produced only 32 per cent stable careers. Although the age distributions amongst the community nurses are not greatly different, there is a strong relationship with marital status, 72 per cent of health visitors being single compared with only 15 per cent of district nurses.

More than half the nurses in the stable career category reported breaks from employment in the NHS. This is true for administrators in particular, showing that breaks are not really prejudicial to promotion. Where respondents had breaks for domestic reasons, both the dual and interrupted career groups, more than half worked exclusively in the NHS, a finding which is particularly marked in the dual career group.

The rather obvious conclusion suggested by this analysis of respondents' work histories and related personal characteristics is that the combination of the nurse's career and her external commitments influences the type of nursing that she will be involved in. Certainly the career implications of marriage and child-rearing are clear, but it should be stressed that the data only describe those nurses who returned to the NHS after a break in service. It was, therefore, thought pertinent to ask all the respondents about inducements which could be offered to nurses who might contemplate returning to the NHS after a break in service and to reconsider the respondent's own reasons for break and return in the light of these inducements.

There have been many valuable studies of recruitment and attrition in nursing and indeed the loss of qualified nursing staff to the NHS is alarming. However, many of the efforts made to find out why, rather than when, nurses leave the profession have tended to be abortive. In the first place it is not easy to trace inactive nurses, and secondly, their stated reasons for leaving the NHS are not necessarily reliable, as they may feel reluctant and embarrassed to give the real reasons for their departure.* It was, therefore, considered appropriate and relevant in this study to ask those respondents who had returned to nursing in the NHS after a break, why they had done so. It is a fair assumption that their reasons might point to incentives for others. The other method which was expected to yield helpful suggestions for recruitment of qualified nurses was a direct multiple choice question on the topic.**

Respondents were first asked to select three items and then to indicate which one they considered the most important. It is appreciated that this question was

---

* A study of inactive nurses and their reasons for having left the profession is currently being undertaken in the Research Unit by Cunningham, C. V., SHHD Training Fellow.

** *Question 60.*[1] As you know there are thousands of qualified nurses in the country who are no longer nursing for various reasons. What do you think would encourage them to return to nursing?

Perhaps you could tell me which three on this list you consider to be the most important. Which one of those that you have chosen do you think is the most important?

Back to nursing courses
Help with transport
Higher salaries
Proper changing and rest rooms
Opportunities for promotion
Facilities for further qualifications
Extra payment for night and/or weekend work
Creches or nurseries
Flexibility of working hours to meet family commitments
Opportunities to specialise
None of these

[1] The incentives presented as options were compiled on the basis of exploratory interviews.

hypothetical; it shared all the known weaknesses of such questions. A further related question asked respondents about advice they might give to a friend who was a qualified nurse but not nursing for one reason or another.* This was also a hypothetical issue for many nurses although some had been involved in talking to such nurse friends about the possibility of returning to nursing.

Reasons for returning to nursing after a break are discussed earlier in this chapter but so far no attempt has been made to relate the replies to the different designation groups.

The administrators were the only designation group among whom more single than married respondents had taken breaks from service. Of 45 single administrators, 25 said that changed circumstances were the reason for their return to the NHS; for many, this meant return from a period spent overseas. Single women other than the administrative grades were less likely to have taken a break in service. Very few unmarried staff nurses, midwives and enrolled nurses had taken breaks from service. Twenty-six unmarried community fieldworkers reported breaks in service. Single women in these designations were also likely to refer to changed circumstances at the time of their return to the NHS.

The replies of the married nurses in different designations showed a gradation in professional motivation and are, therefore, shown in Table 7/12.

TABLE 7/12
The main reason given by married nurses for returning to the National Health Service after a break in service

		Designation			
Reason for return *	Administrators	Sisters/ teachers	Staff nurses/ midwives	Enrolled nurses	Community nurses
Professional motivation	10	10	22	5	25
Career reasons	1	1	3	4	3
Changed circumstances	1	5	10	5	9
Preferred to previous way of life	1	6	16	5	12
Need for income	3	6	17	5	10
Other reasons	1	2	1	1	1
Total	17	30	69	25	60

* These groupings are explained in more detail on p. 102.

More than half of the small number of married administrators who had taken breaks from service gave answers indicating a positive leaning toward nursing and 42 per cent of the married community nurses gave similar replies. About a third of the married sisters/teachers and staff nurses/midwives gave replies suggesting professional motivation, while the enrolled nurses were least likely to answer in such terms.

* *Question 62.* And what about a married friend who has left nursing after becoming qualified. Would you encourage her to return to nursing or not?

In answer to the multiple choice question about incentives for returning to nursing, 52 per cent of respondents considered flexible working hours as the most important factor. Two other suggestions were also frequently selected, the provision of creches or nurseries and 'back to nursing' courses. The points of view of the top managers on the provision of such facilities are described in Chapter 4. Not surprisingly, the provision of creches and nurseries was most likely to be selected by nurses in their twenties and thirties. Some nurses, although expressing the need for creches, realised that they might not provide the complete answer.

'Back to nursing' courses, on the other hand, were favoured most by the administrators, 24 per cent of whom chose this as the most important suggestion as against 13 per cent of staff nurses and 11 per cent of enrolled nurses who considered it of primary importance. It is probable that people who have been out of nursing for a long time particularly appreciate such courses, as they allay their fear of being out' of date'. One part-time staff nurse valued the refresher course she had taken:

> 'I felt I'd been away too long but I didn't want to leave my family any sooner . . . I'd been away for 11 years and things change.'

Many made it clear that while they had felt hesitant before returning to work, they had found their feet very easily in the event.

The only other suggestion which featured strongly was higher salaries, but this was considered important by less than half the number of people who chose 'creches or nurseries'.

After considering the ten listed points on the multiple choice question, respondents were asked if they had any additional suggestions to make. The two most frequent types of reply were, first, that there was scope for improvement in communication, and secondly, that having attracted a nurse back to work, probably on a part-time basis, more could be done to support her at work.* Open days and study days, in addition to 'back to nursing' courses, were also thought to be useful and it was further suggested that these activities could be better advertised; several respondents suggested television advertising as an effective means. For instance:

> 'I don't think we go out advertising enough for married women to come back —in different places in the town, and even radio and television.'

A register of qualified inactive nurses was yet another suggestion.

Finally, as indicated earlier, respondents were asked on a more personal level whether they would encourage a married friend to return to nursing or not. Sixty per cent of respondents said they would encourage a friend to return and half the remainder said they would do so if home commitments permitted it. Only 6 per cent replied that they would not encourage a qualified married woman to return to nursing, but in most cases this was because they felt it must be the friend's own decision. The group with the largest number of those who felt they could not encourage a friend were learners. By contrast, only one staff nurse gave such a negative answer.

---

* Part-time nursing is dealt with more fully in Chapter 9.

In a social climate in which it is increasingly accepted that married women wish to work, especially if they have skills which would otherwise be wasted, it may be expected that the proportion of qualified nurses, who would like to come back, will increase. This trend is likely to be hastened by the current depressed economic climate. In order to derive maximum benefit from this trend, health service managers might wish to consider the suggestions offered by the cross-section of practising nurses in this study.

CHAPTER EIGHT
Job Satisfaction

In spite of the known difficulty in measuring or even assessing a person's level of job satisfaction it was considered appropriate to attempt it in this study. Quite apart from the need to obtain substantive knowledge about nurses' job satisfaction, the method involved in constructing a measure was thought to be a helpful learning experience.

The reputed problems in measuring job satisfaction are related to the tendency for people to give favourable answers when asked whether or not they like their job.

Blauner[1] argued that a worker will find it difficult to admit that he dislikes his job without threatening his self respect. Goldthorpe[2] et al. suggested that there is considerable psychological pressure upon the individual to say that he finds his work acceptable, as to say otherwise implies that he does not find himself acceptable. Other studies have also shown that when individuals are asked to rate the level of their job satisfaction on a scale, they tend to make choices in the positive range although other indices may point to a low level of job satisfaction.

On that basis it can be argued that the findings of the current study, which show that a high proportion of nurses assessed their job positively, are neither surprising nor illuminating. At the same time, results of a study which support general statements such as that made by Blauner, nevertheless, have a value. They strengthen and validate other work and, in the case of this specific study, suggest that nurses are similar to other occupational groups in the appraisal of their own job satisfaction.

The main tool used to measure the nurses' level of job satisfaction was an attitude scale developed from the work of Brayfield and Rothe[3] described in detail in Appendix 5.

In order to get a little closer to a reliable assessment of job satisfaction than attitude scales alone are reputed to achieve, three additional questions were asked. The first of these attempted to elicit the respondents' views of the utilisation of

---

[1] Blauner, R., (1960) Work Satisfaction and Industrial Trends in Modern Society in Galenson, W. and Lipset, S. M., *Labor and Trade Unionism*, John Wiley, New York.

[2] Goldthorpe, J. H., Lockwood, D., Bechhofer, F. and Platt, J., (1970) *The Affluent Worker: industrial attitudes and behaviour*, Cambridge University Press.

[3] Brayfield, A. H. and Rothe, H. F., (1951) An Index of Job Satisfaction, *Journal of Applied Psychology*, 35, pp. 307–311.

their skills.* The second question asked for the nurse's reaction if her teenage daughter—real or hypothetical—decided to become a nurse.** In the third, the nurse was given the opportunity to state her ideal occupation.† These questions were based on the known relationship between job satisfaction and skill utilisation and on the hypothesis that a person's error or regret in his occupational choice is more frequently reflected in his reaction to other people's choices than in an acknowledgment of his own dissatisfaction.

The job satisfaction index was designed to show levels of satisfaction with the respondents' current work which did not necessarily reflect the degree of satisfaction with nursing as such.

The responses given to the statements relating to job satisfaction were scored in three categories as follows:

Score of less than 31 . . . . Low
Score between 31 and 39 . . . . Medium
Score of 40 and over . . . . High

Both the Chi Squared and Kolmogorov–Smirnov tests†† were used to examine the significance and direction of differences between groups of nurses on a number of variables in relation to job satisfaction.

It is not always considered appropriate to publish negative findings but their omission may give a misleading impression. The reader may also justifiably draw the conclusion that findings which are not mentioned have not been obtained. The tests used to establish significant relationships between job satisfaction and other variables related to the respondents resulted, for the most part, in negative findings.

The following variables were tested against job satisfaction:

1 Age
2 Marital status
3 Household composition
4 Reasons for choosing nursing
5 Part-time/full-time employment
6 Day duty/night duty
7 Hospital/community
8 Hospital size
9 Department
10 Designation
11 Length of time in present designation
12 Opinion on working hours
13 Skill utilisation

---

* *Question 63.* In your present appointment do you feel that good use is being made of your skills or not?
Why do you say that?
** *Question 54.* If you had a teenage daughter who had decided to become a nurse would you be pleased or not?
Why (not)?
† *Question 53.* If you were able to choose absolutely any occupation or job in the world, with a guarantee of success in this occupation, what occupation would you choose?
Why?
†† These tests are briefly described in Appendix 1.

The only six of the above items which were, in any way, significantly related to job satisfaction were certain age groups and designations, department, opinion on working hours, reasons for choosing nursing and skill utilisation.

Difficulties in interpretation are immediately obvious. Thus, almost by definition, a person who considers her skills are fully used would probably have job satisfaction. Similarly, it is possible that respondents who have chosen to work in a certain department are satisfied; it would be a function of the choice rather than the department. Age and designation are clearly related to each other, older people often being in senior grades. Social data tend to be interdependent and efforts to isolate them may be unreliable. It is important to bear such problems in mind.

TABLE 8/1
Age groups by job satisfaction levels

	Job Satisfaction Levels						
	Low		Medium		High		Total=100%
Age group	No.	%	No.	%	No.	%	No.
Under 20	6	10.3	43	74.1	9	15.5	58
20–29	34	17.8	145	75.9	12	6.3	191
30–39	20	12.9	112	72.3	23	14.8	155
40–49	20	13.2	109	72.2	22	14.6	151
50 and over	19	14.4	86	65.2	27	20.4	132
Total	99		495		93		687

Respondents who gave inadequate answers and/or those to whom the question was inapplicable are excluded from the totals.

Table 8/1 shows the distribution of job satisfaction levels among the different age groups. The small number of respondents aged 60 years and over called for a merging of the two upper age groups for purposes of comparison.

Within the age group 20–29 years, 6.3 per cent scored high against 17.8 per cent who scored low job satisfaction. In the oldest age group, 20.4 per cent scored high and 14.4 per cent scored low job satisfaction. As suggested earlier, the lower job satisfaction of younger people may be caused by many factors which may be related to age in one way or another, designation and length of time in post being two of the obvious.

Reference to the need for young women to come into the profession is made in Chapter 5. If the lower job satisfaction is linked with learner status it is important to consider ways in which the learning period might be enhanced in order to reduce attrition.

The distribution of job satisfaction scores among the different designation categories is presented in Table 8/2. Among the community nursing staff the difference between health visitors and other community nurses in the proportions of respondents scoring high and low job satisfaction levels must be noted. Table 8/2 shows that health visitors reached only low and medium levels of job satisfaction which must cause concern although, as shown in Chapter 7, their careers are remarkably stable.

Findings from a descriptive study provide merely starting points for exploratory work, but in themselves they have little or no explanatory power. It is, moreover, important to distinguish between research findings and their inevitably subjective interpretation.

When confronted with findings such as a relatively low job satisfaction of health visitors one is stimulated to search for reasons and explanations. In theory, three

TABLE 8/2
Designation by job satisfaction levels

	Job Satisfaction Levels						
	Low		Medium		High		Total=100%
Designation	No.	%	No.	%	No.	%	No.
Administrators	14	12.9	81	75.0	13	12.1	108
Sisters/teachers	15	14.8	66	65.4	20	19.8	101
Staff nurses/midwives	15	12.8	89	76.1	13	11.1	117
Enrolled nurses	17	19.3	56	63.6	15	17.1	88
Students	11	11.7	74	78.7	9	9.6	94
Pupils	7	13.7	37	72.5	7	13.7	51
District nurses	6	13.3	33	73.3	6	13.3	45
Health visitors	8	22.2	28	77.7	0	0.0	36
Other community nurses	6	12.2	33	67.4	10	20.4	49
Total	99		497		93		689

Respondents who gave inadequate answers and/or those to whom the question was inapplicable are excluded from the totals.

main steps are open for such a search. First, one should scan the literature to find if other studies have thrown light on the factors to be explained, secondly, one can draw on personal experience and lastly, one may be able to create an experimental situation in which the effect of certain variables is observed. Although the last step comes closest to establishing causal relationships between variables, experiments in a social setting are not easy to mount, have inherent problems and are not always appropriate.

The findings under discussion were examined along the lines outlined above. The literature suggested that many of the possible factors which make health visitors vulnerable to dissatisfaction have already been highlighted. Thus, identity problems are focused on by Hunt,[4] lack of understanding of the health visitor's role by other members of the health team is discussed by Clark,[5] Hockey,[6]

[4] Hunt, M., (1972) The Dilemma of Identity in Health Visiting *Nursing Times*, 68, Occasional Papers, 17–20, 23–24.
[5] Clark, J., (1973) *A family visitor*, The Royal College of Nursing and National Council of Nurses of the United Kingdom, London.
[6] Hockey, L., (1966) *Feeling the Pulse*, Queen's Institute of District Nursing, London.

Gilmore *et al.*,[7] McIntosh and Reid,[8] and Hobbs[9] suggests that some health visitors may not be able to exercise their teaching role as they would wish, while others are expected to conduct formal teaching sessions in difficult settings or against their will. Unsatisfactory establishments of health visitors resulting in unrealistic inadequate staffing ratios are the subjects of many statements, articles, etc.[10, 11, 12, 13]

Personal experience in the community field leads to other speculations. When comparing health visitors with other community nurses, differences in the type of work are immediately obvious. The health visitor is the only worker who is not using her practical nursing skills in a direct way. Later in this chapter skill utilisation is discussed and it is shown that 10 per cent of the health visitors were uncertain about the use of their skills. Although their uncertainty may have been related to nursing or health visiting skills it does suggest, in any event, that there was an element of diffidence.

Another difference between health visitors and other community nurses is that the tasks of the community nurses are more easily identifiable by patients and, therfore, their patients may be more overtly appreciative, thereby giving the nurses immediate gratification whilst health visitors, on the other hand, tend to deal with problems which take longer to resolve. Results in the preventive sector of the nursing service, which is the main concern of the health visitors, are not so easily seen, at least not by an individual health visitor; their efforts are more striking in their cumulative effect over time.

The mixture of work of dual and triple duty community nurses is another feature which distinguishes them from health visitors; it is possible that it is this which raises the job satisfaction of those workers but it is, of course, equally possible that there is another factor, totally unrelated to the work, which produced the difference. Combined duty community nurses tend to work in rural, rather than urban areas where most health visitors operate, which may be conducive to greater contentment generally. Other reasons can be found; for example, health visitors were less likely to have cars provided by their employing authority. It was also evident that health visitors were more apprehensive of the pending unification of the health service; they might have perceived a greater gap between themselves and the hospital nursing service than their district nursing or midwifery colleagues.

The above lengthy merely speculative discourse is not intended to give excessive emphasis to the lack of high job satisfaction levels among health visitors. The reason for it is to show the difficulty, subtlety and subjectivity of interpretation. Clearly, the reader might well add to the explanations offered and some may

---

[7] Gilmore, M., Bruce, N., Hunt, M., (1974) *The Work of The Nursing Team in General Practice*, Council for the Education and Training of Health Visitors, London.

[8] McIntosh, H. T., Reid, M., (1974) A Study of Wastage in Health Visiting, *Health Bulletin*, Vol. XXXII, No. 2.

[9] Hobbs, P., (1973) *Aptitude or Environment*, The Royal College of Nursing and National Council of Nurses of the United Kingdom, London.

[10] Kemp, I., (1969) Health Visiting in Scotland, *Health Bulletin*, Vol. XXVII, No. 2.

[11] Scottish Home and Health Department, (1973) *Towards an Integrated Child Health Service*, HMSO, Edinburgh, p. 87.

[12] Clark, J., (1974) The Case for Health Visitors, *Update*, p. 602.

[13] Gilmore, M., Bruce, N., Hunt, M., (1974) ibid., p. 59.

lead to further testable hypotheses. This is the way in which one research project leads to another and how a descriptive study might stimulate further, possibly experimental, work.

In a survey such as this, which had an exploratory as well as a descriptive purpose it is wise to take cognisance of findings which miss the acceptable statistical significance level by a narrow margin but are highly suggestive. No reliance should be placed on such data for their descriptive function of a certain happening as, by definition of significance level, it might have had a high probability of being due to chance; for exploratory purposes, however, such data deserve further investigation. In this study, there were two suggestive differences in job satisfaction levels between designations.

As can be seen in Table 8/2 almost one in five of the sisters/teachers and only about one in eight of the learners were recorded as having high job satisfaction. One aspect of this is strengthened by the fact that learners contributed the highest percentage of the group of those respondents who recorded lack of skill utilisation, which emerged as an important component of job satisfaction. The other aspect, namely the relatively high job satisfaction of sisters/teachers, cannot easily be explained in terms of skill utilisation, as one in four of this group felt that their skills were not utilised. The complexity and number of factors related to job satisfaction are as obvious as are the hazards of subjective interpretation of data.

When administrators and staff nurses/midwives were considered together in relation to sisters/teachers, it was evident that the latter group tended to achieve higher levels of job satisfaction than the former. It would not be difficult to advance a wide array of feasible, albeit merely speculative, reasons; the reader may like to indulge in such an activity which may prove productive in terms of a starting point for further research.

Table 8/3 also suggests differences in the proportions of staff scoring different job satisfaction levels related to the departments in which they worked. It may be surprising to the reader that respondents working in geriatric departments tended to score high satisfaction levels more often than those in general areas and much more often than those in maternity departments.

It must be remembered that the type of staff working in the different departments showed inherent basic differences which are discussed in Chapter 5. Therefore, differences in job satisfaction may be related to factors other than the type of department. Notwithstanding this possibility, there are indicators pointing to explanations which are directly related to the area of work. Thus, a staff midwife said:

'One hardly gets to know the mother before she is off again.'

A ward sister in a general surgical department expressed dismay about the pressure of work caused by the rapid patient turn-over. A student nurse also working in a general area in answer to the question, 'Is there anything that would make work easier or more enjoyable for you?' said:

'Yes, just a bit more time to get to know the patients. They are either too ill to talk to, or they are moved.'

As already indicated in the introductory paragraphs of this chapter, job satisfaction, acceptability of working hours and factors such as reasons for choosing
nursing are too closely inter-related to explain singly.

Thus, it cannot be startling to find that nurses who did not like their working
hours tended to score low job satisfaction. However, it is worthy of mention that
the converse was not true, that is, people who liked their working hours were not
necessarily satisfied with their job. Thus, the complexity of factors making up the
concept of 'job satisfaction' becomes apparent once more.

TABLE 8/3
Department by job satisfaction levels

| | Job Satisfaction Levels | | | | | | |
| | Low | | Medium | | High | | Total=100% |
Department	No.	%	No.	%	No.	%	No.
General	37	12.8	218	75.4	34	11.8	289
Maternity	13	20.0	46	70.8	6	9.2	65
Psychiatric	9	16.1	39	69.6	8	14.3	56
Geriatric	14	16.5	53	62.4	18	21.2	85
Not restricted to any one department	3	9.7	22	71.0	6	19.4	31
Teaching	3	15.0	14	70.0	3	15.0	20
Total	79		392		75		546

Respondents who gave inadequate answers and/or those to whom the question was inapplicable are excluded from the totals.

It is fair to assume that reasons for occupational choice and job satisfaction may
be related. Table 8/4 gives a rough presentation of the way in which reasons for
taking up nursing were categorised on the basis of some of the nurses' spontaneous
verbatim comments and in Table 8/5 the job satisfaction levels of the three groups
are presented.

It is not too difficult to see that respondents in the first group, 'vocationals',
scored high job satisfaction. They undoubtedly expected to enjoy nursing, either
because of the opportunity to help people or because of the obedience to their
calling. It is likely that these nurses could and would rationalise any disappoint-
ments in the job and find compensatory rewards.

Group 2, which might be called the 'influenced' might have entered nursing
with pre-conceptions which did not match their actual experience. The largest
number in that group had been influenced by someone else who obviously thought
highly of nursing, others had been influenced by personal experience as assistant,
auxiliary or patient which may have led them to certain expectations which were
not met. The remainder of this group had experienced war time conditions in
which nursing might have featured as a more responsible and prestigious occupation.
It must also be noted that this group, by definition, consisted of older people

who may not now find it easy to be subordinates to those often younger than themselves. Any such feelings of frustration would be increased by their realistic appraisal of the hierarchical structure with its poor long term prospect for professional parity with those of similar age.

The third group may, as 'drifters', be disillusioned on many fronts depending

TABLE 8/4
Reasons for choosing nursing as a job

Categories	Examples of quotes and reasons
'Vocational'	'Always wanted to nurse' 'Vocational/heavenly intervention or direction' 'Desire to help, meet and work with people'
'Influenced'	Experience of being an auxiliary, assistant or nursery nurse Experience as a consumer of nursing services War-time experience Influenced by others in or out of para-medical professions
'Drifters'	Nursing as a second choice to non-medical or para-medical careers 'Drifted into it, as it is as good a job as any' 'Bored with previous job, thought that nursing would be interesting' 'Few job alternatives or opportunities' Lack of education or finance to study medicine Attracted by glamour and uniform

TABLE 8/5
Reasons for choosing nursing by job satisfaction levels

	Job Satisfaction Levels							
	Low		Medium		High		Total	
Categories	No.	%	No.	%	No.	%	No.	%
'Vocational'	46	11.0	308	73.5	65	15.5	419	60.9
'Influenced'	19	15.4	88	72.7	14	11.9	121	17.7
'Drifters'	32	21.7	104	69.7	13	8.6	149	21.7
Total	97		500		92		689	

Respondents who gave inadequate answers and/or those to whom the question was inapplicable are excluded from the totals.

on the influence which caused them to 'try' nursing. Novels about nurses and advertisements tend to present love stories or glamourised nursing. Real nursing may deviate from both.

SKILL UTILISATION

As mentioned earlier, the question of skill utilisation in this study was inserted in order to get a little closer to the meaning of job satisfaction; it was prompted by the exploratory work which elicited remarks from some nurses at all levels implying that they were not using the skills which they had acquired in a lengthy educational process.

Nursing is a diverse and complex occupation. It demands skills of many kinds, ranging from manual skills and dexterity to skills of communication and inter-action. The skills employed by nurses may have been acquired in a variety of ways; some are skills linked with personality factors, others are decision-making skills which may be related to intelligence and knowledge; still others are taught and can be improved by repetitive practice. Thus, it can be assumed that nursing education provides the learner with some, but not all, skills which are needed. Moreover, different skills are needed for different branches of nursing and at different levels of the hierarchical structure.

The question did not specify which skills were being referred to. Thus, an administrator might have interpreted it in relation to administrative or nursing skills, a post-basic psychiatric student might have interpreted it in relation to general or psychiatric nursing skills. It is clear, therefore, that the answers to the question cannot be definitive or general in terms of skill utilisation of nurses; they merely indicate whether each respondent felt that her own individual skills, of whatever kind, were being utilised or not.

The data obtained from hospital staff are presented in Figure 8/1 and those from the community respondents are shown in Figure 8/2. Both sets of information are divided into positive and negative answers.

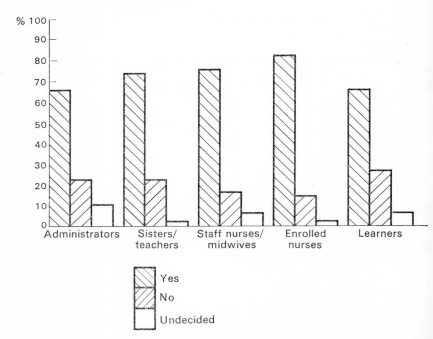

Figure 8/1   Skill utilisation by designation (hospital).

The positive responses from the hospital staff, omitting learners, show a clear pattern. The lower the qualified nurse was in the hierarchical structure, the more likely she was to give a positive answer to the question. Whereas 82 per cent of the enrolled nurses felt that their skills were being used, only 66 per cent of the administrators were of this view regarding their own skills. This finding is consistent with the comparatively lower job satisfaction of the hospital administrators referred to earlier. However, it is possible that the administrators interpreted the question to refer to nursing skills whereas the enrolled nurses had no, or at least

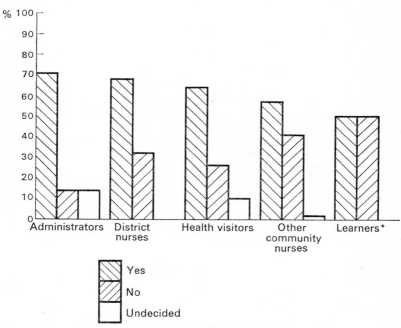

Figure 8/2 Skill utilisation by designation (community).
★ There were only 2 learners in the community.

less, ambiguity to cope with. The fairly high percentage of administrators who were uncertain how to answer, suggests that either they did not know how to interpret, or that they were not sufficiently settled in their job to assess, the question; one-third of that group had only been appointed to their current post within the last year.

It must be of concern to find that almost one-quarter of the sisters/teachers considered that their skills were not being used. This group is generally considered to have sufficient autonomy to generate its own working pattern. It may well be that the constraints of the system and/or extraneous pressures make it difficult for this grade of staff to pursue their appropriate activity.

Learners contributed the highest proportion of their peer group to the respondents who gave negative replies to the question on skill utilisation. Learners were at different stages of their training; therefore it is difficult to argue either that they might have had a higher estimation of their potential skills than the stage of their training justified, or that learners in the final stages of their training might have felt frustrated about the little responsibility they were given. In either case, what matters is that 27 per cent of learners considered that their skills were not being used and this could be a cause of dissatisfaction.

The picture in the community services reflected by Figure 8/2 shows the opposite problem as far as administrators are concerned, in that five out of seven community administrators felt that their skills were being used. In relation to this finding two points must be borne in mind. First, the number of administrators involved is much too small for any conclusion to be drawn; secondly, the community administrators were different from the hospital administrators in the range of their administrative responsibility. As explained fully in Chapter 2, the administrators ultimately responsible for each branch of the community nursing services were interviewed as top managers and are, therefore, not included in this analysis. Although the rationale was identical for the hospital field, there were two clear administrative grades interposed between top managers and field workers which was a result of the Salmon implementation. The only other details in Figure 8/2 which deserve attention are the 1 in 10 proportion of health visitors who were undecided about the utilisation of their skills, already referred to earlier in the chapter, and the 30–40 per cent of all community nurses who felt that their skills were not being used.

TABLE 8/6
Skill utilisation by job satisfaction levels

| Skill utilisation | Job Satisfaction Levels | | | | | | Total=100% |
| | Low | | Medium | | High | | |
	No.	%	No.	%	No.	%	No.
No	43	26.2	106	64.6	15	9.1	164
Yes	49	10.2	357	74.1	76	15.8	482
Qualified answers	6	15.0	32	80.0	2	5.0	40
Total	98		495		93		686

Respondents who gave inadequate answers and/or those to whom the question was inapplicable are excluded from the totals.

Skill utilisation can be taken as one of the components of job satisfaction and the data shown in Table 8/6 are not surprising. As can be seen, a significantly higher proportion of those who considered that their skills were fully utilised also scored higher job satisfaction than the remaining respondents. Again, interpretation is far from straightforward. To begin with, the respondents were active in nursing and, therefore, must in any event be sufficiently satisfied not to have left the profession.

The fact that 1 in 10 of those who felt that their skills were utilised had low job satisfaction and that almost the same proportion showed high satisfaction in spite of their negative answer to skill utilisation, points once again to the complexity of such results and the danger of drawing unsupported conclusions. The possible explanations of the findings advanced above are merely tentative suggestions which deserve further investigation.

A more detailed and sophisticated analysis of the data using factor analysis is planned. Such statistical treatment will show which of the postulated hypothetical factors account for the greatest percentage of variance in job satisfaction levels. It will test some of the suggested ideas for their real power to explain relationships.

DAUGHTER'S CAREER CHOICE

In line with the opening remarks of this chapter which draw attention to the fact that people tend to score high on measures of job satisfaction, people also tend to defend the choice of their own occupation. Wrong choices are reputedly seldom admitted to readily. Sometimes, an acceptable initial choice is made but regretted later. It was felt that a hypothetical question regarding nursing as an occupational choice for a teenage daughter might elicit a reaction which would reflect the respondent's own feeling about herself. Moreover, parental influence might play a real part in the career choices of the next generation. Table 8/7 shows that 87 per cent of all respondents indicated that they would be pleased about a daughter choosing nursing. Differences between sub-groups are negligible. Although the

TABLE 8/7
Reaction to daughter's career choice by designation

| Designation | Pleased | | Not pleased | | Other | | Total = 100% |
	No.	%	No.	%	No.	%	No.
Administrators	99	81.1	16	13.1	7	5.7	122
Sisters/teachers	88	83.0	12	11.3	6	5.6	106
Staff nurses/midwives	107	89.9	4	3.4	8	6.7	119
Enrolled nurses	81	91.0	4	4.5	4	4.5	89
Learners	129	88.0	7	4.8	4	4.0	145
District nurses	42	87.5	6	12.5	0	0.0	48
Health visitors	30	78.9	5	13.2	3	7.9	38
Other community nurses	48	96.0	2	4.0	0	0.0	50
Percentage of total		87.0		7.8		5.3	100
Total No. of respondents	624		56		32		717

health visitors had a higher proportion of answers indicating displeasure, their total sample is small and consists of relatively few actual mothers. However, the finding is consistent with others in the general area of satisfaction/dissatisfaction and, therefore, deserves mention. The analysis of the answers to this question shows perfect consistency with job satisfaction scores. Those respondents, in all categories, who scored a low job satisfaction level were also those who expressed displeasure at a nursing career choice for their daughter.

It would be tempting to conclude that a simple question such as question 54* could replace a complex job satisfaction scale. However, much further validation would be necessary before such a conclusion is warranted. Moreover, a job satisfaction scale is bound to be a more sensitive tool in that it can give a range of values, whereas the question can elicit only three possible answers, namely, yes, no, undecided.

IDEAL OCCUPATION
The third indirect method to test respondents' satisfaction with their job was to ask for their ideal occupation.** A total of 41 occupations were mentioned and they were, somewhat crudely, placed into seven categories:

1 Nursing, any branch of nursing in hospital, community or school.
2 Equal choice between nursing and another occupation such as nursing and missionary work or nursing and teaching.
3 Medicine, including specialties such as psychiatrist or surgeon.
4 Academic, such as lawyer or historian.
5 Caring type work, such as missionary, social work or occupational therapist.
6 Glamorous or creative work, such as musician or author.
7 Other, including hairdressing, clerical work, catering, farming, housewife and mother.

Respondents over 39 years, across all designations, tended to choose caring type work and the highest percentage of nurses choosing academic work also fell into this category. In relation to designation 38 per cent of administrators chose academic work, whereas students and pupil nurses tended to choose glamorous/creative work.

The majority of respondents, 62 per cent, opted to remain in nursing; this category included a small number of respondents who had made an equal choice between nursing and another occupation. The next largest group, amounting to no more than 8 per cent, chose caring type work and medicine. The remaining respondents represented all other types of occupations between them and included a few who were uncertain about another occupation. Eighty-seven per cent of the respondents then gave their reasons for choosing either nursing or non-nursing occupations. The reasons and their distribution are shown in Table 8/8, the reasons are presented in actual quotes and the similarity of reasons is noteworthy.

In conclusion, it is possible to state that the findings of this study point to a considerable measure of job satisfaction taking the sample over all. However, there are deviations which appear to be related to certain variables such as designation and type of work. In view of the reputed shortage of nurses and particularly

---

* *Question 54.* If you had a teenage daughter who had decided to become a nurse would you be pleased or not?
  Why (not)?
** *Question 53.* If you were able to choose absolutely any occupation or job in the world, with a guarantee of success in this occupation, what occupation would you choose?
  Why?

TABLE 8/8 Reasons for choosing specified ideal occupation

| Categories | Nursing Ideal Occupation | | | Non-nursing Ideal Occupation | | |
	Reasons for choosing nursing as ideal occupation	No. of mentions	% of mentions	Reasons for choosing non-nursing occupation as ideal occupation	No. of mentions	% of mentions
Personal/ inherent job interest	Long-term interest in nursing Nursing suits me and I am successful at work Nursing provides: Independence Satisfaction Variety Responsibility Nursing is: Rewarding Interesting Enjoyable	410	75.6	Work involving hobby or interest or creative work, e.g. work involving animals or art Work which I would find: Rewarding Fulfilling Stimulating Challenging Work which I would be successful in	168	75.0
Altruistic factors	Enjoy helping and caring for others Enjoy seeing my work helping people Enjoy meeting and working with others Meets my personal needs	85	15.7	Wish to help specific groups of people, e.g. children Work more suited to meeting my personal needs	35	15.6
Conditions of service and career prospects	Nursing provides: Security Promotion Good pay Opportunities to travel Status Good working hours	35	6.5	Apparent easier success Better status Improved working conditions More highly paid Work involving travel	6	2.7
Other	Nursing provides: Practical active work Good working atmosphere Good company Family trend to nurse	12	2.2	More practical and active work More glamorous type work	15	6.7
Total No. of mentions		542	100		224	100
No. of respondents		425			119	
Don't know		7			6	

of the difficulty in recruiting health visitors, pointers such as these, merit further investigation.

Relationships between variables do not necessarily imply cause/effect relationships. For example, it is just as possible that nurses who are already dissatisfied try health visiting as an alternative, as it is that health visiting itself causes them to be dissatisfied. Moreover, there may well be another factor altogether which causes dissatisfaction and which is also common to health visitors. Marital status, academic preparation, personality factors are but a few of many possibilities. Unfortunately it is extremely difficult to establish causal relationships in the real life situation.

CHAPTER NINE
Part-time Nursing

Part-time employment is an accepted phenomenon in modern society and part-time nursing is no exception.

This chapter is intended to focus more directly on part-time nurses, giving details about their work and about their personal characteristics and problems. It is hoped that information about our part-time respondents might point to features common to all part-time nurses, thereby putting them into the context of the nursing profession and within the framework of working women in general.

DEFINITION OF PART-TIME WORK
Part-time work refers to a total number of working hours which is less than the prescribed minimum for full-time work. The difficulty of finding a common denominator among the wide range of concepts and definitions of part-time employment was emphasised by Janjic[1] when reviewing part-time work in the public service in 1972. In search for an acceptable definition she was driven back to that given by the ILO in 1963:

'Part-time employment is taken to mean work on a regular and voluntary basis, for daily or weekly periods of substantially shorter duration than current normal hours of work.'[2]*

A recent series of publications on women and work[3] show that there is a marked increase in those working part time from 37.5 per cent in 1963 to 49 per cent of all women working in 1973.

PART-TIME NURSING
The upper limit of part-time working hours is bound to be determined by the legislated minimum of full-time hours which has changed over time.

In 1907 nurses in Poor Law Hospitals were expected to work 60 hours each

---

[1] Janjic, M., (1972) Part-time work in the Public Service, *International Labour Review*, Vol. 105, No. 4.

[2] ILO, (1963) An international survey of part-time employment *International Labour Review*, Vol. 88, No. 4, p. 383.

*'Voluntary' in the context of the definition can be taken to mean 'optional' and not 'unpaid'.

[3] Department of Employment, (1974) *Women and Work*, Manpower Papers 9, 10, 11 and 12, HMSO, London.

week but many worked 70 or more.[4] In 1943 the Scottish Nurses' Salaries Committee suggested that a nurse should work a 96-hour fortnight. However, it was not until 1947 that this recommendation was implemented in all hospitals with the addition of overtime pay for grades below that of sister.

In 1948, with the beginning of the National Health Service, England's Rushcliffe and Scotland's Taylor Committees were replaced by the Nurses and Midwives Whitley Council. The Whitley Council on Pay and Conditions of Service of all National Health Service workers has standardised and continues to revise their conditions of service and pay structure.

TABLE 9/1
Changes in nurses' working hours since 1948

Year	Hours per week
1948 to 1959	48
1960	46
1965	44
1971	42
1972	40

Source: Whitley Council (Nurses and Midwives Circular 159).

TABLE 9/2
Changes in working hours in industry since 1951

Year	Average hours per week
1951	44.4
1961	42.1
1966	40.2
1971	40.0
1972	40.0

Source: Central Statistical Office (1973), *Social Trends No. 4*, HMSO London, Table 33.

Table 9/1 shows the decrease in the number of full-time working hours for nurses since 1948, which, in Table 9/2, is compared with similar decreases in working hours in the general industrial field.

The importance of part-time nursing in an era of rising marriage rate of women is obvious. It is, moreover, likely that part-time employment will be increasingly sought, as people in general are endeavouring to raise their earning power. Whilst some married nurses might not have worked at all even five years ago, they now readily accept part-time work providing it is compatible with their home commitments. It would seem, therefore, that nursing may have to compete more seriously with other occupations which a qualified married nurse may be willing and able to pursue.

[4] MacKay, G. A., (1907) *Practice of the Scottish Poor Law*, William Green & Sons, Edinburgh.

Investigations into part-time nursing have been undertaken from time to time either as part of nurse recruitment in general or as specific studies and, as Auld[5] recognises, it is not only necessary to recruit part-time nurses but also to integrate them into the staffing structure without loss of status. It is reported in Chapter 1 that resentment between full- and part-time staff was one of the problems raised in the initial exploratory discussion.

In 1973, 23.3 per cent of the total nursing work force in Scotland were part-time nurses. A recent study commissioned by the Scottish Home and Health Department and undertaken by the Institute for Operational Research[6] shows not only that of the total number who joined the Scottish Health Service in 1972/73 almost 60 per cent were part-timers but also that 79 per cent of these came from within Scotland. Therefore, part-time nursing can be regarded as a topic of some relevance to the Scottish health service.

Although the increase in part-time nursing is marked, it must be noted that it relates to those qualified nurses who are not in administrative positions; only 2.5 per cent of all Scottish administrators were employed on a part-time basis. This finding is consistent with studies of women in top jobs in other professions.[7,8,9] all of which suggest that part-time employment in key positions of administrative or professional responsibility is comparatively rare.

PART-TIME NURSES IN THE STUDY

Our study revealed a wide variety of working patterns all of which are included in the term 'part-time work'.

The most common forms of part-time work are:

1 Work on 5 days a week, but less than the required hours each day to make up a 40 hour week (or 80 hour fortnight).

2 Work on less than 5 days in the week, either regularly on certain days for a specific period, or irregularly to meet demands at work and/or commitments at home.

3 Night duty of mostly two 10-hour shifts.

4 Full-time work, but for a limited time, for example a few weeks in the year only.*

As shown in Tables 9/3a and b the part-time nurses in our study were all qualified fieldworkers except for one administrator and one pupil nurse.

The one part-time pupil in our sample is one of the few remaining participants in a part-time pupil training scheme. Such schemes had been implemented in

[5] Auld, M. G., (1967) An Investigation into the Recruitment and Integration of Part-time Nursing Staff in Hospitals, *International Journal of Nursing Studies*, Vol. 4, pp. 119–169.

[6] Institute for Operational Research, (1975) *The Movements of Hospital Nursing Staff in Scotland*, IOR/834, IOR, Edinburgh.

[7] Jeffreys, M. E. P., (1966) *Women in Medicine*, Office of Health Economics, London.

[8] Fogarty, M., Allen, A. J., Allen, I. and Walters, P., (1971) *Women in Top Jobs*, George Allen & Unwin, London.

[9] Department of Employment, (1974) *Women and Work: a statistical survey*, Manpower Paper No. 9, HMSO, London.

* Although such nurses worked full time during their periods of work they were regarded as part-time workers by their employing authority and in this study.

Scotland on an experimental basis for an initial trial period of five years from 1964.** Between July 1969 and May 1973 part-time training was gradually phased out, the reason being poor recruitment and a high wastage rate.†

In the hospital service, staff nurses, midwives and enrolled nurses had the highest proportion of part-timers in their ranks; in the community services, where part-time employment generally is far less prevalent, district nurses and school nurses contributed the highest proportions to part-time workers.

TABLE 9/3a
Part-time or full-time employment by designation (hospital)

Designation	Full-time	Part-time
Sisters	81	14
Teachers	11	0
Staff nurses	44	64
Staff midwives	5	6
Enrolled nurses	53	36
Total	**194**	**120***

* 1 part-time administrator and 1 part-time pupil nurse should be added to the total of part-time nurses in the hospital.

TABLE 9/3b
Part-time or full-time employment by designation (community)

Designation	Full-time	Part-time
Community nursing officers	7	0
Health visitors	37	2
District nurses	35	8
Domiciliary midwives	11	0
School nurses	0	7
Combined duty nurses	30	7
Total	**120**	**24**

Part-time workers in industry are often associated with the temporary or short-term work force. Table 9/4 shows that the patterns of stability of full- and part-time nurses are almost identical, both groups contributing the highest proportion to those who had been employed by the same authority between 3 and 10 years. The two groups show a slight divergence when the periods of time over which they remained at the same designation are compared. Whereas 72 per cent of part-timers had remained in a static grade for longer than 3 years, the comparable proportion for full-time qualified staff was only 55 per cent. As administrators are excluded from this comparison it reflects a somewhat slower upward

** Made possible by The Nurses (Scotland) Act, 1951, Section 21(2).
† Source: General Nursing Council for Scotland (private communication).

mobility of part-time staff which can be partially explained by their breaks in service.

It is impossible to separate the effects of qualifications and type of employment on upward mobility. Our data show that part-time nurses tended to hold less qualifications than their full-time colleagues. As shown in Table 9/5 over half the part-time nurses had only the one basic qualification which gave them licence to practise, compared with only one-third of full-time nurses who had such a bare minimum. Career aspirations and patterns are discussed in Chapter 7, where the

TABLE 9/4
Length of time employed by hospital group or local authority★

Length of time	Part-time No.	Part-time %	Full-time No.	Full-time %	Total
Under 1 year	23	16	48	11	71
1 year, less than 3 years	32	22	84	20	116
3 years, less than 10 years	57	40	155	36	213
10 years or more	32	22	142	33	174
Total= 100%	144		429		574

★ excluding learners.

TABLE 9/5
Number of qualifications by full- or part-time employment★

	Number of Qualifications										
	1 No.	1 %	2 No.	2 %	3 No.	3 %	4 No.	4 %	5 or 6 No.	5 or 6 %	Total= 100%
Full-time	108	33.2	98	30.2	82	25.2	24	7.3	13	14.0	325
Part-time	80	55.5	45	31.2	16	11.2	3	2.1	0	0.0	144

★ excluding administrators and learners.

point is made that part-timers may have less motivation, but also less opportunity, to acquire further qualifications.

Four main areas of activity were, somewhat arbitrarily, identified within the hospital service; these were general, maternity, psychiatric and geriatric areas. Table 9/6, presenting the distribution of part-time and full-time staff among these four main areas, shows that the largest proportion of available part-time staff is deployed in the general field. A detailed analysis of part-time and full-time deployment within the hospital departments showed that the proportional allocation of all staff to the various departments is remarkably similar.

Table 9/7 has relevance for nursing administrators, in that it shows the relative importance of part-time staff in hospitals of different sizes. Apart from the smallest hospitals of less than 20 beds, with their small number of staff, the contribution of part-time staff to the total labour force is seen to be inversely correlated with the hospital size. Hospitals of medium size were those which had the largest proportion, 35 per cent, of all learners. It is fairly obvious, therefore, that part-time nurses especially in these medium sized hospitals fulfil an important teaching function in addition to the direct service they provide.

TABLE 9/6
Hospital department by type of employment★

Department	Part-time %	Full-time %
General	60	53
Geriatric	18	18
Maternity	13	17
Psychiatry	9	12
Total=100%	113	261

★ teaching staff and learners are excluded.

TABLE 9/7
Employment of part-time, full-time qualified and learners by hospital bed numbers

Type of staff	Less than 20 beds	20–29	100–499	500–999	1000+	Total
			Number of Beds			
Full-time nurses	15	31	100	54	95	295
Part-time nurses	5	14	53	18	32	122
Learners	0	3	49	28	63	143
Total	20	48	202	100	190	560
Part-time staff as % of all staff	25	29	26	18	17	

Predictably, part-time employment in the hospital service is seen to be more prevalent in the urban than in the rural study areas. Figure 9/1 shows the proportions of full-time qualified staff, part-time qualified staff and learners in each of our four hospital groups and their adjacent local authority areas and emphasises the small component of part-time staff in the community. The other point worthy of mention is the marked difference in full-time qualified staff as a proportion of all staff between Hospital Groups A and C. As explained in Chapter 3 it was not our concern to compare the four areas with each other. Differences are stressed merely to show that our respondents represented different staffing patterns, as it can be assumed that their views, attitudes and relationships might be influenced by the general staffing structure and policy of their areas.

Given the need to integrate part-time nurses into a service committed to the

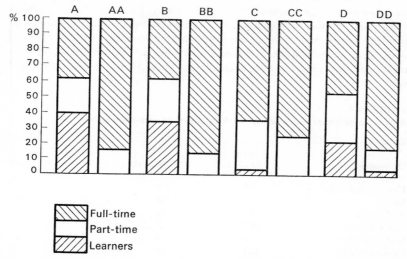

Figure 9/1 Proportion of full- and part-time qualified staff and learners in the research areas.

provision of full-time coverage, an analysis of the number and arrangement of part-time working hours is relevant.

Table 9/8 gives a detailed picture of the average number of hours worked by the different groups of part-time nurses.

Apart from the two 'unusual' part-timers,* it seems that part-time nurses, as a group, work on average more than half the full-time hours but the records completed by the top managers (Chapter 4) indicated that in most cases two part-timers were regarded as one whole time equivalent. It may be that this method of calculation of part-time nurses compensated for change-over periods and double reporting time.

The part-time nurses were asked to state their contracted hours. The few part-time community nurses' contracted hours amounted to an overall average of 22.2 hours against their recorded average of 23.7 hours. Hospital nurses reported a contracted average of 24.6 hours against a recorded average of 24.5 hours. The Halsbury Committee Report[10] states, however, that in a survey carried out by the Health Departments part-time nurses in hospital worked just under 30 hours per week, and those in the community worked about 20 hours per week. In our study hospital and community part-timers showed a greater similarity between their working hours than the official survey report.

---

* The one and only 'part-time' administrator as well as the one and only 'part-time' pupil nurse were obviously part-timers in theory rather than in practice.

[10] Department of Health and Social Security, (1974) *Report of the Committee of Inquiry into the Pay and Related Conditions of Service of Nurses and Midwives* (Chairman: The Earl of Halsbury, FRS), HMSO, London, para. 47.

As far as the distribution of part-time working hours is concerned, the peak day for part-timers in the hospital service is Wednesday, followed closely by Friday. In line with all other staffing levels, the week-end shows the smallest numbers of part-time nurses, Sunday being the lowest when two-thirds of the Wednesday work force were on duty. Part-timers, therefore, do not seem to completely replace full-timers at week-ends, although they obviously contribute to week-end work.

TABLE 9/8
Average number of one week's* working hours of part-time nurses

Designation	Average hours for one week	No. working	No. not working	Total
Unit nursing officer	40.8	1	0	1
Sisters	22.9	11	3	14
Staff nurses	23.4	59	5	64
Staff midwives	15.1	3	3	6
Senior enrolled nurses	32.3	3	0	3
Enrolled nurses	27.1	29	4	33
Pupil nurse	41.5	1	0	1
District nurses	23.6	8	0	8
Health visitors	19.0	2	0	2
School nurses	23.9	6	1	7
Triple duty nurse	32.5	1	0	1
Relief district nurses/ health visitors	19.6	4	1	5
Triple duty and school nurse	20.0	1	0	1
Total		129	17	146
Mean Average	24.38			

* Week immediately before the interview.

Part-time nurses on day duty in hospital were slightly more likely to work morning than afternoon or evening shifts, but as can be seen from Figure 9/2 part-timers as a group provided a fairly stable labour force throughout the day. Part-time nurses in the community were overwhelmingly most likely to work in the morning period. The working pattern of part-time nurses is closely related to their domestic commitments, that is their dual roles, which are discussed below.

The Finer Report, though not intended specifically for nurses, draws a picture which is relevant to the nursing scene:

'Longer life, a sex ratio near unity, more and younger marriages and small consciously planned families, with fertility compressed into a narrow band of years, have resulted in revolutionary alteration in women's lives as wives, as mothers and workers.'[11]

[11] Department of Health and Social Security, (1974) *Report of the Committee on one-parent families* (Chairman: Sir Morris Finer), Cmnd. 5629, HMSO, London, p. 33.

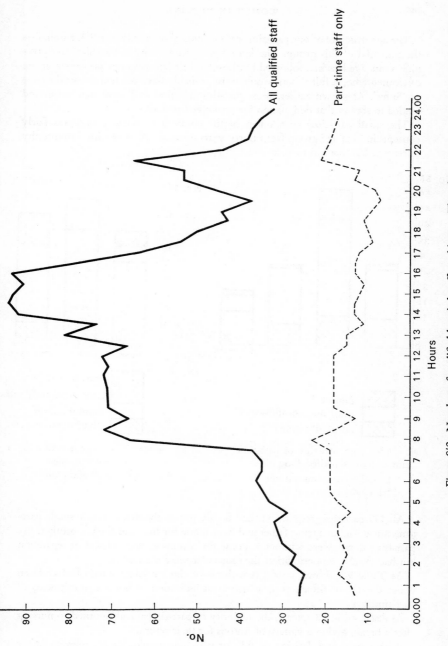

Figure 9/2 Number of qualified hospital staff working on Thursday.

The age structure of our part-time respondents, shown in Figure 9/3, emphasises the potential of this group. The largest proportion being in the thirty to thirty-nine years age bracket, followed by those in their late twenties presents a group of women who, as full-timers, would most probably have reached at least the level of 'Sister'. As shown earlier, most part-time hospital staff were staff nurses and tended to stay in that designation for prolonged periods.

The small part-time component of the community nursing staff was fairly constant in each age group from thirty years onwards. No part-time community nurse was less than thirty years old.

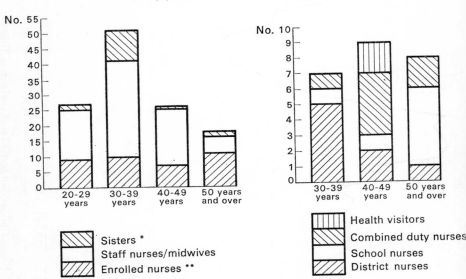

Figure 9/3a   Age structure of part-time nurses by designation (hospital).

* Includes one administrator.
** Includes one pupil nurse.

Figure 9/3b   Age structure of part-time nurses by designation (community).

All 147 part-time respondents had family responsibilities, the only single part-time nurse had an ageing father and kept house for him and for her brother. Six part-time nurses were without a spouse for reasons of widowhood or separation but had family responsibilities; the remainder were married.

As Table 9/9 shows, nearly two-thirds of the part-time nurses had children under the age of fifteen years which is an indication of home commitments of part-timers.

As discussed in Chapter 7, the majority of part-timers had returned to nursing after a break, giving a variety of reasons for their return.

With regard to a decision on full- or part-time employment a relevant factor might be the husband's occupation and the family income. Of our respondents, 35 per cent of part-timers against 12 per cent of full-timers had husbands in white collar or professional grades and, whereas over half the husbands of part-time nurses earned more than £1500* per annum, only one-third of full-time nurses' husbands came into this higher income bracket. As most part-timers earned less than £1000, the difference in family incomes between full- and part-time staff was to some extent balanced.

Part-time nurses must be viewed as an important current, as well as a potential full-time, work force. Our study, in line with others, showed the contribution, in terms of working hours, made by part-time staff, highlighting the fact that they are a necessary component of the hospital staff.

TABLE 9/9
Number of children under 15 years of age of part-time nurses

Designation	Number of Children				
	0	1	2	3	4
Sisters	5	3	2	4	0
Staff nurses/midwives	17	16	23	10	4
Enrolled nurses	16	11	7	2	0
Health visitors	1	1	0	0	0
District nurses	2	2	3	1	0
Other community nurses	8	3	2	1	0
Total	49	36	37	18	4

It is, moreover, pertinent to note that conventionally designated unsocial hours, such as night duty and week-end rotas are not infrequently worked by part-time nurses.

As a potential full-time work force the earlier quotation from the Finer Report is relevant. Nurses, like other women, tend to plan their pregnancies within a relatively short span of their life thereby giving themselves greater freedom sooner than previous generations.

Although there is evidence to show that a greater proportion of women return to full-time teaching after a break than to full-time nursing, this is clearly related to full-time school teaching hours being more compatible with family responsibilities than full-time nursing hours; this statement is supported by comments such as:

'I'd like to work full time, but can't be out when children come home.' or

'If it weren't for school holidays I could cope full time.'

The Committee on Nursing[12] claimed that in striking contrast to casual impressions over half of all married nurses and midwives returned to the profession.

---

* Data were obtained in 1973.

[12] Department of Health and Social Security and Scottish Home and Health Department, (1972) *Report of the Committee on Nursing* (Chairman: Professor Asa Briggs), Cmnd. 5115, HMSO, London, para. 413.

From our and other data it seems obvious that most of those who return to nursing seek part-time employment in the first instance, although they proceed to full-time work later.

In order to assess the relationships between full- and part-time staff it seemed relevant to attempt an assessment of nurses' attitudes to part-timers. The scale designed to make this assessment and the treatment of the resulting scores are described in detail in Appendix 5. Table A5/10 shows the distribution of nurses' responses to statements on the part-time scale. In the interpretation of the results it must be emphasised that a high score indicates a positive attitude to part-time nurses and a low score a negative attitude. As can be seen from Table A5/7 the distribution of low, medium and high scores on the part-time scale for all nurses was perfectly symmetrical. When separating hospital from community staff it seems that the former tend to have a more positive attitude to part-time staff than the latter. In the interpretation of this finding it must be remembered, however, that few community nurses were part-timers and that full-time community nurses were, therefore, unlikely to have had recent experience of working with part-time colleagues.

This study, unfortunately, included only working nurses and the part-timers were, therefore, those who wanted to work and could fit into the system. They are less well qualified than full-timers and less likely to advance to senior positions in the hierarchy. They are, however, predominantly under forty years of age with twenty years of potential service before them. The fact that they are working at all, albeit part time, must be viewed as a valuable transition stage toward full-time work, during which they are maintaining their nursing practice.

The profile of a part-time nurse emerges as one who is likely to be under forty years of age, married with one or two children less than fifteen years old, having returned to nursing after a single break in service to the NHS in the last 10 years, the purpose of the break having been to bear and raise a family. The nurse is likely to have only one qualification and be working as a staff nurse in a medium-sized general hospital for 24 hours a week, either 2 nights a week or on a morning shift. She is likely to be working closely with student nurses.

It seems that the potential of this group might be considerably enhanced by opportunities to acquire further qualifications during their part-time working phase. They would then eventually be more ready for a full-time post, commensurate with their age and experience, which may not only be an incentive for part-time nurses to remain in the profession, but may also raise the ultimate value of their contribution. The urgent need to provide facilities for part-time courses at many levels is repeatedly stressed by the Committee on Nursing.

CHAPTER TEN
Working Hours

Hours of work are of importance to any working person, not least to women who, more often than not, have domestic commitments in addition to their work. Many employers are not dependent on any specific hours of work by their employees for successful functioning and are able to 'close down' for periods of the day, night, week or year without difficulty. It may indeed be advantageous for them to do so as complete closure of premises may reduce overhead costs. Thus, many industrial concerns have fixed holiday periods for all their workers and, of course, many close at nights, week-ends and public holidays. They are free to open or close as they wish.

The health service does not have this freedom and is committed to the provision of a 24 hour service for seven days a week for the majority of the patients. For any one patient, there is a large number of health personnel involved in both the hospital and the community setting but the nursing staff provides the largest single group attending to the varying needs of the patients.

The nursing service, therefore, has to ensure that an appropriate number and mix of nursing personnel are available at all times. Inability to procure such a staffing level may undermine the quality of patient care.

No attempt was made in this study to calculate appropriate staffing levels, which has been and currently is the concern of many research workers and policy makers.[1-5] This investigation applied itself only to the number and distribution of hours worked by the sample of nursing staff in order to discern not only broad patterns of work but also to focus on details and individual problems.

The complexity of the nursing staffing problem with the inherent conflicts between service needs and societal trends toward a shorter working week was highlighted by the Committee on Nursing.[6] In its Report, the Committee recom-

---

[1] Auld, M., (1974) *A Method of Estimating the Requisite Nursing Establishment for a Hospital*, M.Phil. Thesis, University of Edinburgh, unpublished.

[2] Rhys Hearn, C., (1974) Evaluation of patients' nursing needs: prediction of staffing, 1-4. *Nursing Times* Occasional Paper, Vol. 70, Nos. 38-41.

[3] Oxford Regional Hospital Board, (1967) *Measurement of nursing care*, Operational Research Unit, Oxford Regional Hospital Board.

[4] Bryant, Y. M., Heron, K., (1974) Monitoring patient-nurse dependency, *Nursing Times* Occasional Paper, Vol. 70, No. 19.

[5] Grant, N., (1975) Nursing Care Plan—2, *Nursing Times* Occasional Paper, Vol. 71, No. 13.

[6] Department of Health and Social Security and Scottish Home and Health Department,

mends that three issues should be considered in deliberation on shifts and working hours:[7] first the efficient working of the hospital and community service and the best possible provision of service for patients; secondly the preferences and welfare of the nursing staff; thirdly the programme of education for students.

The concern, which surrounds the provision of adequate health service round the clock, emphasises the importance of obtaining a full and detailed picture of nurses' working hours. It was, therefore, considered prudent to attempt initially to construct such a picture in this study.

Several obvious methods for collecting the information were considered; first the nurses could have been asked to record their own duty periods for a given time span during the survey; secondly, a mechanical timing device could have been used; thirdly, an observer could have 'shadowed' a nurse throughout her working day or, lastly, nurses could have been asked to recall their working periods in an interview.

The first three methods were discarded for the following main reasons. Self-recording was considered to be prone to distortion and to missing information; for example, a nurse, seeing her working hours for a whole week adding up to less than 40, might have been tempted to adjust them; incomplete returns are another hazard of such a method. The second option, in the form of a mechanical clocking on and off device, would have had to be specially introduced as even in hospitals where time clocks are used they do not usually apply to full-time workers; moreover, such devices would have been difficult to use in the domiciliary field. Continuous observation, the third alternative, may not only be liable to produce abnormal behaviour in the observed person, but would have been prohibitive in terms of time and money for the number of people involved in our study. For these reasons the last method was adopted; each nurse was asked to state the times at which she went on and off duty during the seven day period immediately preceding the interview.* In the pilot studies, when this question was tested, it became apparent that the respondents found it easier to begin the week's recall with the day prior to the interview and to work back.

Breaks were recorded as well as periods 'on call'. Emphasis was placed on recording actual, rather than scheduled, times. Although it would be unrealistic to believe that the information was totally accurate, the interview situation did not give time for deliberate misrepresentation.

Once the data were collected a decision on their presentation had to be made. The specially written computer programmes** aided by graphical output,† generated much detailed information not only for the total sample but for any desired sub-group within it.

(1972) *Report of the Committee on Nursing* (Chairman: Professor Asa Briggs), Cmnd, 5115, HMSO, London.

[7] Department of Health and Social Security and Scottish Home and Health Department, (1972) ibid., para. 570.

    * See page opposite.

    ** Written in IMP language for IBM/158 computer.

    † CALCOM 563 driven by a PDP8 computer attached to the IBM/370/158, using a special graph plotting package.

Question 38. Can you tell me your duty time for the last week starting yesterday and working backwards? For each day I would also like to know when you had your main meal breaks and any periods when you may have been on call?

Code each working period. Record night duty for day in which shift started. Use 24-hour clock. Tick right hand column if on call.

	Start	Finish	On call
Sunday			
Monday			
Tuesday			
Wednesday			
Thursday			
Friday			
Saturday			

It was decided to divide the 24-hour day into 48 half-hour segments. A nurse was considered as being on duty during any of the half-hour periods if she worked 15 minutes or more within it. It could happen, for example, that any half-hour was said to be staffed by two people although one of them worked for only 15 minutes of it, but this bias was likely to be balanced by periods within which several people worked less than 15 minutes none of which was recorded.

The pattern of working hours unfolded by the analysis can be taken as a fairly reliable picture. The nature of the data and the allowance for breaks result in slightly more uneven patterns than scheduled shifts and rotas would suggest, which is an asset in that actual peaks, troughs and overlaps are revealed more clearly.

OVERALL PICTURE

Predictably, the hospital and community nursing staff show clear differences between them as far as the pattern of working hours is concerned. The reason is, no doubt, in the provision of a round the clock service in the hospital sector. Thus, there is first, a night staffing level which is absent in the community and secondly, there is a staggering of meal breaks in the hospital whilst community staff tended

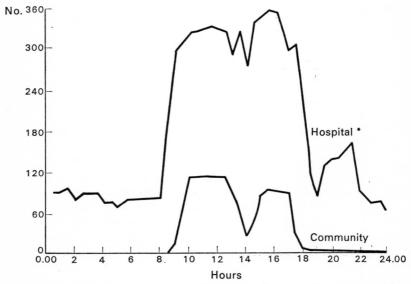

Figure 10/1   Comparison of numbers of hospital and community nurses working on a Monday.

★ Adjustment made for sampling difference.

to take their main lunch break at the same time. Although, or perhaps because, these points are self-evident, it is reassuring to find that our method for recording the information resulted in such a clear picture, especially of the lunch break patterns. In Figure 10/1 these differences are illustrated.

Table 10/1 shows the proportion of different designation groups of respondents who were on duty on each day of a week. It gives a presentation of the fluctuation in staffing levels throughout the week and the differences in fluctuation between the designation groups.

Most striking is the week-end decline in every single group of staff, though it is more marked in some groups than others. Within the hospital structure, adminis-

TABLE 10/1

Percentage of designations who were working on individual days of one week

Designations	No.=100%	Percentage of Totals Working Each Day							Average percentage for the 5 weekdays %
		Monday %	Tuesday %	Wednesday %	Thursday %	Friday %	Saturday %	Sunday %	
Hospital administrators (excluding tutors)	102	78	75	69	75	63	45	42	72
Sisters	95	70	58	56	55	58	53	54	59.4
Staff nurses/midwives	119	49	51	53	48	55	42	35	51.2
Enrolled nurses	91	51	52	57	51	54	43	45	53
Learners	143	72	64	66	69	73	51	52	68.8
Health visitors	39	87	89	87	87	77	3*	0	85.4
District nurses	43	93	95	83	79	65	40	34	84.6

* 1 person only.

This table deliberately excludes some designations, for example, teachers and some community nurses such as school nurses.

trators showed the sharpest drop both on Saturday and on Sunday but staffing in general was decreased at week-ends.

In the community, well over twice the number of district nurses were on duty on Monday and Tuesday than at the week-end. Only one of the health visitors in our sample worked on Saturday and none worked on Sunday.

The working pattern of staff is bound to be affected by the type of employment in terms of full-time or part-time. Part-time employment, as a crucial issue in modern society, is discussed in Chapter 9. It is relevant here to view the hours worked by part-timers in relation to their full-time colleagues, in order to obtain a clearer picture on overall nursing coverage.

Figures 10/2a, b and c show the proportion of part-time and full-time nurses working during each segment of selected days both in the hospital and the community. As a 'typical' week-day Thursday was chosen and the two week-end days are presented separately.

Figure 10/2a, which presents the Thursday pattern, shows that part-time nurses contribute more than half the qualified nursing staff to the hospital night shift. The irregularity of the curve during the night is due to meal breaks and not to staff changes within that period. As can be seen part-time nurses became a less prominent component as the day shift came on duty. Thus, there is a sharp drop in the proportion of part-timers to full-time staff between 07.00 and 09.00 hours remaining at that lower level throughout the day but increasing again from 20.00 onward.

The pattern of community part-time employment is, of necessity, different in that there is no regular night nursing service provided. As Figure 10/2a shows, the part-timers make up no more than 20 per cent of the total community nursing staff at any time of the day, with the proportions in hospital averaging 21 per cent during the day shift period.

The general trend described is maintained on Saturday (Figure 10/2b) which shows slight deviations in detail only, whereas the Sunday pattern (Figure 10/2c) presents a different picture, especially in the community. In the hospital, the overall proportion of part-timers is roughly 10 per cent smaller throughout the 24-hour period on Sunday than on the week day. In the community, the total number of all staff was small on Sunday and within that group the part-time component becomes disproportionately important especially late in the day. In fact, during the one hour period 18.00 to 19.00 hours there was no full-time community nurse of any type actually working, although some were on call.

Because of the marked differences in the working pattern between hospital and community nurses they are considered separately.

HOSPITAL NURSING STAFF

The working hours of all designation groups were analysed separately but not all analyses are presented in this section.

It must be stressed that auxiliaries are not included in any of the analyses, although their contribution to the work force is clearly recognised.*

---

* Because of the accepted importance of the nursing auxiliary in the health service a detailed study of this occupational group is currently being planned by the Nursing Research Unit.

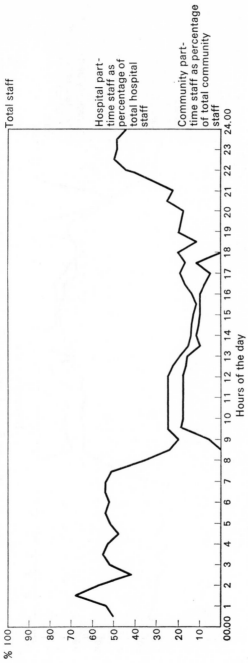

Figure 10/2a Relative full- and part-time staffing levels over 24 hour period (Thursday).

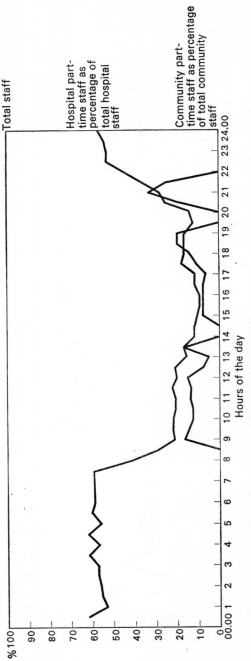

Figure 10/2b   Relative full- and part-time staffing levels over 24 hour period (Saturday).

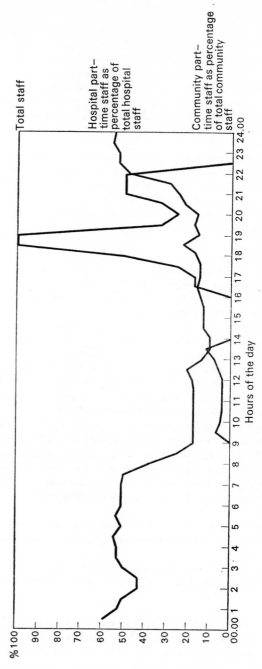

Figure 10/2c Relative full- and part-time staffing levels over 24 hour period (Sunday).

Figures 10/3a, b, c, d show the average apportionment of different grades of staff at four selected half-hour periods of the day and night. Each period was deliberately chosen first, because each was seen to be relatively stable in as much as there were few meal breaks or shift changes, and secondly, because each appeared to reflect the working norm for that period. The full circle represents the total staff, apart from administrators and teachers. As can be seen, learners contribute the highest proportion of personnel in all shifts excepting night duty. The early afternoon period has the largest proportion of learners on duty mostly due to overlap of shifts.

Enrolled nurses, a group which includes both enrolled and senior enrolled nurses, seemed to contribute a stable and consistent staff component. As Table 10/1 shows, the number of enrolled nurses did not fluctuate greatly throughout the week and from Figure 10/3 it can be seen that they make up between 17 and 19 per cent of staff during the day but appear to compensate for the smaller number of learners on night duty, when over 22 per cent of staff were enrolled nurses.

Hospital administrators

Because of the sampling method adopted it is necessary to consider the administrators as a separate group. As explained in Chapter 2 they constituted the total population and, by virtue of the high response rate achieved from that group, they included almost all administrators in post.

Administrators, in the context of this analysis, are Nursing Officers and Senior Nursing Officers, excluding those with teaching responsibilities only; 101 administrators interviewed were employed on a full-time basis.

As Table 10/1 shows, just under half the nursing officers worked at the week-end, whereas 78 per cent were on duty on Monday. When separating SNOs from UNOs, some differences in their working patterns emerge. Whereas most SNOs worked a straight shift from around 08.00 hours the UNOs were divided among two shifts with an overlap in the early afternoon period. Therefore, the maximum number of SNOs would be on duty in the morning and early afternoon and the maximum number of UNOs also in the early afternoon, this being the overlap period. The early afternoon period, is, therefore, a part of the day during which most administrators are at work; they seem to coincide with each other and with ward sisters as to the timing of their lunch break which tended to be no longer than half an hour.

Predictably, a smaller proportion of administrators than of any other group was on night duty, 16 per cent on permanent night duty against 75 per cent who never worked at night.

The number of administrators who were on call for shorter or longer periods was minimal, that is, less than 1 per cent, a point which is further discussed below.

Sisters

Our sample included 95 sisters, most of them employed full time. Although they were working in different types of hospital and a wide variety of different departments a fairly clear working pattern emerged for the total group.

The sisters' full-time weekly working hours averaged just about 40, although this average distorts the real picture for some of them. Thus, 6 respondents had in fact worked over 50 hours, whereas others, though full-time employees, had been on duty for less than 30 hours during the week. It must be stressed that the Whitley Council lays down 80 hours work a fortnight rather than 40 hours a week, which accounts for the variations among our respondents. The average weekly hours for the few part-time sisters was 23.

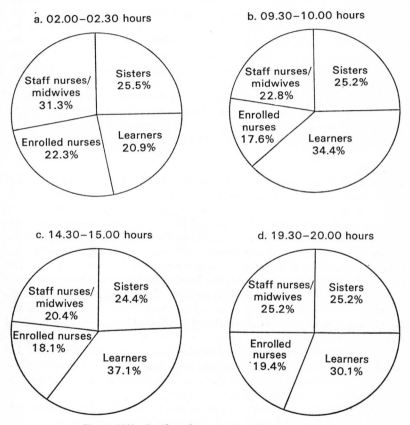

a. 02.00–02.30 hours

Sisters 25.5%
Staff nurses/midwives 31.3%
Enrolled nurses 22.3%
Learners 20.9%

b. 09.30–10.00 hours

Staff nurses/midwives 22.8%
Sisters 25.2%
Enrolled nurses 17.6%
Learners 34.4%

c. 14.30–15.00 hours

Staff nurses/midwives 20.4%
Sisters 24.4%
Enrolled nurses 18.1%
Learners 37.1%

d. 19.30–20.00 hours

Staff nurses/midwives 25.2%
Sisters 25.2%
Enrolled nurses 19.4%
Learners 30.1%

Figure 10/3 Staff on duty at selected time periods.

Apart from night duty, there were basically two shifts worked by sisters, the most common shift commenced between 08.00 and 09.00 hours and applied to just over half of all sisters working on any one day. A further 20 per cent started work at 14.00 hours which resulted in a concentration of sisters' working hours between 14.00 and 17.00 hours. The other shift was night duty which tended to commence after 21.30 hours. The few remaining sisters did not fit clearly into any of the three shifts.

Staff nurses and midwives

This group consisted of 108 staff nurses and staff midwives; for the purpose of this section they are referred to as 'staff nurses'.

The working pattern for the group as a whole seemed to be largely determined by the relatively high proportion of part-timers, in which respect they differed from the sisters.

The other two main differences between staff nurses and sisters were first, the larger proportion of the former being on night duty and secondly, that the day when most staff nurses were on duty was Friday, as against Monday for sisters. Within the day, staff nurses also worked basically two shifts, early and late, resulting once again in an overlap in the early part of the afternoon which was, however, less marked than that of sisters. Predictably, staff nurses alternated their meal breaks with sisters.

Similar to enrolled nurses, staff nurses seemed to provide a fairly stable core of staff at all times, fluctuating only slightly. The increase of staff nurses at the beginning of the morning shift is an indication of a higher staffing level maintained by them throughout the day, rather than a short-term overlap.

Learners

The group of 143 learners in this study consisted of student and pupil nurses as well as post-basic students. The criterion for inclusion in the group was that the person's prime aim was to learn in order to become qualified in the respective field of nursing. On the one hand, a learner, especially in the early stages of training, requires qualified supervision and guidance; on the other hand, it is important for learners to gain appropriate experience in independent nursing. Although value judgments, regarding the supervision and experience of learners, are not warranted on the basis of our data, it is helpful to know how learners fit into the general staffing picture, analysing their working hours in relation to those of qualified staff. Working hours, in this analysis, refer only to hours spent in clinical areas and exclude any time spent in the school. Roughly 1-in-5 of all learners were in school on any one week day.

The peak days for learners to be in the clinical areas were Monday and Friday and the weekly average of their working hours was just about 40, with a slight excess for pupil nurses. Because of the usual shift arrangements, the overlap of learners in the early afternoon period is marked.

Figure 10/4 shows the working pattern of learners and all qualified staff excluding administrators. The main features demonstrated by this figure are first, the small number of learners on night duty and secondly, that their working pattern follows that of all other clinically involved nurses. In other words, they do not stand out as a group whose purpose in clinical involvement is different from that of other nursing staff, a statement which is not intended to imply criticism. The figure shows that the proportion of learners to qualified staff is roughly 1-to-2,* except on night duty.

---

* This statement conceals variation among different sizes and types of hospital; for example, there were only 3 learners in hospitals of less than 100 beds, while the greatest concentration of learners was in the hospitals of 1000 beds and over.

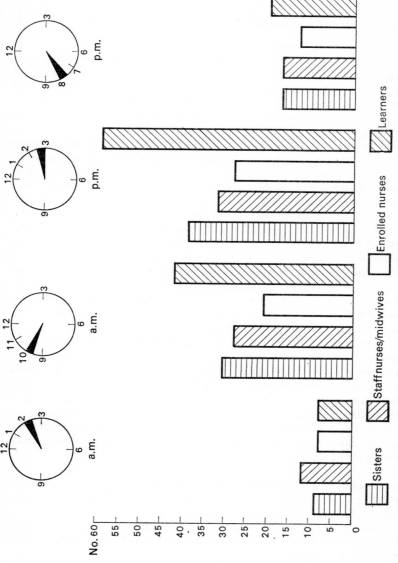

Figure 10/4 Average number of each group of nurses on duty at selected periods of the day (excluding administrators).

Teachers

The working hours of teachers are not commented on as they fitted in perfectly with the predictable timetable of a school with its normal 09.00–17.00 hours day.

COMMUNITY NURSING STAFF

District nurses and health visitors

As the nature of the work of district nursing staff differs considerably from that of health visitors, their work patterns can be expected to differ also. It must be stressed that working hours in this analysis do not include on call periods, which would increase the working day considerably. This point is further discussed below.

The district nurses employed on a full-time basis worked an average of 35 hours, the part-timers an average of 24 hours, whilst the 32 full-time health visitors recorded a weekly average of 36 hours, against the 19 hours of their two part-time colleagues. The distribution of the working hours through out the five weekdays was remarkably consistent, almost all community nurses, in whatever branch, commenced work between 08.00 and 09.00 hours; irrespective of whether they worked broken shifts, part-time hours or full-time straight shifts, they were all at work by 09.00. Similarly, most community nurses in all fields tended to have finished work by 17.30 hours, although around 5 per cent of district nurses and 3 per cent of health visitors worked on at least one evening in the week. As mentioned earlier, there was a general reduction of staff on Saturday, which was accentuated on Sunday, the reduction on both week-end days being more marked for the health visiting than for the district nursing staff.

Tables 10/2a and b show the number of district nurses and health visitors who were working at selected time periods throughout the week and highlight the sharp decline of the work force at the week-end.

The reader who is familiar with the work of district nurses, may justifiably question the wisdom of selecting 19.30–20.00 hours as an appropriate evening period to gauge district nursing staffing levels. Most of the evening visits by district nurses are for the purpose of giving sedation and settling patients for the night, which is usually done later than 20.00 hours. Our data showed, however, that of any evening hours the selected period was the one during which the largest number of district nurses worked, although many short working periods were reported intermittently right up to 22.00 hours. One district nurse worked throughout one night.

Combined duty nurses and domiciliary midwives

Predictably, combined duty nurses showed a different work pattern, largely due to the fact that they were employed predominantly in rural areas.

The major sub-groups within the sample of 37 combined duty community nurses were 19 triple duty workers and 8 district nurses/midwives. The others represented almost every combination of duties with small numbers in each. It is pertinent to emphasise that all but 7 of this sample had a midwifery component in their work. Responsibility for midwifery in a rural community implies prolonged periods on call and this was one of the two factors which distinguished combined duty nurses' working pattern from that of health visitors and district nurses mentioned earlier. The other difference lay in their tendency to work a little later in the evenings.

The 11 full-time single duty domiciliary midwives worked in urban areas only. Predictably, they were the one group of community nurses whose periods on call feature most prominently in their work pattern. Thus, whereas the average number

TABLE 10/2a
Number of district nurses on duty at selected time periods

Days of the week	Hours of the Day			
	02.00–02.30	09.30–10.00	14.30–15.00	19.30–20.00
Monday	0	39	31	3
Tuesday	1	41	32	1
Wednesday	0	36	29	2
Thursday	0	34	26	1
Friday	0	28	20	0
Saturday	0	17	7	0
Sunday	0	10	1	2

Total number of district nurses=43.

TABLE 10/2b
Number of health visitors on duty at selected time periods

Days of the week	Hours of the Day			
	02.00–02.30	09.30–10.00	14.30–15.00	19.30–20.00
Monday	0	34	34	2
Tuesday	0	35	34	1
Wednesday	0	33	34	0
Thursday	0	34	32	2
Friday	0	30	30	0
Saturday	0	1	0	0
Sunday	0	0	0	0

Total number of health visitors=39.

of hours actually worked by them was only just 22 hours, almost exclusively in the morning, they were on call for the full 24-hour period of any working day.

School nurses

The analyses of school nurses' working hours are not presented. By virtue of the type of their employment they worked during school hours only and enjoyed school holidays. There were only 7 school nurses in our sample, all of whom were part-timers. Although one would expect this sort of post to be held by young women with school children, for whom it seems ideally suited, only one of the

7 nurses had children who were under fifteen years of age; the other respondents in this group were women over forty-five years, 2 being over sixty.

Having established the working pattern of all grades of nursing staff within the limits of the method adopted, it is now relevant to consider the three points made by the Committee on Nursing which were mentioned earlier. The first of these was the efficient working of the hospital and community services. As already indicated this study did not set out to evaluate the nursing services. Therefore, it is merely possible to use the pattern of working hours of different grades of staff as one, albeit crude and debatable, indicator of efficiency of service or, perhaps preferably, as a pointer to further investigations. For example, it seems reasonable to look for explanations when confronted with marked fluctuations in working hours on certain days of the week or at certain periods of the day. Similarly, irregular changes in staff mix, that is in the combination of different grades of staff, would lead one to search for reasons. The data presented in this chapter, particularly the week-end trough and after lunch peaks, should be viewed in this light.

The second point stressed by the Committee on Nursing was the need to pay attention to the preferences and welfare of the nursing staff.

Our respondents were asked whether they liked their present working arrangements or not.★

TABLE 10/3
Opinions on arrangements of working hours

	Administrators	Sisters/ teachers	Staff nurses/ midwives	Enrolled nurses	Students	Pupils
Like	102	91	107	68	70	30
Dislike	20	13	12	16	20	18
Other	1	2	0	5	3	2
Totals	123	106	119	89	93	50

Table 10/3 shows the responses. As can be seen, the overwhelming proportion of all staff were happy with their working arrangements, at least on day duty. They were satisfied with the number, as well as the distribution, of their working hours. The respondents were asked how long in advance they knew about their off-duty and whether the period of notice was satisfactory or not.★

Table 10/4 shows the staff's advance knowledge of their off-duty, as can be seen, a substantial proportion of enrolled nurses had only short notice of their off-duty and, understandably, some of them were not happy about this, especially as it was not always easy to change:

★ *Question 19.* I realise that this is just one week's working pattern which may not be typical. On the whole do you like the arrangement of your working hours or not?
★★ *Question 40.* How far in advance do you know your off-duty/time off?
Question 41. Is this sufficiently in advance to arrange your life outside work or not? How far in advance would you like to know?

'It depends on the sister in charge and you have to find someone to change with.'

Even some of the administrators found it difficult to make changes in their off-duty. A Nursing Officer said:

'You have to go cap in hand to people, it causes too much discussion and you feel it's not worth the bother.'

The only group who voiced fairly consistent dissatisfaction was the learner category, most of whom knew their off-duty no more than one week in advance, sometimes even less than that. The reason for such short notice of off-duty was, however, not always due to lack of consideration; for example, a sister said:

'I make it up . . . (off-duty list) . . . and I don't do it very far ahead because people invariably want something special.'

As the most senior grades of staff tend to work out their own off-duty times with each other, their satisfaction in this respect is not surprising. Similarly,

TABLE 10/4
Knowledge of off-duty by designation

Knowledge of rota in advance	Administrators	Sisters/ teachers	Staff nurses/ midwives	Enrolled nurses	Students	Pupils
Fixed duties	47	32	47	19	1	0
Less than one week	8	16	27	28	63	30
1 week, but less than 2	16	26	24	20	25	10
2 weeks, but less than 3	15	16	11	7	1	3
3 weeks, but less than 4	9	5	3	9	3	1
4 weeks or more	28	11	7	6	0	7
Total	123	106	119	89	93	51

Respondents who gave inadequate answers and/or those to whom the question was inapplicable are excluded from the totals.

community nursing staff tend to arrange their rotas among themselves by mutual consent. Although the respondents were invited to indicate changes, if any, they would like to see in the advance knowledge of their off duty, their comments were too few to merit presentation in this report.

Nurses on night duty consist of three different groups and, when discussing their reaction to night duty, these differences are pertinent. The first group are those on permanent night duty, the second are those who merely take their turn for limited periods and the last group consists of those nurses who work basically on day duty but are on call during the night.

One hundred and one nurses in our sample worked on permanent night duty and more than half were part-time staff. All grades of staff were represented in this group but the staff nurses contributed 33 per cent of their total number to permanent night duty staffing; administrators and sisters were equal in having 16 per cent of their numbers on permanent night duty. Predictably, staff on permanent night duty had chosen to work during the night and were happy about it; it is relevant to note that three-quarters of these nurses were married.

'I'm going on permanent nights . . . for the off-duty. You know every week when you're off and when you're on.'

'I prefer it to day-duty. I think the number one reason for anyone liking night duty would be that you can sleep during the day. The whole working of night-duty is smoother in a way. You don't have your interruptions, doctors' rounds. It has its busy times, of course. Basically I'm a nocturnal person.'

The average number of working hours for the part-time nurses was 23.4 which could represent only two nights per week. Whilst it was seen by the nurse as a distinct advantage to fulfil her weekly working commitment in two nights, such a system requires frequent staff changes with their inherent administrative complexities. It seems also fair to question whether this particular staffing pattern might have an adverse effect on patient care if continuity is thought to be important.

Reasons why permanent night staff liked night duty were of a professional kind, such as greater autonomy, responsibility and interest, and personal reasons such as family or social convenience and greater financial reward. Nurses on temporary night duty concurred with the professional reasons for liking night duty. The reason most frequently advanced by all grades of staff for not liking night duty was difficulty in sleeping during the day.

The third group, which consisted of those nurses who were on call during the night, is also the group whose members tend to be on call for varying periods during the day. Three distinct patterns of on call periods emerged. First, there were those nurses who were on call for periods of 24 hours, secondly some respondents were on call for shorter periods which might have included meal breaks, thirdly, there were some who reported being on call during meal breaks only. Whilst the long periods of being on call related almost entirely to the community nursing staff, only hospital respondents were likely to be on call during meal breaks only.

Within the community, it was nurses with midwifery responsibilities who recorded the longest and most frequent periods on call during the week. Such extended periods on call applied predominantly to single duty domiciliary midwives in urban areas and to a lesser extent to combined or triple duty nurses working in rural areas. Some were not too happy about the constraints on their social activities which on call periods imposed, but the interviews, on the whole, conveyed the general impression that the advantages of their working conditions outweighed the disadvantages. One triple duty nurse said:

'It's rather tying. You aren't able to go out anywhere when you're on call. You sit in the house for hours and no calls come.'

although one domiciliary midwife commented:

'I quite like being on call. It's part of the job, I suppose. The patients see you coming in the middle of the night and they're so grateful. It's nice.'

If hours on call are added to working hours, some of these community nurses could easily 'clock up' 70 hours per week. Although single duty district nurses in the cities reported less and shorter periods on call, an average of one-third of all community nurses were on call for extended periods at least once during the week.

In the hospital service, 1 per cent of the administrators were on call for a period of 24 hours and no other grades of staff gave a 24 hours call service.

On call periods during meal breaks were recorded by 7 per cent of qualified nursing staff in the hospital service, but did not seem to be unacceptable to them.

As already indicated, the only way in which our data can throw any light on educational programmes for learners is to examine the hours worked in the clinical areas in relation to time in the classroom and to view the ratio of learners to qualified staff. The recorded number of hours worked by pupil nurses has already been mentioned as appearing excessive; if the recorded hours are accurate at all, and given that the week during which they were recorded was typical, it would not leave much time for private study. As seen from Figure 10/3 learners made up around one-third of all staff, excluding administrators, during the day-time hours overall, and exceeded that proportion in the afternoon overlap period. Whilst it is known from many descriptive studies of work in hospital that the overlap period tends to be used for teaching purposes, the value of that period of time might be undermined if the proportion of qualified staff decreases as the proportion of learners increases. Our data give no evidence in that direction but point to a possible area deserving vigilance.

The only other finding relevant to the needs of learners relates to night duty. Although Figure 10/2a shows that learners made up one-fifth of the total staff on night duty, it must be pointed out that, unlike sisters on day duty, night sisters may not be specific to any one ward or department. Therefore, the immediate support given to the learners on night duty must come from the other grades, namely enrolled nurses and staff nurses. In view of the finding, commented on earlier, that over half the qualified staff on permanent night duty are part-timers, working something like two nights a week, their potential to teach learners on the basis of detailed knowledge of individual patients may be limited.

It is also worthy of mention that the reduced number of learners during the night period was made up by enrolled nurses, which suggests by implication, that learners provide part of a work force which, in any event, must be kept constant. Clearly, if learners should become supernumary in the wake of the Briggs' recommendations, recruitment of other staff in larger numbers for day as well as night duty is imperative.

CHAPTER ELEVEN
Nursing Auxiliaries

The number of nursing auxiliaries employed in Scottish National Health Service hospitals is considerable. In 1973 it represented 33.6 per cent of all hospital nursing staff. In the decade 1960–1970 the percentage of nursing auxiliaries in the total nursing labour force was increased from 28.6 per cent to 33.2 per cent.* The high proportion of part-time workers in this group of staff is worthy of note.

In the community nursing services, the increase of auxiliary staff was more rapid in England and Wales than in Scotland. Between 1968 and 1971 the number of this grade of staff south of the border doubled, reaching 4.7 per cent of the labour force compared with 1.9 per cent in Scotland. Geographical characteristics may partly account for this difference as distances and difficulties of travel in the scattered rural areas of Scotland are bound to be a hindrance to supervision and support of unqualified staff. Another reason may lie in the fact that district nursing continued to be organised for a longer period by a voluntary body acting as agent of the local health authorities. The existence of this voluntary body, the Queen's Institute of District Nursing, which has a long tradition of providing a fully qualified domiciliary nursing service, may have delayed a change in policy.

To consider the impact of the auxiliary worker it is necessary to view the whole picture and to compare the changes in the employment of both auxiliaries and other nursing staff. However, the lack of a clear definition of 'nursing auxiliary' as discussed below, militates against a precise comparison between hospital and community services.

The statistical information suggesting the importance of the auxiliary, was, of course, available before this study was set under way. Equally clearly recognised was the absence of an acceptable unambiguous definition, which was the main reason for the decision to use this study as a means to obtain a little more informtion about nursing auxiliaries from other members of the nursing staff. It could then serve as a possible preliminary to a more detailed study of the nursing auxiliary herself.

DEFINITION OF NURSING AUXILIARY

Within the hospitals selected for the study the title 'nursing auxiliary' referring to unqualified members of the nursing staff, other than learners, was familiar to everyone interviewed, although 'nursing assistant' was the designation most often used in psychiatric hospitals. There is some general confusion about the exact definition of the term 'nursing auxiliary' both in the U.K. and internationally.

---

* DHSS and SHHD statistics. Annual Reports, etc., 1961–73.

Discussions in the 1950s and 1960s by the World Health Organization on the use of auxiliary nursing personnel related to those giving supplementary care less exacting than that given by professional nurses, the former being described as:

'paid workers in a particular technical field with less than full professional qualifications in the field and who assist, and are supervised by professional workers' (unpublished United Nations report/R 170)

This grade of staff is somewhat analogous to the enrolled nurse grade in the United Kingdom and it is worthy of note that some registered community nurses in this study misunderstood the use of the title 'nursing auxiliary'. They were accustomed to referring to all members of staff who did not have an RGN qualification, as auxiliary help, thereby including enrolled nurses and untrained staff.

The Royal College of Nursing and National Council of Nurses of the United Kingdom (Rcn) in preparation for the 1973 International Council of Nurses in Mexico, questioned member countries on their use of auxiliary nursing personnel and usefully classified nurses into three categories. Category three, equivalent to the nursing auxiliary was defined as:

'Nursing personnel able to perform specific tasks related to patient care that require considerably less use of judgment. They should be able to relate well to patients and carry out dependably under supervision, the tasks for which they have been trained.'[1]

Of 35 countries who responded, 22, including the United Kingdom, had no officially approved training schools for this grade of staff, while the remainder varied from 1 to 338.

The last few years in this country have seen a radical change of thought on the role of the nursing auxiliary. The Central Health Services Council in 1968 recognised that nursing auxiliaries would continue to be needed for the immediate future but predicted:

'. . . as the number of enrolled and pupil nurses increases and if housekeeping teams become established, the composition of ward teams will change and less reliance will need to be placed on the services of nursing auxiliaries.'[2]

The Committee on Nursing reported in 1972 and using the term 'aide' to encompass nursing auxiliaries, nursing assistants and ancillary (nursing) staff in the community, recommended that maximum use of aides should be made both in hospital and in the community:

'To us they appear as indispensable members of health teams, but their place in those teams should be to support professional nurses and midwives,'[3]

[1] World Health Organisation, (1966) Report of the Expert Committee on Nursing, World Health Organisation, Geneva.

[2] Central Health Services Council, (1968) Relieving Nurses of Non-Nursing Duties in General and Maternity Hospitals, HMSO, London.

[3] Department of Health and Social Security and Scottish Home and Health Department, (1972) Report of the Committee on Nursing (Chairman: Professor Asa Briggs), Cmnd. 5115, HMSO, London, para. 45.

Nursing auxiliaries are seen as those who enable professional nurses and midwives to exercise their role more effectively.

Evaluations of auxiliaries' capabilities and competence tend to be made on an individual basis in the given situation they enter and little has been done to determine how the greatest job satisfaction and cross matching of skills can be accomplished. Scottish Hospital Memorandum No. 70/1970[4] acknowledges this variation succinctly:

> 'The word "assist" (in the list of duties considered appropriate to nursing assistants which followed) is used to imply that the specific duties will vary with the type of ward, the degree of patient dependency and the experience and training of the nursing auxiliary. She may also assist with other procedures and techniques at the discretion of the ward sister.'

This particular memorandum does not refer to the use of auxiliary nursing personnel in the community nursing services.

Although the Scottish Home and Health Department provides some guide to the duties and training of nursing auxiliaries, discussion continues on the inclusion of 'nursing' in the title 'nursing auxiliary' and on the exact functions of this grade of staff. It would appear, however, that the dependence of the nursing services on the auxiliary is now well recognised and viewed as permanent. The Committee on Nursing (1972) therefore investigated existing training provisions of nursing auxiliaries.[5] It obtained details of 594 courses, all in-service schemes, and noted many variations in the number of hours involved and in the amount of emphasis on orientation or training. In the present study provisions ranged from an in-service training scheme arranged by a nursing officer specially designated for that purpose to a two-day orientation programme. The recommendation was made by the Committee on Nursing (1972) for a nationally agreed outline syllabus of a practical nature for both hospital and community auxiliary staff and for the award of a certificate on successful completion of the course.

While variation can as easily reflect flexibility as it can a lack of definition, it was fairly obvious in this study that the roles, functions and titles of auxiliary personnel varied considerably. Titles given to auxiliary personnel included the following: nursing auxiliaries, nursing assistants, bath attendants, nurses' aides, nursing aides. Also, more specific designations of community health aides, operating room aides and psychiatric aides were mentioned in addition to 'allied health personnel'. These more specific designations describe where or in what environment the nursing auxiliary works as opposed to the type of work required in the situtaion.

For the purpose of this study, interviewers were asked to establish the use of the term 'auxiliary' for 'unqualified nursing staff' in the respondent's hospital or local authority, and the term continued to be used in this sense in the interview context and throughout the study.

---

[4] Scottish Home and Health Department, (1970) *Duties and Training of Nursing Auxiliaries and Nursing Assistants*, Scottish Hospital Memorandum No. 70/1970, Scottish Home and Health Department, Edinburgh.

[5] Department of Health and Social Security and Scottish Home and Health Department, (1972) ibid., p. 101, paras. 336–341.

NURSING AUXILIARIES IN THE RESEARCH AREAS

The material discussed in this chapter is entirely based on information obtained from respondents in answer to a series of questions about nursing auxiliaries and not from nursing auxiliaries themselves.

The questions covered the following points:

the number of auxiliaries in employment

the method of their allocation

nursing staff's opinions about nursing auxiliaries

nursing staff's opinions about the measure of responsibility given to nursing auxiliaries and about the advisability of including them in official ward reports on patients

nursing staff's views on auxiliary employment in relation to patient care.

As described in Chapter 2, the top managers in the research areas provided statistical information about number and type of staff.

Tables 11/1a, b and c show the total staffing picture of nursing auxiliaries in the research areas. The staffing ratio between nursing auxiliaries and other nursing staff is presented in a number of ways in order to facilitate comparison with other parts of the country, where the recording of staffing figures may follow a variety of patterns. Tables 11/1a and b show that there is little difference in the overall effect between counting auxiliaries as whole time equivalents, that is on the basis of hours worked, and counting them as total numbers of staff. Only in Hospital Group B was the ratio significantly altered, thereby indicating considerable part-time employment of auxiliaries. The number and proportion of auxiliaries in Hospital Group A is striking, 5 auxiliaries to every 7 other nursing staff and it is worthy of note that, as shown, in Table 11/1c, the adjacent Local Authority AA had by far the lowest number and proportion of nursing auxiliaries working in the community. Comparison between Table 11/1b and c also shows that in Hospital Group D and its local authority area the picture was reversed; the hospital nursing service was the one with the smallest proportion of nursing auxiliaries, 30.2 per cent, whilst the local authority had the largest proportion, 16.7 per cent, of this grade of staff.

It almost seems that there is a given potential number of nursing auxiliaries in an area who, all things being equal, might be shared between the hospital and community nursing services; if one service does not offer employment the other tends to absorb this labour force.

NURSING STAFF'S WORK CONTACT WITH NURSING AUXILIARIES

As explained earlier, no nursing auxiliaries were interviewed for this particular study; it was deemed important, however, to establish the extent of personal knowledge of their work by nurses. Fifteen per cent of the nurses had themselves been nursing auxiliaries before their professional training. For 6 per cent of the sample, this had been the sole job between leaving school and taking up nursing. Five per cent numbered auxiliary nursing as one of the two jobs they had held, and 4 per cent had two or more other posts between school and nurse training.

TABLE 11/1
Nursing auxiliaries in relation to other nursing staff

(a) Nursing Auxiliaries in Relation to Other Hospital Nursing Staff★

Hospital groups	No. of auxiliaries	No. of other nursing staff	Total no. of nursing staff	Proportion of auxiliaries to other nursing staff	Percentage of auxiliaries in total nursing staff	Proportion of auxiliaries to total nursing staff
A	858	907	1765	1:1.1	48.6	1:2.1
B	719	1401	2120	1:1.9	33.9	1:2.9
C	82	184	266	1:2.2	30.8	1:3.2
D	355	821	1176	1:2.3	30.2	1:3.3
Total	2014	3313	5327	1:1.6	37.8	1:2.6

★ Part–time staff counted as whole members of staff.

(b) Nursing Auxiliaries in Relation to Other Hospital Nursing Staff★

Hospital groups	No. of auxiliaries	No. of other nursing staff	Total no. of nursing staff	Proportion of auxiliaries to other nursing staff	Percentage of auxiliaries in total nursing staff	Proportion of auxiliaries to total nursing staff
A	599	828	1427	1:1.4	42.0	1:2.4
B	465	1234	1699	1:2.6	27.4	1:3.7
C	66	172	238	1:2.6	27.7	1:3.6
D	307	762	1069	1:2.5	28.7	1:3.5
Total	1437	2996	4433	1:2.1	32.4	1:3.1

★ Part–time staff counted as whole–time equivalent.

(c) Nursing Auxiliaries in Relation to Other Community Nursing Staff★

Community areas	No. of auxiliaries	No. of other nursing staff	Total no. of nursing staff	Proportion of auxiliaries to other nursing staff	Percentage of auxiliaries in total nursing staff	Proportion of auxiliaries to total nursing staff
AA	3	80	83	1:26.7	3.6	1:27.7
BB	14	130	144	1:9.3	9.7	1:10.3
CC	4	37	41	1:9.3	9.8	1:10.3
DD	18	90	108	1:5.0	16.7	1:6.0
Total	39	337	376	1:8.6	10.4	1:9.6

★ Part–time staff counted as whole members of staff. Whole–time equivalents not available in all areas.

Of the 104 nurses who had previously done this work, 84 per cent were now working in wards, departments or districts with nursing auxiliaries. This is a slightly higher percentage than was found in the whole sample, in which 79 per cent of all nurses interviewed worked with nursing auxiliaries. It is worth noting that there was no significant difference in answers to questions concerning auxiliaries between those who had been and those who had not been nursing auxiliaries themselves.

Nurses working in hospital, whether administrative staff, students or pupils, were more likely to be working in situations where auxiliary workers were also employed than were nurses in the community posts. None of the health visitors was aided in her work by auxiliary nursing personnel, although several studies[6] [7] [8] [9] have suggested that some of the health visitor's activities, especially at clinics, might lend themselves to auxiliary support. Over 84 per cent of hospital nurses in each job designation, or an average of 92 per cent of all hospital nurses, worked with auxiliary nurses. Forty-two per cent of district nurses and 36 per cent of other community nurses also had working contact with auxiliaries. Table 11/2 shows the number of nurses in the different designations who were working with auxiliaries at the time of the study.

TABLE 11/2
Designation of staff in working relationship with nursing auxiliaries

Designation	Working with nursing auxiliaries		Not working with nursing auxiliaries		Total=100%
	No.	%	No.	%	No.
Administrators	108	88	15	12	123
Sisters/teachers	90	85	16	15	106
Staff nurses/midwives	110	92	9	8	119
Enrolled nurses	83	93	6	7	89
Students	88	94	6	6	94
Pupils	50	98	1	2	51
District nurses	20	42	28	58	48
Health visitors	0	0	39	100	39
Other community nurses	18	36	32	64	50
Total	567	79	152	21	719

[6] Marris, T., (1971) *The work of health visitors in London*, Greater London Research Department of Planning and Transportation, Research Report No. 12, Greater London Council, London.

[7] Hockey, L., (1972) *Use or Abuse? A study of the state enrolled nurse in the local authority nursing services*, Queen's Institute of District Nursing, London.

[8] Clark, J., (1973) *A Family Visitor—A Descriptive Analysis of Health Visiting in Berkshire*, The Royal College of Nursing and National Council of Nurses of the United Kingdom, London.

[9] Gilmore, M., Bruce, N. and Hunt, M., (1974) *The Work of the Nursing Team in General Practice*, Council for the Education and Training of Health Visitors, London.

Nurses who were not currently working with auxiliaries were asked whether they thought nursing auxiliaries would be helpful or unhelpful to their work. Since few hospital nurses fell into this group, the answers mainly reflect the opinions of community nursing personnel.

Fifty-seven per cent of those stating that auxiliaries would not be helpful, indicated that the work was not suitable for them and over four-fifths of this group were community nurses. Unsuitability of the work referred mainly to complex technical/confidential aspects in hospital and to the practice of patient assignment in the community. Many community nurses felt that the responsibility of the type of total patient care in the home which often also involved advice to the family was too great for auxiliary staff. Other reasons given were that no extra help was presently required, 24 per cent, trained personnal would be preferred, 15 per cent, and that auxiliary nurses would require supervision, 4 per cent.

Almost half of those who considered that nursing auxiliaries could be helpful thought that they would relieve nurses of some tasks altogether, a quarter thought that they would assist nurses with some skilled tasks and the same proportion that they would help nurses by doing some of the less skilled tasks. The remainder gave a combination of these answers.

ALLOCATION OF NURSING AUXILIARIES

Various methods of organising the allocation of nursing auxiliaries are in operation up and down the country and in different hospitals. Sometimes a 'pool' of these workers is established so that allocation to areas of need is made from a central point; such allocation may be for varying periods but is usually for one shift at a time. It is possible, however, that even in a pool system nursing auxiliaries may remain in one area for a long period; it would seem reasonable to retain pool labour in a familiar setting as long as additional labour is required there, rather than to exercise an indiscriminate daily allocation. 'Relief' in this context means that the nursing auxiliary fills gaps which arise in the permanent staffing situation. Often nursing auxiliaries are allocated to specific areas, that is wards or departments, on a more long-term basis. This enables the auxiliary to identify with a particular setting and in a nurse training hospital ensures some continuity in a situation where student and pupil nurses are frequently changing. Occasionally, auxiliaries may be recruited to a specific ward or department on a permanent basis. Combinations of methods are often operated especially in larger hospitals.

The nurse administrators were asked how auxiliary nursing personnel were assigned to their ward or department, and within their work areas. Only in one hospital was it indicated that a 'pool' was their sole system of auxiliary assignment and this was a hospital with over a thousand beds.

By far the most commonly mentioned method seemed to be the allocation of a nursing auxiliary to a particular ward, department or area as a permanent or semi-permanent staff member. Eighty-one per cent of respondents from differently sized hospitals reported this as the only system.

The remaining 17 per cent respondents were in hospitals where both systems operated simultaneously; all but one of these had 100 beds or more.

NURSING STAFF'S OPINIONS ABOUT NURSING AUXILIARIES

In an attempt to gain some insight into the nursing staff's opinions about nursing auxiliaries, respondents working with them were asked to assess the appropriateness of the responsibility the auxiliaries were given.* The assessment can only be subjective as neither 'auxiliary' nor 'responsibility' have been defined so that, inevitably, criteria for measurement are lacking. There is, moreover, little, if any, agreement on the apportionment of responsibility to specific nursing tasks.

TABLE 11/3
Opinions of nurses about the amount of responsibility given to nursing auxiliaries

		Amount of Responsibility			
Designation	No.	Too much %	Too little %	Just about right %	Other answer %
Administrators	108	9	2	82	7
Sisters/teachers	90	10	8	75	7
Staff nurses/midwives	110	19	8	65	8
Enrolled nurses	83	5	11	79	5
Students	88	9	5	83	3
Pupils	50	8	4	78	10
Community nurses*	38	5	0	95	0
Total**	567	10	6	78	6

* This group consists of district nurses and other community nurses; no health visitors in the sample were working with auxiliaries.
** Includes only those respondents who were currently working with nursing auxiliaries.

Table 11/3 shows the views on this matter of the 567 nursing respondents who were currently working with nursing auxiliaries. It is probably not too surprising that over three-quarters of that group considered the responsibility given to nursing auxiliaries about right. Senior personnel would, themselves, organise the work and thus, no doubt, use their judgment in giving responsibility to different grades of staff; learners could perhaps not be expected to evaluate measures of responsibility.

Of all groups of staff, community nursing respondents were most homogeneous in their view that the 'right' amount of responsibility was given to nursing auxiliaries. This may also reflect the fact that many of them were directly responsible for deploying the auxiliary workers.

Of those who did not feel that the responsibility of auxiliaries was just about right, the tendency was to say that they had too much rather than too little responsibility. Only one group of nursing personnel, the enrolled nurses, showed

* *Question 56.* Do you feel the responsibility that nursing auxiliaries/nursing assistants are given is too much, too little, or just about right?

the reverse tendency by saying that auxiliaries had too little responsibility. Although this difference did not prove statistically significant, it may be of interest to study the work of these two groups more closely; historically they had the most in common, enrolled nurses having been known as 'assistant nurses' until 1961.

A statistically significant difference was found between the full-time and part-time nurses on the question of auxiliaries' responsibility. Eighty one per cent of all full-time nurses thought that the responsibility was just about right, with 9 per cent saying auxiliaries had too much and 4 per cent that they had too little responsibility and 6 per cent giving other answers. Only 66 per cent of part-time nurses, however, considered that auxiliaries had about the right amount of responsibility, 15 per cent feeling they had too much, 11 per cent too little and 8 per cent giving other, qualified, answers.

The fact that part-time nurses question the responsibilities more closely, may reflect uncertainty as to how the work of the auxiliary relates to their own work. Not infrequently, part-time nurses complain of their own relative lack of responsibility due to their part-time status. The respondent's age group did not seem to influence answers in this respect. If the increased usage of part-time nurses and auxiliaries is to continue, it may be important to study the respective levels of responsibility as they may overlap and conflict.

REASONS FOR OPINIONS CONCERNING LEVELS OF RESPONSIBILITY

Respondents were asked to give reasons for their judgment on the level of responsibility given to nursing auxiliaries. Of those who considered the level to be just about right, 46 per cent related it to the auxiliaries' capabilities and amount or absence of training. A higher percentage of sisters and teachers held this opinion than those in other job groups and this might be seen to relate closely to their own greater responsibilities in the setting of suitable tasks. Roughly 1-in-5 of the respondents considered it right that nursing auxiliaries were not given any responsibility and approximately 1-in-10 considered their level of responsibility suitable as they were working under the supervision of trained staff. Eight per cent felt that nursing auxiliaries knew their jobs well and had useful experience from their own life or home situation. Because responsibilities could be adjusted to the individual and the task at hand, 9 per cent considered them about right. Seven per cent gave combinations of these reasons.

Of the 58 respondents who stated that nursing auxiliaries had too much responsibility only 2 were community nurses. Reasons given for this view were fairly evenly distributed between 4 categories. Thirteen said that nursing auxiliaries were sometimes left in charge of a ward or given similar considerable responsibility, 11 considered that nursing auxiliaries worked without supervision and took too much on themselves; 15 saw them as having to undertake responsible nursing duties due to staff shortages, and 11 were of the opinion that their responsibilities exceeded their training. Eight gave other qualified answers.

The main reasons given by the 32 respondents for the responsibility of nursing auxiliaries being too little were that their capabilities were being under-used and that they worked mostly as domestics, the implication being that they were capable of more responsible work.

The fundamental weakness in the above information is that the 'right' level of responsibility is not defined. This was clearly a concept that cannot easily be generalised while the group of nursing auxiliaries is far from homogeneous and while there is no uniform training scheme. In fact, a small group of respondents in each of the groups tied their judgment to the present working situation only, qualifying their answer by saying that the level of responsibility would depend greatly on the person or ward or job assignment.

NURSING AUXILIARIES' PRESENCE AT FORMAL WARD REPORTS

The formal 'ward report' is a commonly used method for one shift to transmit to the next shift verbal information about the patients. In asking nursing staff's views on the presence of nursing auxiliaries at 'formal ward reports about patients'* the term was used in the above sense although a precise definition was not given; it included, therefore, all types of group reports whether or not they had a teaching content. Such ward reports are by no means the only method of conveying information and practice varies not only between hospitals but also between wards.

It may be customary for only the person in charge of one shift to hand over to the next person in charge; this possibly, but not necessarily, being followed by a further session at which the rest of the team are given a partial report with particular attention to nursing care directions. In some wards it is the practice for only qualified staff to be present at the formal report, in others for qualified staff as well as those in training to attend. In such situations nursing auxiliaries may be given a special report or they may receive no structured information or directions. Another alternative is the presence of all nursing staff, including auxiliaries, at the formal reporting session.

Common practice in psychiatric hospitals is a written report which each member of staff reads at the beginning of a duty; this may engender a general discussion and verbal exchange of information or may be a solitary exercise. This is by no means an exhaustive list of the varied organisational practices with regard to reports about patients.

Many arguments can be raised against the presence of the nursing auxiliary at a formal reporting session. It is sometimes the case that staff from one shift do not remain on the ward until the report has been given. However, an unattended ward may not be considered desirable by all nursing staff and the nursing auxiliary may be considered to be a suitable person to remain available to the patients on the ward.

Although the question was basic and couched in somewhat pedestrian terms it was considered that the answers would reflect an important policy regarding the involvement and integration of the nursing auxiliary in the ward team.

As can be seen from Table 11/4 the number of respondents stating that nursing auxiliaries were not present at formal reports was slightly higher than the number who gave the opposite answer. This does not necessarily mean that more nursing

---

* *Question 57.* Are nursing auxiliaries/nursing assistants usually present at formal reports about patients or not?

auxiliaries were excluded from report sessions than were present, as it is possible
that several answers related to the same situation. Table 11/4 also shows the number
of respondents who agreed or disagreed with the respective ward practices. The
extent of disagreement was significantly greater where auxiliaries were not present
at formal ward reports.

Sisters and teachers, the group who would be expected to have particular
influence in ward/area policy decisions, reflected the highest level of agreement
with current policy regarding the presence of auxiliaries at ward reports. In the

TABLE 11/4
**Opinions of hospital nurses (currently working with auxiliaries) about presence of
auxiliaries at formal reports on patients**

Current practice in ward/area	Nurses' Opinions							
	Agree		Disagree		Other answer		Total	
	No.	%	No.	%	No.	%	No.	%
Auxiliaries present at report	195	83	32	14	8	3	235	48
Auxiliaries not present at report	124	48	126	49	7	3	257	52
Total*	319	65	158	32	15	3	492**	100

* Includes only those respondents who were currently working with nursing auxiliaries.
** Thirty respondents stated that no formal ward reports were given.
The remaining hospital nursing staff gave inadequate or unclassifiable answers.

two oldest age groups there was a significantly greater agreement with current
policies than was shown by the two youngest age groups. This difference may again
reflect the seniority and decision-making power of the older groups. A slightly
higher percentage of full-time nurses agreed with present policies than did part-
time staff.

Setting aside whether respondents agreed or disagreed with current policies, it
is perhaps more important to examine the reasons given for their opinions.

By far the most common reason given for favouring the presence of nursing
auxiliaries at the formal report session was that they too ought to know about the
patients—the reply given by 87 per cent of the 190 nurses who were working in
areas where this was the practice. Exactly the same reason was advanced by 90
per cent of the group of 126 respondents who disagreed with the exclusion of
nursing auxiliaries as practised on their wards. In both these groups the second
most popular reason, by 7 per cent and 5 per cent respectively was that nursing
auxiliaries were members of the nursing team and, therefore, should be present.
All the people who gave this reason were full-time staff.

Those who did not agree with the presence of nursing auxiliaries at report
sessions varied more in their replies. About half the respondents who at present did
receive reports jointly with auxiliaries, but did not agree with the arrangement,
said that the auxiliaries tended to gossip about patients and were not committed

to the same standards of professional integrity as nurses. Seven respondents thought that auxiliaries did not understand the report or the medical terminology used; four considered that auxiliaries required no or limited information in order to perform their duties. A special report for them was suggested by three nurses and one nurse gave a combination of the above reasons.

TABLE 11/5
Reasons for excluding nursing auxiliaries from formal ward reports

Primary reason	No.	%
Auxiliaries are likely to gossip about patients	37	31
Auxiliaries need limited information only	34	29
Auxiliaries don't understand medical terminology/information	22	18
Auxiliaries should have their own separate report	20	17
Other reason	6	5
Total★	119★★	100

★ Includes only those respondents who were currently working with nursing auxiliaries.
★★ This figure represents only those nurses who agreed with the policy of their wards excluding auxiliaries from ward reports on patients.
Five respondents gave inadequate answers which have been excluded.

Table 11/5 shows that the 119 nurses who agreed with the exclusion of nursing auxiliaries, as practised in their areas, spread their reasons even wider. It is possible that experience of auxiliaries being present at ward reports tends to make people well disposed to the idea. As can be seen 83 per cent of such nurses considered that auxiliaries should be present at ward reports whereas only 14 per cent of the other group held this view. Clearly, it is equally possible that nurses who thought that auxiliaries should share the ward report session gave them the opportunity to do so.

Arguments in favour of the presence of nursing auxiliaries at reports are seen to centre on the necessity for a team approach to patient care and on the important contribution made by the auxiliary.

BETTER CARE FOR PATIENTS/CLIENTS

Nurses were asked whether any of the following courses of action relating to auxiliaries★ would help in the care of patients/clients. They were invited in the first instance to choose the three most important from a card. The alternatives were:

More nursing auxiliaries
Fewer nursing auxiliaries
Adequate initial training for nursing auxiliaries

★ *Question 58.* Which three on this list do you think would help most in the care of your patients/clients?

Replacement of nursing auxiliaries by nurses in training
Close supervision of nursing auxiliaries
Regular refresher courses for nursing auxiliaries
Rotation of nursing auxiliaries between wards or districts
Good selection of nursing auxiliaries
None of these.

Respondents were then asked which course of action they would consider the most important of those they had chosen. Under 1 per cent of respondents thought that none of these proposals would help patients. The proposals which were thought to be the most important were in order of preference:

1 Good selection of nursing auxiliaries
2 Adequate initial training for nursing auxiliaries
3 Regular refresher courses for nursing auxiliaries.

Table 11/6b shows the choices made by nurses in the various job designations. There was a fair degree of agreement on the part of hospital staff as to those proposals, a substantial proportion of nurses in each category giving choices (1) and (2) above, as preferred choice.

The difference in choice made by administrators and sisters/teachers as opposed to the remainder of hospital nursing staff was highly significant. Administrative nursing personnel, sisters and nurse teachers were substantially agreed that initial selection of nursing auxiliaries was the most important factor which would aid patients/clients. The other grades of nursing personnel agreed with each other that the most important factor was adequate initial training.

TABLE 11/6a   Most important factor likely to help patient care

Designation	Adequate training of nursing auxiliaries	Good selection of nursing auxiliaries	Other answer	Total
Administrators sisters/teachers	53	86	58	197
Staff nurses/midwives enrolled nurses students pupils	138	89	105	332★
Total	191	175	163	529★★

★ Discrepancy of 1, owing to error in coding.
★★ Includes only those members of the hospital nursing staff who were currently working with nursing auxiliaries.

This finding was also supported by the information gained from the interviews with top managers. Better selection of nursing auxiliaries was given by 14 of that group of 22 respondents as the one most important factor likely to be helpful in the care of patients/clients. Figures 11/1a and b present the above information for all respondents. The irony of the situation appears to be that in the first place selection is not always possible and that, secondly, selection criteria have not yet been identified.

TABLE 11/6b
Nurses' opinions on most important factor in nursing auxiliaries usefulness to patient care

Designation	No.	Factors in Improvement of Patient Care								
		More auxiliaries %	Fewer auxiliaries %	Adequate initial training %	Trainee nurse instead %	Close supervision %	Refresher courses %	Rotation between wards/districts %	Good selection %	None of these %
Administrators	107	3	1	22	18	6	4	0	47	0
Sisters/teachers	90	1	1	32	17	2	4	2	40	0
Staff nurses/midwives	110	2	0	36	14	8	9	2	28	2
Enrolled nurses	83	5	0	45	4	4	11	1	31	0
Students	88	2	0	41	16	6	8	7	20	0
Pupils	51	4	0	51	2	2	12	2	27	0
Community nurses	38	0	0	47	8	5	3	3	29	5
Total	567	3	0	37	12	5	7	2	33	1

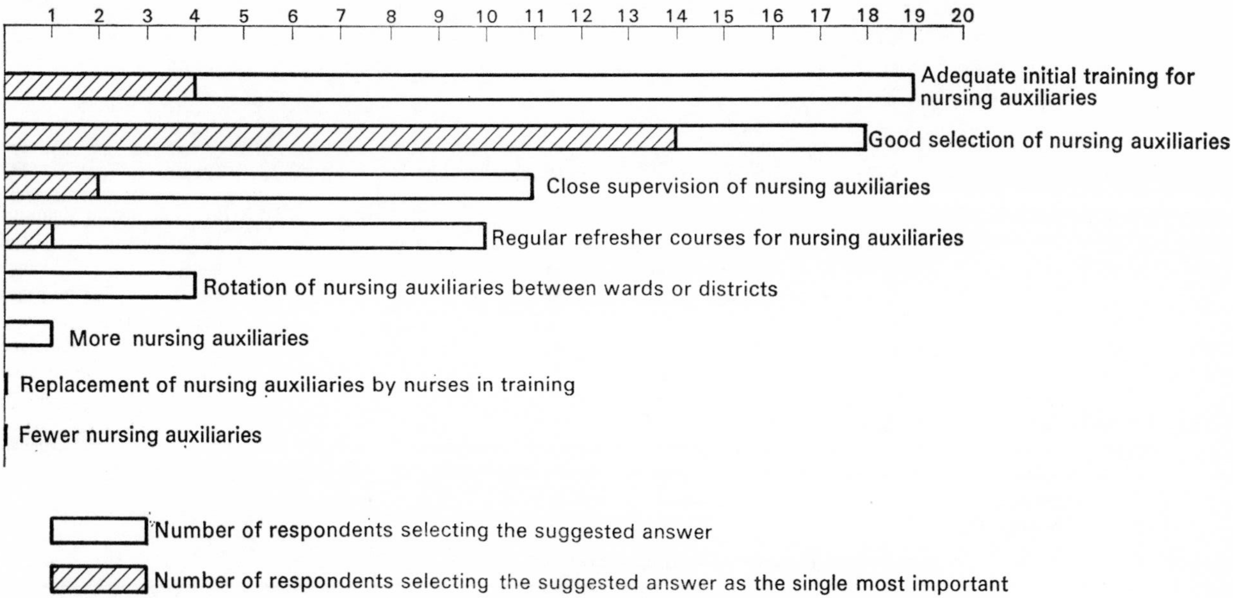

Figure 11/1a Respondents' views on nursing auxiliaries. Top managers'* views on nursing auxiliaries.**

* One respondent did not answer.

** *Question 58* Which three on this list do you think would help most in the care of your patients/clients? Which one of those that you have chosen do you think is the most important? One respondent gave two answers only.

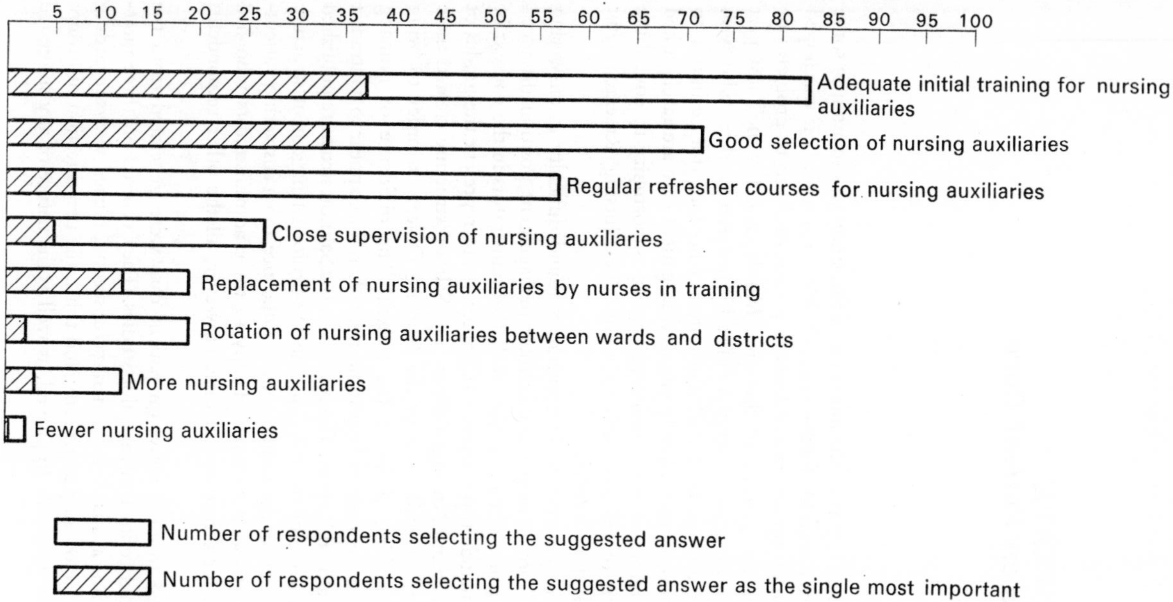

Figure 11/1b Respondents' views on nursing auxiliaries. All other nursing staff's★ views on nursing auxiliaries as a percentage.★★

★ 152 nurses did not answer as they did not work with auxiliaries.

★★ Question 58 Which three on the list do you think would help most in the care of your patients/clients? Which one of those that you have chosen do you think is the most important?

CHAPTER TWELVE
Nurses' Views on Patient Care

As explained in Chapter 1, part of the intention of this study was to attempt some identification of priority areas for further research. More particularly it was hoped to direct the attention of nursing respondents to patient care and to problems or weaknesses, if any, in the practice of this care. Mostly, and for the most part inevitably, research projects are generated either by research workers who wish to pursue their own interest or by administrators who look for solutions to organisational problems. Nurses directly engaged in patient care are rarely asked for their views. Therefore, it was considered that an opportunity to contribute ideas to the direction of research activity within the Nursing Research Unit should be given to all those interviewed.

The pilot study had shown that administrators found difficulty in answering questions on patient care as they felt that their management position distanced them from patients. It must be remembered that administrators in the context of this chapter do not include top managers (Chapter 4) but represent the grades of Senior Nursing Officer and Nursing Officer. The Salmon structure created these administrative grades, especially that of the Nursing Officer, in order to bring managerial decision-making closer to the patient. The diffidence of Nursing Officers in answering patient centred questions may, therefore, appear to contradict the intention of the Salmon Report. The review on the Salmon structure published by SHHD[1] discusses some of the role issues in the Senior Management structure more extensively. In view of the administrators' diffidence about answering patient-orientated questions, these were directed only to three administrators who had some responsibilities for direct patient care. However, all the other respondents were included.

Questions designed to elicit views on patient care were generated from the exploratory work and refined in the pilot studies. They centred on three inter-related issues: first, time available for patient care; second, nurses' views regarding the most important factors in patient care; and third, the identification of groups of patients whose care might be improved, as well as the nature of any suggested improvements.

---

[1] Scottish Home and Health Department, (1974) *Review of the Senior Nursing Staff Structure (Salmon Report)*, SHHD, Edinburgh.

TIME FOR PATIENTS

Exploratory work had pointed clearly to concern experienced by nursing staff about shortage of time. The question* aimed to elicit the nurses' generalised responses about their ability to give adequate care to their patients.

Of the 588 respondents, just over one-third stated that they had enough time to give to their patients, whilst the remainder indicated that they would like more time. These answers convey no information about the quality of care actually given but they reflect the nurses' feelings about the care they were giving.

TABLE 12/1
Nurses' opinions about time for patients

Designation	Have enough time No.	%	Need more time No.	%	Have mostly enough time No.	%	Other No.	%	Total= 100% No.
Administrators*	2	66.7	1	33.3	0	0.0	0	0.0	3
Sisters/teachers	39	40.6	50	52.1	2	2.1	5	5.2	96
Staff nurses/midwives	46	38.7	70	58.8	1	0.8	2	1.7	119
Enrolled nurses	24	27.0	65	73.0	0	0.0	0	0.0	89
Learners	32	22.2	111	77.1	0	0.0	1	0.7	144
District nurses	23	47.9	24	50.0	1	2.1	0	0.0	48
Health visitors	13	33.3	25	64.1	0	0.0	1	2.6	39
Other community nurses	28	56.0	20	40.0	1	2.0	1	2.0	50
Total	207	35.2	366	62.2	5	0.9	10	1.7	588

* The three administrators invited to give answers to the patient oriented questions had some responsibilities for direct patient care.

Table 12/1 relates the respondents' answers to their designation. As can be seen, it appears that the need for more time was more frequently expressed by hospital nurses; however, further analysis shows that there is little difference between qualified staff, whether working in hospital or in the community. The apparent difference arose from the fact that the need for more time was expressed by 77 per cent of learners and 73 per cent of enrolled nurses, most of both groups being hospital staff.

The finding that learners' and enrolled nurses' views are so different from those held by registered nurses working in either hospital or community would be worth pursuing.

It is reasonable to assume that learners feel the need for more time as they are less experienced and therefore slower in carrying out their assigned duties. Learners

* *Question 64.* What about the care of patients/clients. Do you feel that on the whole you are able to give enough time to them or would you like to be able to give more time?
IF MORE TIME What sort of things would you like more time for?

are also less likely to be familiar with 'legitimate' short-cuts when working under pressure. Moreover, there is evidence to show that learners tend to find difficulty in practising procedures in the way they have been taught in the classroom.[2] Clearly all these points are inter-related.

Enrolled nurses are also more likely to be involved in the patients' basic care and in the light of their experience are able to recognise the individual needs of the patient beyond basic nursing and technical care.

It appears that with hospital nurses the expressed need for more time decreases with the ascent up the nursing hierarchy; possibly, the lower the position in the hierarchy the less autonomy exists as regards the apportioning of time. As a group, only 50 per cent of community nurses wanted more time, though health visitors deviated from this, 64 per cent voicing a need for more time.

Health visitors attempt to advise, support and counsel, which implies listening rather than doing. Further, compared with other nurses, the health visitor's functions, if they are to be successful, are not amenable to strict time rationing. Some clients' needs are difficult to judge and the health visitor may feel in these cases that she requires much more time to make an accurate assessment of the situation and needs. Other studies have discussed the allocation of health visitor's work.[3],[4]

TABLE 12/2
Views on time for patients by nurses' age groups

Age groups	Enough time		More time		Mostly enough		Other		Total= 100%
	No.	%	No.	%	No.	%	No.	%	No.
Under 20	9	15.5	48	82.8	0	0.0	1	1.7	58
20–29	62	32.1	127	65.8	0	0.0	4	2.1	193
30–39	45	34.4	81	61.8	3	2.3	2	1.5	131
40–49	51	45.5	59	52.7	0	0.0	2	1.8	112
50–59	34	41.5	45	54.9	2	2.4	1	1.2	82
60 and over	5	55.6	4	44.4	0	0.0	0	0.0	9
Total	206	35.2	364	62.2	5	0.9	10	1.7	585

Respondents who gave inadequate answers and/or those to whom the question was inapplicable are excluded from the totals.

As is apparent from Table 12/2, there was a decrease in the expressed need for more time with an increase in nurses' age. A significantly greater proportion of nurses under forty years stated that they required more time than did nurses over that age.

[2] Hunt, J. M., (1974) *The Teaching and Practice of Surgical Dressings in Three Hospitals*, Series 1, No. 6, Royal College of Nursing and National Council of Nurses of the United Kingdom, London.
[3] Clark, J., (1973) *A Family Visitor*, The Royal College of Nursing and National Council of Nurses of the United Kingdom, London.
[4] Kemp, I., (1969) Health Visiting in Scotland, *Health Bulletin*, Vol. XXVII, No. 2.

The need for more time was expressed most strongly by the nurses under twenty years, all of whom would be learners. This finding is consistent with those relating to designation. Upward mobility in the hierarchy with progressive withdrawal of responsibility for direct patient care may cause the expression 'time for patients' to be interpreted in a different way; it may be considered alongside general administrative duties undertaken in the service of patients. Possibly, also, mature nurses expressed less demand for more time, not only because they were able to use more discretion as a result of their experience and might, therefore, devote enough time to their patients, but also because they were more realistic about attainable standards of patient care.

TABLE 12/3
Views on time for patients by department

Department of work	Enough time No.	%	More time No.	%	Mostly enough No.	%	Other No.	%	Total= 100% No.
General	70	27.2	181	70.4	0	0.0	6	2.3	257
Maternity	23	46.0	25	50.0	2	4.0	0	0.0	50
Psychiatric	22	43.1	29	56.9	0	0.0	0	0.0	51
Geriatric	17	23.9	52	73.2	1	1.4	1	1.4	71
Covers all hospital	6	54.5	5	45.5	0	0.0	0	0.0	11
Teaching	0	0.0	1	50.0	0	0.0	1	50.0	2
Total	138	31.2	293	66.3	3	0.7	8	1.8	442

Respondents who gave inadequate answers and/or those to whom the question was inapplicable are excluded from the totals.

Table 12/3 relates the respondents' views regarding time for patients to their branch of nursing. Over 70 per cent of nurses working in general or geriatric wards felt that they required more time, whereas only 50 per cent of nurses in maternity and 57 per cent in psychiatric wards expressed this view. Neither the respondents' marital status nor whether they were employed on a full- or part-time basis appeared to be associated in any way with their views on need for more time for their patients.

Nurses' views on time for their patients were compared in relation to the size of hospital in which they were working. The only difference worthy of mention concerned those respondents working in very small hospitals, those with less than twenty beds, where only half as many nurses expressed the need for more time in comparison with those working in larger hospitals. This finding may suggest that staff, working in autonomous units, may feel able to give their patients more time as there is no risk of having to 'help out' in other busier departments in a large hospital. The data did not give information on whether the patients in the very small hospitals were actually given more time.

In attempting to identify the 'type of nurse' most likely to feel pressure with regard to available time for patients, the data suggest the picture of a young nurse under the age of thirty years working as a learner or junior member of the hierarchy in a fairly large hospital and, more particularly, in either a geriatric or general ward.

Findings suggesting that nurses would like more time for their patients may seem irrelevant, when nursing time is considered a scarce resource which cannot be increased during a period of economic stringency and a generally reputed nursing shortage. However, the findings may provide pointers for further investigation and might be helpful to nurse managers. Some nurses, frustrated because they feel they are not able to give enough time to their patients, may become disenchanted and leave the profession, thereby reducing available nursing manpower. Certainly, disappointment with nursing soon after qualification has been documented in British and American literature,[5,6,7] and the high wastage rate amongst newly qualified nurses must cause concern.

USE OF TIME

As the need for more time is a general and rather vague complaint, nurses were asked specifically what tasks they would like more time for.* Although the pilot work had shown that answers to this open-ended question were likely to be diffuse and present problems in analysis, the disadvantages of forcing answers into pre-determined categories were thought too great, and so the open-ended approach was adopted. Predictably, this resulted in a wide array of responses, which served a useful exploratory purpose as far as further research is conerned, but which did present some immediate problems in terms of categorisation. Broadly speaking, respondents' thoughts on the use of time were directed to communication with the patients, improved organisation and methods of care. More than one answer could be given and the nurses were not asked to rank their answers in order of importance. All responses were given equal weighting, though in fact only 27 per cent of respondents gave more than one answer.

Table 12/4 shows the replies to the question on the use of time and demonstrates strikingly nurses' awareness of the importance of communication with the patient. Further, by 'communication' they did not mean merely explanation and reassurance; over three times the number who mentioned explanation and reassurance specifically cited talking and listening. This suggests nurses' appreciation of the patient as a person, rather than as just a 'renal failure' or a 'prostatectomy'. Perhaps this concern, which emerged most strongly on the part of hospital nurses, reflects the fact that on a busy ward where there is a lot of pressure on time, communication has to take second place to direct nursing care.

As already indicated, there were differences in the response patterns of hospital and community staff. Hospital staff were more like-minded in their views and,

---

⁵ MacGuire, J. M., (1969) *Threshold to Nursing. A Review of the Literature on Recruitment to and Withdrawal from Nurse Training Programmes in the United Kingdom*, Occasional Papers on Social Administration No. 30, G. Bell & Sons Ltd., London.

⁶ Kramer, M., (1974) *Reality shock: why nurses leave nursing*, Mosby, St Louis.

⁷ Scott Wright M., (1968) *Student Nurses in Scotland, Characteristics of Success and Failure*, Scottish Health Service Study No. 7, SHHD, Edinburgh.

* *Question 64b.* IF MORE TIME What sort of things would you like more time for?

irrespective of designation, their answers followed a common pattern. Communication was the need they most frequently mentioned, followed by methods of care, then organisation and teaching. Percentages between the designation groups giving the replies differed, but the order of importance remained the same. Thus, whereas 62 per cent of learners mentioned the use of time for communication

TABLE 12/4
Tasks for which nurses want more time

Categories	Tasks included in categories	Hospital No.	%	Community No.	%	Total	%
Communication	Talking and listening to patients	179		26		205	
	Reassurance and explanation	55		7		62	
	More personal contact	16		0		16	
Total		250	57.7	33	31.1	283	52.6
Methods of care	General nursing care	54		9		63	
	Performance of procedures and techniques correctly	29		2		31	
	Diversional therapy	24		1		25	
	Extra non-basic care	19		0		19	
	Rehabilitation	11		2		13	
Total		137	31.6	14	13.2	151	28.1
Organisation of care	Attention to specific groups (elderly, handicapped, children)	32		26		58	
	Care at peak times	8		1		9	
	Home visiting	0		16		16	
Total		40	9.2	43	40.6	83	15.4
Teaching	Teaching patients and relatives	3		10		13	
	Preventive and health education	2		5		7	
Total		5	1.2	15	14.1	20	3.7
Other		0	0.0	1	0.9	1	0.2
Total		**432**		**106**		**538**	**100.0**

purposes against only 45 per cent of staff nurses, for both groups, and indeed all groups, that category of answer achieved the highest number of mentions.

Community nursing staff gave a greater number and diversity of replies. They expressed the need for more time in relation to organisational aspects and this was most often followed by communication. The main difference between hospital and community staff concerned the need for more time which was mentioned so consistently by the hospital staff and less by community nurses. This difference might be explained by the pattern and organisation of work in the community field where the nurse gives her undivided attention to one patient at a time and her relationship with the patient is more coherent and less fragmented. Further, as the patient is in his natural environment, the nurse does not have to allay the anxieties frequently aroused by the strangeness and unfamiliarity of the ward setting. Moreover, the community nurse is in control of her time and therefore has more scope for flexibility in coping with the needs of her patients.

The analysis of answers on the use of more time by age groups gives 'communication' the top frequency with each age group, but in some other respects there were significant differences. Those under forty years gave more replies indicating the need for time in relation to nursing care methods, whereas the older nurses tended to mention organisational aspects more frequently. This is probably due to the fact that junior nurses are more involved in the giving of direct nursing care and less aware, by virtue of their position, of organisational implications. The size of the hospital seemed to make no significant difference to the general pattern of opinion on ideal allocation of time.

IMPORTANT CARE ELEMENTS

As stressed throughout this report, the study was designed, at least in part, to elicit the views of all grades of nurses on aspects of patient care. The question which appeared to cause the greatest diffidence and hesitation amongst the respondents was one asking for their opinions regarding the most important factors in the care of their patients.[*] The answers have been grouped as shown in Table 12/5. Only nurses with 'direct' patient care responsibilities, 81 per cent, were invited to answer and they offered 857 views on patient care. The pattern of community nurses giving multiple replies more often than hospital nurses was repeated, but the difference did not reach statistical significance.

Respondents readily expressed a concern for the comfort of their patients and Table 12/5 shows, as the first priority, the need for care to be patient centred, with three different, yet intertwined aspects of care emerging within this category—personalised care, communication and attitudes. Because of their close inter-relationships, the boundaries between these aspects are open to debate. The findings have, therefore, been organised so as to highlight main aspects without suppressing and blurring individual components.

It is apparent that many nurses saw their responsibilities as not merely confined to technical nursing and vague kindness, but as embracing a positive attitude toward communications and supportiveness based on an understanding of the patients' psychological and social needs. Other studies[8,9] have suggested that patient anxiety does not always seem to be responded to, which, on the basis of these findings, could be the result of time pressures rather than of lack of awareness.

[*] *Question 65.* Can you tell me what you consider to be most important in the care of your patients/clients?

[8] Franklin, B. L., (1974) *Patient Anxiety on Admission to Hospital*, Series 1, No. 5, Royal College of Nursing and National Council of Nurses of the United Kingdom, London.

[9] Stockwell, F., (1972) *The Unpopular Patient*, Series 1, No. 2, Royal College of Nursing and National Council of Nurses of the United Kingdom, London.

TABLE 12/5
Nurses' opinions as to most important aspects of patient care

	Categories	No. of mentions	% of mentions
Patient centred care	*Personalised care*		
	Comfort and well-being of patients	161	
	Kindness to patients	57	
	Respect for patients	19	
		237	27.6
	Communication		
	Support and reassurance	118	
	Time for communication	62	
	Education of relatives	17	
		197	23.0
	Attitudes		
	Acceptance and understanding of patient's needs and appreciation, by nurses, of the importance of the nurse/patient relationship	85	
	Concern for the family unit and support of relatives	20	
		105	12.3
		539	62.9
Technical care	Nursing care	123	
	Observation of patients and execution of treatments	38	
	Cleanliness	25	
	Nursing skill	22	
	Relief of pain	12	
	Attention to diet	11	
		231	26.9
Improved facilities	Physiotherapy, occupational and other therapies	16	
	Regular frequent visiting by community nurses	8	
	Provision of services and facilities	5	
		29	3.4
Other	Everything is important	17	
	Relaxed ward atmosphere	9	
	Teamwork	5	
	Others, including combined answers	27	
		58	6.8
Total		857	100.0

Hospital and community staff differed as to their second priority in care. Hospital staff gave technical care the next highest frequency of mention, whereas community nurses reiterated aspects of patient-centred care as their second choice. As can be seen from Table 12/5 the category of technical care includes direct physical care as well as complex nursing procedures, although the emphasis was on the former.

Compared with the older nurses, the younger half of the sample, those under the age of forty, placed their opinions more frequently in the technical care category than in the attitude component of patient-centred care. The importance of attitudes toward patients may be recognised more by the older nurses because of their acquired confidence in nursing procedures and their greater experience of the total needs of the patient; this suggestion is consistent with the finding that community nurses, who tend to be in the older age group, placed a greater emphasis on attitudes and relationships, whereas younger nurses expressed a need for more time for attending to physical needs.

Nurses working in psychiatric wards and departments were the only group mentioning the importance of the nurse-patient relationship almost as frequently as other aspects of patient centred care. Such concern for the patients' environment is probably a result of the training and orientation of psychiatric nurses, and it is reassuring that according to the findings presented in Table 12/5, nurses in other fields are also beginning to develop this awareness.

PATIENTS WHOSE CARE COULD BE IMPROVED

The identification of vulnerable groups in the community is a perennial problem for policy makers in the health and welfare services. Although the sick as a total group might always qualify for a measure of priority attention, there is no unanimity on the needs, met or unmet, of the component subgroups. Professional and political factions tend to compete for resources to improve the care of whatever clientele they have a particular interest in and those with the greatest success are often those who are the most vocal.

It was decided to give all the nursing respondents, including the administrators, the opportunity to voice their views on the types of patients/clients whose care they felt could be improved.*

The answers fell into three identifiable categories: those defining groups in terms of age, those mentioning broad generally acknowledged groups such as psychiatric or post-operative patients, and those singling out more specific conditions such as cerebro-vascular accidents.

Table 12/6 shows the categories of replies and the number of specific mentions within each category. Almost one-third of all respondents considered that no one group of patients required more care than any other. However, this does not carry the implication that nurses were necessarily satisfied with the standards of care, but rather that they could not identify any particular group of patients as outstanding in their need for improved care.

---

* *Question 66.* Are there any particular types of patients/clients whose care you feel could be improved?

Of the 775 mentions, specific age groups received 34 per cent of mentions, general broad groups 21 per cent, and specific diseases and conditions 9 per cent. Within the largest category, the most frequently mentioned groups were the elderly and geriatric.

TABLE 12/6
Patients seen to require improved care

Type of answer	Specific mention of patient groups	No. of mentions	% of mentions
Age groups	Elderly	86	
	Geriatric	149	
	Children, adolescents, young chronic sick	25	
	Premature/newborn	1	
Total		261	33.7
General groups	Physically and mentally handicapped	33	
	Patients with social problems	25	
	All patients	24	
	Psychiatric	22	
	Psychogeriatric	2	
	Seriously ill	13	
	Medical	10	
	Terminally ill	10	
	Post-operative	10	
	Long-term	10	
	Convalescent/post-discharge	8	
Total		167	21.5
Specific groups	Cerebro-vascular accidents	29	
	Maternity	24	
	Ante-natal		
	Labour		
	Post-natal		
	Bedridden/incontinent	8	
	Paralysed	7	
	Cancer	6	
Total		74	9.2
Other and combined answers		29	3.7
None require improved care		244	31.6
Total		775	100.0

Some respondents referred directly to the difficulty of nursing geriatric patients in the same ward as others. In fact, of the 88 nurses working in geriatric units or wards only 38 cited this group of patients as needing improved care, the majority of mentions for 'geriatrics' coming from staff on medical and surgical wards. Further examination of the data showed that where patients in the elderly age bracket were mentioned, it was less in terms of unmet need than that their needs should be met elsewhere, that is, in appropriate hospitals or the community, and not in medical and surgical areas. As one nurse put it:

'It is the geriatric patients—we have such a lot of social admissions that we can't nurse the medical cases—so neither are looked after properly—particularly the young stroke patients.'

While another nurse said:

'heavy medical wards with so many geriatrics—they should be cared for separately.'

Again from the medical ward, the complaints:

'it's the people waiting for geriatric beds.'

and:

'I feel our general and medical wards are left with an awful lot of geriatric patients and they are not being nursed as they should.'

It is reasonable to conclude that geriatric wards are organised in a way which is compatible with their patients' needs. General medical and surgical wards, however, also house an increasing number of elderly patients. There, the organisation and environment may be less well suited to the care of elderly people. In addition, younger patients hospitalised nowadays tend to be those who, because of their condition, require a considerable proportion of nursing time, thereby creating conflicts for the nurse in the apportionment of her time between them and the elderly. The elderly and geriatric patient received, as could be expected, more mention from hospital nurses working within wards where elderly patients are present and also from district nurses with a case load bias toward the older age groups. However, 10 per cent of learners also mentioned the need for improved care for the elderly patient. Until 1973 pupil nurses were required to spend twenty-six weeks of their training in chronic sick/geriatric areas but student nurses, whilst not required to have geriatric experience within their training period, were permitted to gain up to four weeks experience in this area. Therefore, some of the student nurses' experience of elderly patients had been within medical and surgical areas with a mix of patients of all ages, whereas pupil nurses would have gained the experience in strictly geriatric areas.

It is clearly impossible to distinguish between informed comment and that determined by current trends and publicity. It is relevant to note, however, that nurses consider geriatric patients to warrant improvement in care, at a time when much concern is focused on this field by the media, conferences and research projects. It could be that there is a tendency to adopt prevailing points of view indiscriminately or alternatively, that publicity is effective in promoting a deeper concern for areas of unmet need.

POSSIBLE IMPROVEMENTS IN PATIENT CARE

An open-ended question* explored further the types of improvements for those patient groups who were seen to require improved care. Of those 461 nurses identifying such groups, 457 suggested 698 actual improvements they would like to see. It was, of course, understood by the researchers categorising the replies, as well as by the respondents themselves, that in many cases, one improvement may depend on other pre-requisite conditions. For example, improved nursing care may be inextricably linked with staffing, staff attitudes and ward organisation. The investigators concentrated on the respondents' primary concern rather than attempting to pursue all the necessary components required for a particular improvement.

Table 12/7 gives the frequency of mentions of needed improvements suggested by nurses. A high agreement on order of frequency was evident in the community nursing groups with the health visitors making the highest number of suggestions per respondent. The hospital nurses were more diverse in their suggested improvements.

The stock reply of nurses, when asked about the frustrations of their work, tends to be shortage of staff; however, at least in this study, this shortage did not refer only to nursing staff; 37 per cent of respondents expressed a need for more occupational therapists and physiotherapists, and this was the largest single need nominated in the staffing shortage category.

The respondents' emphasis on the need for more occupational therapists and physiotherapists deserves further attention. It shows an appreciation of the need and potential of rehabilitation which again supports nurses' awareness of their patients' total needs. It also suggests that nurses, who tend to fill gaps in a variety of allied professions, physiotherapy and occupational therapy among them, realise that such makeshift arrangements are not in the patients' best interests.

Other improvements commanding a high percentage of mentions were in the organisational category, where the need for better accommodation received the highest percentage of mentions of all single categories.

The popular choice for community nurses was for improved home and community care and there was a significant, but understandable, difference between the proportions of hospital and community staff who devoted mentions to this. It would be of interest to observe whether the reorganised health service and a greater emphasis on community experience within nursing education, recommended by the Committee on Nursing, will eventually balance the views of hospital and community nursing staff, giving both a wider perspective. Community nurses placed 32 per cent of their opinions in this category against only 4 per cent of hospital staff. Equally understandably, given their special perspectives, administrators and teachers tended to concentrate their suggestions within the area of accommodation, equipment and money.

The improvements wanted by hospital nurses were analysed in relation to the department in which they worked, using the same categories as in Table 12/7. With the exception of teachers, most of the specialty groups gave increased staffing

---

* *Question 66b.* What improvements would you like?

TABLE 12/7
Improvements wanted by nurses

Group	Combined categories	No. of mentions	% of mentions
Staffing	More staff	69	
	More staff to give more time	36	
	More occupational therapists and physiotherapists	87	
	More staff for holiday relief	13	
	More staff for night visiting	28	
Total		233	33.4
Time	Time to talk	29	
	More time	23	
Total		52	7.4
Education	Explain and reassure	12	
	Patient instruction	12	
	Health education	11	
	Attention to diet	3	
Total		38	5.4
Patient care	Attitude to patients	30	
	Basic nursing care	31	
	Reorganisation of patient care	4	
	Teamwork	6	
	Rehabilitation	32	
	Social/psychological	24	
Total		127	18.2
Organisational	Better equipment	45	
	Better accommodation	101	
	More money	8	
	Day care facilities	13	
	Welfare service	36	
	Longer stay in hospital	11	
Total		214	30.7
Other	Research	5	
	Other	24	
	Combined	5	
Total		34	4.9
Total	Responses	698	100.0
	Respondents	461	

as the major component of improved care, whereas the teachers saw the greatest need for changes relating to organisational factors. Nurses from maternity and psychiatric areas were equally divided over their second priority, each group giving the same number of mentions to patient care and organisational practice. Teachers, however, gave increased staff as their second choice.

The plea for more staff, better accommodation and equipment came strongly from all nurses in all departments while factors concerned with time, education and patient care were mentioned less frequently.

CONCLUSIONS

Throughout the series of questions on patient care, respondents offered many suggestions for improvements, the most vocal group being health visitors. Overall, respondents tended to indicate lack of time and organisational problems, such as staffing and accommodation, as the main obstacles in attaining their ideal of good patient care.

Time for communication with patients was the primary need stated by the entire sample. Points related to communication arose in answer to all questions, and this need was expressed most strongly when nurses were asked directly which tasks they would like more time for, and which aspects of patient care they considered to be the most important.

This finding would seem to contradict Stockwell's contention[10] that both patients and nurses felt that conversation was not part of a nurse's responsibility, and further, that the nurses in her sample considered they already had enough time for communication within the scope of their normal contacts with patients.

Obviously the series of questions that forms the basis of this chapter relates, in an oblique fashion, to nurses' perception of what constitutes good or ideal standards of patient care. Various sub-groups emerge as having differing views on this subject. Thus the psychiatric nurses, compared with other groups, stressed the importance of the nursing environment and the quality of the nurse/patient relationship. There were the expected differences in emphasis between hospital and community nurses, and younger nurses emerged as having preoccupations within the sphere of nursing care differing from those of their older colleagues.

One is tempted to speculate to what degree the differences between the various branches of nursing are the outcome of self-selection for specialties, of different orientations and approaches in the specialist training courses; or, alternatively, to what degree these differences manifest themselves spontaneously as a result of experience of particular patient groups. Similarly, it may be of value to enquire further into the differences between older and younger nurses in order to see how far these differences reflect a contrast in the attitudes the two generations bring to patient care—a kind of 'generation gap' effect; or, alternatively, how much they are a result of one group of nurses being the more newly qualified—nurses who in the course of time may follow the lead of their older colleagues for whom idealism is perhaps already tempered with experience, maturity and realism.

---

[10] Stockwell, F., (1972) *The Unpopular Patient*, Series 1, No. 2, Royal College of Nursing and National Council of Nurses of the United Kingdom, London.

CHAPTER THIRTEEN
Concluding Discussion

It is usual practice for the last chapter of a research report to summarise findings and, if appropriate, to make recommendations. Unfortunately, it is often only the last chapter which is read at all and which forms the basis of any reviews. One of the ways to avoid such cursory reading is to curtail the repetition of information in the concluding chapter and to use it for other purposes.

In line with the initial intent of the report of our study, its concluding section takes the form of an appraisal of the work in terms of achieved and non-achieved aims, suitability of method, outcomes and application. The introductory chapter describes why and how the choice of research topic 'Women in Nursing' was made. It is shown that it was the outcome of an objectively handled 'customer* enquiry' which gave a project into staffing of nursing services a clear majority over other possible research topics. The results of our study validate this priority need. In reply to a general question** toward the end of interviews from all grades and types of nurses and midwives there was an entreaty for more staff.

The decision to focus our attention on *women* in nursing proved reasonable in view of the need to limit the parameters of the study. In addition, the longitudinal cohort investigation of men in nursing is still being pursued by the University of Hull and a historical sketch of the Association of Male Nurses is also being prepared which provides useful supplementary information.[1] The nursing profession is still predominantly female and of the 2203 newly qualified nurses who were placed on the Scottish Register of Nurses in 1974, 1835 (83.3 per cent) were women. A study of women in nursing can, therefore, be assumed to throw some light on nursing staff in general.

The study was designed as a social survey using the interview as the main tool for data collection. Basic descriptive information and pointers for further research were obtained. The descriptive data make some relevant additions to the national manpower study initiated by SHHD[2] after our study was launched, by virtue of inclusion of the learner group and by more detailed information on specific

---

* 'customer' refers to the members of the nursing profession in whose interest the Nursing Research Unit hopes to function.

** *Question 67.* Is there anything at all that would make work easier or more enjoyable for you? *If yes* could you please tell me what this is.

[1] Edwards, G., *Men in Nursing*—The Society of Registered Male Nurses: An Era of Nursing History and Development (unpublished).

[2] Scottish Home and Health Department (1974) *Nursing Manpower Planning Report No. 1,* RE 34884 TBL(3), SHHD, Edinburgh.

issues. However, our study has an obvious limitation in terms of the population it studied which was confined to four hospital groups and their adjacent local authority areas. Based on the national manpower study a further Report was published during the period of our investigation.[3] Again our data make a relevant contribution to that Report by providing some of the detailed information about breaks in nursing service. For example, the IOR Report states:

'The analysis has highlighted the importance of this group (. . . domestic reasons) of losses and the lack of reliable more detailed information.'

and further on:

'We do not know about the pattern of returning.'

Chapter 7 of our report gives some, but by no means all, of the needed answers. The method of sampling adopted in our study is fully explained in Chapter 2. It enables us to generalise the findings from our sample to the total nursing population in the research areas within the limits of the calculable sampling error. In addition, our detailed interviews can serve as useful case study material not only for our sample survey but also for the Scottish National manpower and Staff movement studies. Our sampling method, whilst fulfilling its purpose, had some disadvantages due to the different sampling ratios we adopted for administrators, for other hospital staff and for community staff. Although the three samples resulted in adequate numbers in each group, they militated against inter-group comparisons. In such situations the relative advantages and disadvantages of alternative sampling methods must be carefully considered.

Our nursing respondents spanned over half a century in their age and it is revealing to let one of the oldest nurses in the study record her observation:

'The nursing of tomorrow is much different to the nursing of yesterday. There is no such things as scrubbing floors and chairs and sweeping. And look at the equipment they have in hospital. . . .'

Thus, in a present nurse's professional experience the most profound changes have taken place, both in the type of work expected from nurses and in their role perception.[4] The changes in the nurse's professional role are accentuated by the introduction of functional nursing management and by the change in the role of women generally. It is the interface between the roles of the nurse as a woman and of the woman as a nurse which was identified as a major part of our investigation. Added to the complexity of this dual role pattern which nursing managers have to accommodate is the radical extension of a nurse's role into the technical and managerial fields. At the same time, the need for direct personal nursing care is likely to increase rather than decrease as medical and technical advances result in survival of seriously damaged patients and the trend of general longevity continues. The above combination of circumstances would not in itself constitute

[3] Institute for Operational Research (1975) *The Movements of Hospital Nursing Staff in Scotland*, IOR/834, IOR, Edinburgh.
[4] Anderson, E., (1973) *The Role of the Nurse*, Series 2, No. 1, Royal College of Nursing and National Council of Nurses of the United Kingdom, London.

nursing staffing problems if nursing recruitment kept pace with increasing demands. However, attrition during training and loss of qualified staff from the service result in constantly diminishing proportions of qualified staff, both enrolled and registered, in relation to nursing auxiliaries.

In Scotland an overall proportion of roughly one-third of all learners discontinue their training.[5] There appears no prospect of an increase in the number of student nurses in the remainder of this decade and even less so in the 1980s. There has been a consistent trend of increase in the number of pupil nurses but a decrease in that of students. Although the number of student nurses in Scotland in 1972 was higher than in 1970 it was lower than ten years before that.[6]

The most recent Annual Report of the General Nursing Council for Scotland[7] shows an increase of 239 nurses placed on the Register. However, the increase of enrolled nurses during the same year was 1033, more than four times that of registered nurses. While the number of young student nurses may be maintained during the 1970s, the picture is likely to change after 1980. In Scotland, as in the remainder of Great Britain, births were at a peak in 1964 and have been declining steadily since then.[8] Therefore, the number of school leavers will begin to decline markedly after 1980 and, in order to maintain even the current recruitment rates, an increasing proportion of these school leavers will need to be attracted to nursing.

Whilst recruitment to student nurse training is steadily declining, at least in the field of general nursing, the number of entrants into training for enrolment is on the increase. The Scottish Nursing Manpower Planning Report[9] states:

'By 1968 about 26 per cent of all qualified staff were enrolled nurses and only five years later the proportion had risen further to about 31 per cent.'

Our study shows in Chapter 6 that enrolled nurses, as a group, differ in many personal characteristics and other ways from registered nurses. The common portal of entry envisaged in the Briggs recommendations will, therefore, merge two different groups of people and recruitment under the new system should be carefully monitored in awareness of this difference. It may be that the prospect of advancing from certification to registration will be an added attraction but our data would suggest that for many nurses such advancement will remain a theoretical rather than a practical possibility. It is not unreasonable to wonder whether the type of nurses who now enter for enrolment and stay the course to become fully qualified might become unsettled when overtaken by their peers who proceed to registration. Similarly, nurses who obtain a licence to practise after eighteen months may not take the trouble to pursue a further course whereas they would under the current system have become student nurses and completed the three years

---

[5] General Nursing Council for Scotland, (1973, 1974) *Annual Reports*, GNC, Edinburgh.
[6] General Nursing Council for Scotland (1973), ibid.
[7] General Nursing Council for Scotland (1974), ibid.
[8] Office of Population Censuses and Surveys, (1974) *Population projections*, No. 4, 1973–2013, HMSO, London.
[9] Scottish Home and Health Department, (1974) *Nursing Manpower Planning Report*, No. 1, RE 34884 TBL(3), SHHD, Edinburgh.

training period. Moreover, some nurses with good educational qualifications could be discouraged by the 'broad' gateway into the profession. Clearly, career guidance for school leavers will need to be based on good up-to-date information on the range of opportunities within the nursing profession.

The potential problem of recruiting school leavers having been recognised, one must make attempts to retain qualified nurses and to attract back those who have left the service. For these reasons it was considered prudent to assess the job satisfaction of practising nurses. Within the constraints and limitations of such an assessment, which is described in Chapter 8 and Appendix 5, the crude indicators which emerged deserve to be heeded.

National statistics for Scottish hospitals for the year from July 1972 to June 1973 show the present pattern of losses and returns to employment of qualified nurses.[10] The net loss of young staff, that is up to the age of thirty, but especially under the age of twenty-six years, is greater than the loss due to retirement. Our data supported the national findings that those young women who return to nursing after a break are likely to seek part-time employment. The gross loss rate for the service as a whole is about 20 per cent, half of the loss being due to domestic reasons. As neither our nor the national studies included qualified professionally inactive nurses, our knowledge about this potential work force is limited. We asked all our respondents for their views on inducements to such inactive nurses to cause them to return. Overwhelmingly, flexibility of working hours emerged as the first choice and further investigations regarding the feasibility of flextime in nursing are indicated. In this context it is worth paying attention to the reasons given by our respondents for having returned to nursing, which are shown in Chapter 7.

Job satisfaction and working hours were found in our study to be related. Thus, those members of staff who were satisfied with the arrangement of their working hours were more likely to attain higher job satisfaction scores. Considering that our respondents were all practising it may be that others could be brought back if their working hours could be arranged in a more acceptable way. The Committee on Nursing recommends that shift systems should take account of the quality of the service, the welfare of the staff and the educational needs of learners. Our data in relation to the above recommendations are discussed in Chapter 10, from which the conclusions can be drawn that there is room for improvement on all three fronts.

Faced with nursing staffing problems the increase in the employment of nursing auxiliaries is not surprising; whilst the absolute increase could be beneficial to the service, the increase of this occupational group in relation to qualified staff and learners warrants vigilance. The Committee on Nursing was fully aware of the growing importance of the nursing auxiliary and commissioned an enquiry on the current position regarding the deployment and training of this grade of staff. Our study included an exploratory section on various aspects of the relationship between the nursing auxiliary and other members of the nursing team, which

---

[10] Institute for Operational Research, (1975) *The Movement of Hospital Nursing Staff in Scotland*, IOR/834, IOR, Edinburgh.

forms the substance of Chapter 11. The urgent need for further research on various aspects of the employment of nursing auxiliaries including their preparation, job satisfaction and integration within the nursing team was perceived in the exploratory and planning stages of our own study. The data gathered from all grades of nurses about the nursing auxiliary will be used in the design of a more detailed project which the Unit hopes to undertake.

As stated in the introductory chapter it was hoped to give the nursing respondents in our study the opportunity to point us to priority research areas in nursing and patient care. For this reason a deliberately leading section was built into the interview. Chapter 12 presents the analysis of this part of the study and is intended to give us the basis for a further project. It is appropriate to repeat the major plea voiced by the cross-section of our nursing respondents which was 'more time for talking to patients'. One could legitimately be accused of presenting and emphasising findings which, in view of the reputed staffing shortage, are not likely to be remedied. In answer to such a reproach two points must be made. In the first place nurses who feel pressurised and frustrated about not being able to 'communicate' with their patients may eventually become disillusioned and leave the profession, thereby aggravating the situation. Secondly, and more importantly, research findings have shown the therapeutic effect of relevant communication such as the giving of information. As this report was being completed Hayward's study 'Information—a prescription against pain' appeared.[11] It makes an appropriate conclusion to acknowledge his study as a welcome contribution to nursing and as a support for the study on 'Communications' which we are planning. Information being an important aspect of communication, findings, such as those presented by Hayward, augur well for further work in that area which was prompted by the nurses themselves. Maybe the 'customer' knows best after all.

---

[11] Hayward, J., (1975) *Information—A prescription against pain*, Series 2, No. 5, Royal College of Nursing and National Council of Nurses of the United Kingdom, London.

APPENDIX ONE
Statistical Approach

The purpose of Appendix 1 is two-fold.

First, it gives a basic explanation of significance and discusses calculable and incalculable errors in relation to the reliability of the data.

Second, it is intended to give the reader details about the statistical tests used in the analysis of the study and some additional information to facilitate their interpretation.

The concept of probability underlies most of the commonly used statistical methods. It is not an easy concept to define and is, therefore, usually introduced by illustration rather than by definition. For a study of probability theory and statistical methods text and reference books must be consulted, and a selection of comparatively simple texts is suggested at the end of this appendix.

Probability may be expressed either as a percentage or in decimal form: thus $p < 5$ per cent and $p < 0.05$ are equivalent statements indicating that the probability of an event occurring by chance is less than one in twenty cases.

Significance tests determine levels of probability, thereby assessing the reliability of numerical results. A result considered to be statistically significant is relatively unlikely to have arisen by chance. Significance levels may be set differently for different purposes, the most frequently used level in social research being 5 per cent. A statistically significant result at 5 per cent level of probability means that the confidence that can be placed upon it is 95 per cent, which is reasonably high. Such a 95 per cent confidence level was set in this study; therefore, any result which does not reach at least that level is deemed as 'not significant'.

A highly significant result is one which is extremely unlikely to have arisen by chance and tends to be used when the probability is 1 per cent or less, or the confidence level is 99 per cent—both statements being equivalent. The higher the significance level the more confidence may be placed upon a statement derived from those results.

There is, however, an important difference between statistical significance and meaning. If the wrong questions are asked it is easy to produce statistically significant results which have no meaning. Equally, many observations are meaningful without being statistically significant. A unique event may be important but has no statistical significance and, where samples are small, apparent differences may well have meaning without being statistically significant. It is important in a study designed to provide pointers for future research to notice features which may not have been reliably established but which warrant further investigation.

Many statistical tests make assumptions about the parent populations from which the samples have been drawn; these are called parametric tests. Such assumptions are rarely appropriate in the present type of study and, therefore, non-parametric tests have been preferred.

RELIABILITY OF ESTIMATES
The estimates given in this report are based on the results obtained from a sample of female nurses working in four hospital groups and seven local authority areas in Scotland using a single stage sample design. The estimates given do not represent the whole of Scotland but only the selected research areas in Scotland. As with all sample surveys, the results are subject to various forms of error. Some errors arise from sampling variability and are calculable; other errors may arise from various forms of non-response. Non-response can be due to such factors as subjects refusing interviews, leaving the employing authority before being interviewed, prolonged sickness or a misunderstanding of questions asked by the interviewer. Some factual questions, used in this study, such as the hours worked by subjects in previous weeks are subject to error in memory. The effects of this non-response are not known and are not calculable, whilst errors due to sampling variability are measurable.

STANDARD ERRORS
Statistical data are always taken from a population. The data may come either from the entire population or from a sample of that population. In describing the population N, the statistics most frequently used are the mean (or average), μ; the standard deviation (σ) or variance (σ^2); and the standard error, SE. The symbols μ and σ are used to represent the true values for the whole population; estimates derived by sampling are usually represented by other symbols, usually $\bar{x}$ and s. Standard errors may be calculated for means, standard deviations, proportions and other types of measures. When based on sample results, they estimate the relationship of those results to the ideal results from the whole population; they are used as estimates of reliability or precision.

The standard error of the mean is often described as $\dfrac{\sigma}{\sqrt{n}}$ or $\dfrac{s}{\sqrt{n}}$. This formula is convenient but is not always strictly correct unless a true value for σ is available. Where only an estimate, s, is available it may be a useful approximation if the sample does not exceed 10 per cent of the population.

Thus, the reliability of the sample mean, which is unlikely to be exactly the same as the true mean of the entire population, is indicated by stating the standard error of the mean. In a normal distribution of the data, there is a 95 per cent probability that the true mean lies within a calculable range expressed as follows:
$$[\bar{x} \pm 2SE(\bar{x})]$$
When a sample is big enough the sample average or mean is unlikely to provide a misleading estimate of the true mean. Estimates may be obtained from a pilot survey and used to determine the necessary sample size for the main study.

There is no rule of thumb for the optimum size of a sample; it is determined by two factors, which are first the variability or standard deviation of the sample and, secondly, the size of sampling error the researcher is prepared to accept. The formula $SE=\dfrac{\sigma}{\sqrt{N}}$ relates these factors to each other and shows that in order to halve the standard error, SE, it is necessary to quadruple the sample size, N. The variability σ, being a property of the sample itself, is given and cannot be altered. Thus, to obtain a given reliability from a heterogeneous population a larger sample is needed than to obtain the same reliability from a homogeneous population.

Moreover, the more heterogeneous the population, the more variables one could probably wish to isolate and relate to each other. A small sample might produce inadequate numbers in the available categories for each variable, to carry out statistical tests. In this study the reason for selecting a 3 in 5 sample of community nursing staff as against a 1 in 5 sample of hospital staff was the need to achieve an adequate sample size of community nursing staff.

SAMPLING PROBLEMS

Sampling might produce problems which are not related to size but representativeness.

As explained earlier, the population in this study, statistically speaking, were the female nurses employed in the research areas.

Two separate samples were drawn from the hospital population, not including the top managers.

A 1 in 1 sample of administrators, i.e., the total population, was approached and a 1 in 5 sample of other hospital staff. The administrators formed a fairly homogeneous group as far as their designation was concerned. The 1 in 5 sample of other hospital staff was compiled from an alphabetically ordered sampling frame. This method of sampling resulted, inevitably, in random variations in the representation of the different designations.

The sampling problem in the community nursing services was similar in that the sampling frame consisted of an alphabetical list of all staff from whom a 3 in 5 sample was drawn.

Stratification by designation was deliberately avoided.

Random bias due to the above sampling technique is calculable, at least within a definable margin of error.

The incalculable error is due to non-response as non-respondents may be different from respondents in important respects.

NON-RESPONSE

It was possible to obtain a 100 per cent response rate for administrative grades 8, 9, 10, but not for other grades of staff.

Tables A1/1a and b present the complete sampling and response pattern for hospital and community nursing staff respectively.

A hypothesis that there would be no marked variability in the response rates by different grades of staff was tested.

On the basis of chi-squared tests the hypothesis was refuted; different grades showed different response rates. The most significant difference was between the

TABLE A1/1a
All hospital groups (female nursing staff only)

Designation	Whole population	Sample	Non-participants	Respondents No.	Percentage of sample
Open interviews (grade 9 and 10)	13	13	0	13	100.0
Nursing officers (grade 8)	33	33	0	33	100.0
Nursing officers (grade 7)	103	103	11	92	89.3
Sisters	424	110	13	97	88.2
Staff nurses	704	142	34	108	76.7
Staff midwives	114	14	3	11	(78.6)★
Senior enrolled nurses	25	7	1	6	(85.7)★
Enrolled nurses	558	111	28	83	74.8
Student midwives	98	15	6	9	(60.0)★
Student nurses/ post-registration students	531	102	19	83	81.4
Pupil nurses	390	66	15	51	77.3
Total	2993	716	130	586	81.5

★ Brackets indicate a percentage of a total number which is less than 20.

TABLE A1/1b
All local authority areas (female nursing staff only)

Designation	Whole population	Sample	Non-participants	Respondents No.	Percentage of sample
Open interviews (administrators)	8	8	0	8	100.0
District nurses	78	51	6	45	88.2
Health visitors (including community nursing officers)	81	46	4	42	91.3
Midwives	16	13	0	13	100.0
District nurses/health visitors	1	1	0	1	100.0
District nurses/midwives	16	9	1	8	(88.9)★
Health visitors/midwives	3	1	0	1	100.0
Triple duty nurses	29	21	2	19	90.5
Student health visitors★★	2	2	0	2	100.0
All other nurses†	30	15	0	15	100.0
Total	264	167	13	154	92.2

★ Brackets indicate a percentage of a total number which is less than 20.

★★ There were no student district nurses or midwives in the sample.

† Includes 18 school nurses, 9 relief district nurses, 2 triple duty nurses also doing school nursing and 1 nurse who worked both in the hospital and the local authority area.

numbers of sisters and other hospital field workers who were interviewed. It showed that sisters were over-represented in the sample, a point which must be borne in mind in the interpretation of the data.

Response rates were also tested for inter-hospital group variations; only the smallest group was omitted as the numbers were below the minimum necessary for statistical treatment, leaving three groups for comparison. Response rates in one group differed significantly from the two others.

TABLE A1/2a
Overall sampling and interview numbers in the hospitals (female nursing staff only)

Hospital groups	Whole population	Sample	Non-participants	Respondents No.	Percentage of sample
A	849	208	29	179	86.1
B	1308	307	74	233	75.9
C	137	33	4	29	87.9
D	699	168	23	145	86.3
Total	2993	716	130	586	81.8

Staff nurses and enrolled nurses formed the largest group of non-respondents both in absolute and relative terms.

TABLE A1/2b
Overall sampling and interview numbers in the local authority areas (female nursing staff only)

Local authorities	Whole population	Sample	Non-participants	Respondents No.	Percentage of sample
AA	41	27	2	25	92.6
BB	102	63	6	57	90.5
CC	33	21	1	20	95.2
DD	88	56	4	52	92.9
Total	264	167	13	154	92.2

TABLE A1/2c
Total overall sampling and interview numbers

Total of hospital groups	2993	716	130	586	81.8
Total of local authorities	264	167	13	154	92.2
Grand Total	3257	883	143	740	83.8

In situations like these where response rates differ more than can be explained by chance factors, one must search for possible reasons.

Table A1/3 shows the known reasons for non-response for hospital staff.

It is always desirable to obtain as much information as possible about non-respondents. The data which could be collected in this study were designation and, for the two larger hospital groups, part-time/full-time employment. This indicated that there was a greater loss of part-time staff in some designations, staff nurses/midwives and enrolled nurses being the designations in which part-time working was frequent. Part-time enrolled nurses in these two hospital groups were clearly under-represented.

There was a high proportion of part-time staff in the hospital group from which there was a significantly low response rate, and there was a higher rate of non-response among part-time than among full-time staff in the same designation. However, the response rate of full-time staff in this hospital group was also low and this remains unexplained.

Thus it can be seen that it is desirable, in a study of this type, to obtain the highest possible response rates. It is the incalculability of the non-response error which may confound research results.

STATISTICAL TESTS USED IN THE ANALYSIS

The choice of statistical tests is not always straightforward. It is usually advisable to seek advice on statistical matters at an early stage in the design of a project. The most frequently described methods are suitable for handling quantitative data, but methods for handling qualitative data are also available.

Two significance tests which have been most frequently used in this study are described below. The chi-squared test is widely used in many different contexts and an account of the test can be found in most statistics text books. The other test used in the analysis is the Kolmogorov–Smirnov test which is less well known; where applicable it has advantages which are explained below. Kendall's Coefficient of Concordance was applied to some of the ranked data in the study but as that specific section is not presented in this report, the test is not described.

Chi-squared Test

This test is generally used to examine the distribution of population members among independent samples. One sample or several samples may be compared with a theoretically expected distribution; for example, when discussing data on births, one may expect a distribution of equal numbers of males and females. Alternatively, samples may be compared with each other on the null hypothesis that the observed results show only fortuitous rather than significant differences between them. Thus, as described earlier, different sub-groups in our sample of respondents were compared on the null hypothesis that there was no significant difference between their response rates. The chi-squared test was suitable for this purpose and it was shown that the null hypothesis in that case was refuted; the

TABLE A1/3
All hospital groups—detailed reasons for non-participation

Designation	A*	B*	C*	D*	E*	F*	G*	H*	Total	Percentage of non-respondents in grades
Open interviews (administrators)	0	0	0	0	0	0	0	0	0	0.0
Nursing officers (grade 8)	0	0	0	0	0	0	0	0	0	0.0
Nursing officers (grade 7)	1	0	0	0	6	2	2	0	11	(8.5)**
Sisters	2	0	0	0	4	4	2	1	13	(10.0)**
Staff nurses	2	3	3	3	8	9	2	4	34	26.2
Staff midwives	1	0	0	0	1	0	0	1	3	(2.3)**
Senior enrolled nurses	0	0	0	0	1	0	0	0	1	(0.8)**
Enrolled nurses	5	1	0	4	4	7	2	5	28	21.5
Student midwives	0	0	0	0	3	2	0	1	6	(4.6)**
Student nurses/ post-registration students	1	0	0	0	4	7	4	3	19	(14.6)**
Pupil nurses	0	0	0	0	3	4	1	7	15	(11.5)**
Total	12	4	3	7	34	35	13	22	130	100.0
Percentage of non-respondents for various reasons	9.2	3.1	2.3	5.4	26.2	26.9	10.0	16.9	100.0	

Consistently, both among hospital and local authority staff, the most frequent reasons for non-response were 'E' (retiring shortly/leaving shortly/left) and 'F' (no reply to letters). The impending organisational changes may be at least partially responsible.

*Detailed reasons for non-participation

A	Personal reasons/off sick (long-term)/maternity leave.
B	Just returned to nursing after long absence/new to area.
C	Working part-time.
D	Working night-duty/evenings.
E	Retiring shortly/leaving shortly/left.
F	No reply to letters.
G	Other (fed up with research, hospital closing, on extended service, nothing of interest to say, away on a course, too much studying to do).
H	No reason given.

** Brackets indicate percentage of a total number which is less than 20.

observed differences in response rates were unlikely to have been due to chance.

The usual formula is:

$$X^2 = \Sigma \frac{(O_i - E_i)^{2\star}}{E_i}$$

where O_i represents the number of observations occurring in groups O_i, and E_i denotes the corresponding number to be expected under the hypothesis to be tested. The summation indicated by the symbol Σ is taken over all groups. The above formula is appropriate only when the observed and expected frequencies in a group exceed 5. When such frequencies are equal to or less than 5, appropriate adjacent groups can be merged with each other for the purpose of the test.

When the above formula is applied to a 2 by 2 contingency table on the assumption of independence between row and column characteristics with the number of observations in each cell represented by A, B, C, D, whose sum equals N, the expression can be simplified to:

$$X^2 = \frac{N(AD - BC)^2}{(A+B)\,(C+D)\,(A+C)\,(B+D)} \qquad 1$$

Other refinements and adaptations of the chi-squared test are available and before its use statistical advice should be sought.

Kolmogorov-Smirnov Test

This test is restricted to a comparison of two independent samples, but in this situation has some advantages over the chi-squared test, one being that the arithmetic is simpler and another, that it can accommodate small groups, thereby obviating the need for the merging of groups.

The null hypothesis for this test is that two population distributions are identical in all respects. If an extreme value of the test statistic is observed, it indicates that the two distributions differ at at least one value of the variable in some important respect.

The two-tailed version of the test is sensitive to differences of mean, dispersion or skewness, while the one-tailed test can be used to show not only that results from sample A are different from those obtained from sample B but that, at a given point, they are greater or smaller.

The procedure requires a cumulative presentation of the data from which the cumulative step functions are calculated.

The test statistic focuses on the largest difference between the cumulative step functions of the two samples.

$\star$ The approximation of the distribution of X^2 to that of a chi-squared (X^2) statistic is improved by using the square of $\mid O_i - E_i \mid -\frac{1}{2}$ in place of $(O_i - E_i)^2$ in the formula. Other requirements of the formula are available for certain specific conditions.

[1] Siegel, S., (1956) *Nonparametric Statistics for the Behavioural Sciences*, International Student Edition, McGraw-Hill Kagakusha Ltd. Tokyo. (A continuity correction may be necessary and was used frequently in our analysis.)

For large samples, that is where the sample sizes n_1 and n_2 are greater than 40, the test statistic, based on the formula

$$4D^2 \; \frac{n_1 \, n_2}{n_1 + n_2}$$

is distributed approximately as χ^2 with two degrees of freedom.

For small samples the procedure must be modified and a special table used.

Where applicable, this test can be more sensitive than the chi-squared test but the rules for testing large or small samples, and for using the one-tailed or two-tailed version of the test are complex and statistical advice should be sought before its use.

In our study the test was used mainly in the comparisons of job satisfaction levels.

A clear account of the test and its use is presented by Siegel[2] whose book also contains the necessary tables with directions for their use.

Suggested Texts

1 Cormack, R. M., (1971) *The Statistical Argument*, Oliver & Boyd, Edinburgh.
2 Maxwell, A. E., (1961) *Analysing Qualitative Data*, Methuen Monographs, London.
3 Moroney, M. J., (1951) *Facts from Figures*, Penguin Books, London.
4 Moser, C. A. and Kalton, G., (1971) *Survey Methods in Social Investigation*, 2nd Edn., Heinemann, London.
5 Siegel, S., (1956) *Nonparametric Statistics for the Behavioural Sciences*, International Student Edition, McGraw-Hill Kagakusha Ltd., Tokyo.

---

[2] Siegel, S., (1956) ibid.

APPENDIX TWO
The Definition of Social Class

Occupational status tends to correlate with most other indicators of social status; income, wealth, education or place of residence. The usefulness of the variable in analysing data is generally and officially recognised:

'Apart from the possibility of detecting specific occupational hazards, knowledge of a man's profession gives some idea of his income, his intelligence and education, his leisure pursuits, diet, hygiene and other features of his existence.[1]

It is not always possible to use occupation in this way, for example, a housewife working a few evenings a week in the local public house will have a different kind of home background if her husband is a coal miner than if he is a doctor. Similarly, it makes little sense to classify a retired bank manager according to his present occupation if he now runs a newspaper shop. It is usual to classify married women by their husband's occupation and retired persons according to their main occupation or husband's main occupation.

Of the important background variables about individuals in this study, 'social class' was probably the most difficult to code. This was not unexpected as many other research workers who have used 'social class' as a variable have experienced difficulty in classification and coding. The use of 'social class' requires not only precise information about a person's job, which is often difficult to elicit and sometimes not available, but also a classification scheme which can cope with a wide and subtle variety of occupations. However, it is essential to use the social class variable not only if there is to be comparability of findings with other research, but also if a study is to make a pertinent contribution to knowledge and social theory.

During interviews an attempt was made to obtain precise information about the occupations of husbands, fathers and mothers of respondents. By using only four interviewers, two of whom had experienced the difficulties of coding occupations before, and then giving them all a week's training in interviewing technique, it was hoped that sufficient information would be collected to make fairly accurate coding possible.

Unfortunately this was not the case. Not only did the interviewers sometimes omit to probe when, for example, 'engineer' was given as an answer by respondents, but some respondents had difficulty in expressing exactly what their spouse

[1] Office of Population Censuses and Surveys, (1971) *The Registrar-General's Decennial Supplement, England and Wales, Occupational Mortality Tables*, HMSO, London, p. 18.

or father did as they appeared to have only a rough idea themselves. As a result, some responses could not be classified at all and some occupations were classified on the basis of 'informed guesses'. It would seem desirable for interviewers to have an intimate knowledge of the classification scheme to be used, but even this cannot overcome the lack of knowledge on the part of respondents.

In Britain, the most frequently used classification of occupations is that adopted by the Registrar General for Census purposes.[2] Since the 1911 Census it has been customary to arrange the large number of occupational groups into six broad categories called social class as follows:

1. Professional occupations
2. Intermediate occupations
3. Skilled occupations
   (a) Skilled—non-manual
   (b) Skilled—manual
4. Partly skilled occupations
5. Unskilled occupations

The use of this classification scheme of social class has two main advantages; first, it is widely used and allows direct comparison with Census data and other Government statistics and secondly, it has been well documented,[3] which makes its use relatively easy.

However, for the purposes of this study it was felt that this classification of social class was not the most suitable. Although the classification of skilled occupations, manual and non-manual, partly skilled and unskilled occupations was considered satisfactory, it was felt that the intermediate and professional occupations did not discriminate sufficiently between non-manual jobs. In particular, it was noted that a nurse, whether she be a chief nursing officer or pupil nurse, would fall into social class II (intermediate occupations). It was felt that the life style of a nurse would vary according to her status and that a system of classification with greater discrimination was required.

The classification of social class selected, is a revised version of that developed by Hall and Caradog Jones.[4, 5] This scale has unusual merit in that it is based on the prestige ratings given by a representative British sample and expanded by the judgments of expert sociologists. Since the original scale was an occupational prestige scale for males the version was amended so that it could be used equally for both men and women. The eight-fold classification is as follows:

1. professionally qualified and high administrative,
2. managerial and executive with some responsibility for directing and initiating policy,
3. inspectional, supervisory and other non-manual higher grade,

---

[2] Office of Population Censuses and Surveys, (1970) *Classification of Occupations 1970*, HMSO, London.

[3] Office of Population Censuses and Surveys, ibid.

[4] Hall, J. and Caradog Jones, D., (1950) The Social Grading of Occupations, *British Journal of Sociology*, No. 1, pp. 31–55.

[5] Moser, C. A. and Hall, J. R., in David V. Glass, ed., (1954) *Social Mobility in Britain*, Routledge and Kegan Paul, London, pp. 29–50.

4. inspectional, supervisory and other non-manual lower grade,
5. routine grades of non-manual work,
6. skilled manual workers,
7. semi-skilled manual workers,
8. routine manual workers.

A list of jobs classified by Oppenheim[6] using this method was followed and additional jobs not included in his list were held over for discussion and subsequent allocation to the above categories. The following is a complete list of occupations classified in the study. In all, 41 answers from respondents, 2.2 per cent, were unclassified.

1. Professionally qualified and High Administrative

Accountant
Architect
Army (major upwards)
Author
Bank manager
Civil servant, administrative: chief executive officer, chief inspector of taxes, inspector of schools
Colliery manager
Company registrar
Consultant engineer (textiles)
Doctor

Engineer (qualified)
Farmer (self-employed with employees)
Lawyer
Medical Officer of Health
Nurse (top manager)
Physicist
Planter (tea plantation owner)
Quantity surveyor
Research scientist
Surveyor (qualified)
University lecturer

2. Managerial and Executive (with some responsibility for directing and initiating policy)

Area manager (British Rail)
Area manager (Gas Board)
Army (captain, and commissioned officers below)
Bank clerk (senior)
Book valuer
Broker (insurance)
Civil engineer (Water Board)
Civil servant (senior executive officer, inspector of taxes)
Colliery manager (deputy)
Commercial artist
Estate agent (self-employed with employees)
Fishing proprietor
Headmaster (elementary school)

Hospital secretary
House property manager
Interpreter
Lecturer (technical college)
Minister of Religion
Missionary
Nurse—other administrator
Pay officer (airline)
Pharmacist
Police—Chief inspector
Restaurateur
Sea captain
Shipping manager
Squadron leader
Statistician
Teacher (secondary school)

[6] Oppenheim, A. N., (1966) *Questionnaire Design and Attitude Measurement*, Heinemann Educational Books Ltd., London, pp. 275–284.

3. Inspectional, Supervisory and other Higher Non-manual

Air traffic controller
Animal pharmacist
Area supervisor (building company)
Army: W.O.
Assistant manager (knitwear)
Bank clerk (junior)
Brewery manager
Butcher (self-employed with employees)
Buyer (wholesale and retail)
Civil servant: executive officer
Clerk of works
Colliery engineer
Commercial traveller
Contracting supervisor (building)
Dairyman (self-employed with employees)
Departmental manager
District superintendent (British Rail)
Draper (self-employed with employees)
Draughtsman (qualified)
Engineer: heating (self-employed with employees)
Engineer—machine
    ,,   mining
Executive officer (GPO engineering)
Export manager
Farm bailiff/grieve/manager
Farmer (self-employed without employees)
Fish curer (self-employed with employees)

Fisherman (self-employed with employees)
Food inspector
Garage proprietor
Grocer (self-employed with employees)
Haulage contractor (self-employed)
Head clerk
Hotel keeper/manager(ess)
Hospital administrator
House factor
Inspector (insurance)
Lay Preacher
Librarian (assistant, qualified)
Marine engineer
Master baker
Nurse (other qualified)
Photographer
Piano teacher
Produce marketing manager
Radio officer (Navy)
Restaurant manageress
Social worker
Station master
Teacher (elementary school)
Traffic inspector
Transport manager
Wholesale confectioner (self-employed with employees)
Work study engineer
Works manager

4. Inspectional, Supervisory and other Non-manual

Accountant's clerk
Army: Sgt. and S/Sgt.
Beautician
Book-keeper
Chef or hotel cook
Chief clerk
Engineer—planning
    ,,   ships
Estimating clerk

Estimator (machine costs, re-wiring)
Furrier
Herbalist (self-employed with employees)
Insurance Agent/claims official
Landscape gardener (self-employed with employees)
Manageress—shop
Marine engineer (merchant navy)

Matron/House mother
Master shoe-maker
Master Tailor (self-employed with employees)
Merchant Navy: Midshipman
Nurse—in training
Police: sergeant
Post mistress

Publican (Inn-keeper)
Shop owner (small, unspecified)
Shop supervisor
Sub-postmaster
Superintendent (Old People's Home)
Student
Welfare Officer

5. Routine Grades of Non-manual Work

Accountancy Assistant
Civil Service: Tax officer
Clerk (routine)
Comptometer operator
Credict inspector
Dispatch clerk
Dock checker (supervisor)
Estate agent (clerk)
Governess
Hairdresser
Janitor
Nanny
Nursing auxiliary
Police: constable, special
Postal and telegraph officer

Post office clerk
Proof reader
Receptionist
Secretary
Security officer
Shop assistant: Chemist, confectioner, draper, florist, grocer, ironware, furniture, stationer, tailor
Storekeeper
Supply officer
Telephone operator
Valet
Wages clerk
Wireless operator

6. Skilled Manual

Baker
Blacksmith
Boiler maker
Brass designer
Builder (employed craftsman)
Burner (and brazer)
Bus driver
Butcher
Cab driver
Carpet fitter
Caulker (ship-yard)
Chauffeur
Checker
Chemical worker (foreman)
Chief technician (R.A.F.)
Coachbuilder (British Rail)
Coachman

Coal merchant
Colliery electrician
Colliery engineer
Cook
Cowman
Dairyman (skilled farm worker)
Dressmaker
Electrician (employed craftsman)
Engine driver
Engineer—dairy
    ,,   —employed craftsman
    ,,   —marine (ordinary worker)
    ,,   —mechanical (armaments factory)
    ,,   —metal work
    ,,   —refrigeration
    ,,   —service

Engineer—telephone
Farm worker (skilled)
Fireman (leading)
Fitter
Food processing manager
Forester
French polisher
Game-keeper
Ganger
Gardener
Glass blower
Groom
Golf-club maker
Head gardener
Horseman
Hosiery trimmer
Housekeeper
Inseminator
Inspector (Gas Co., Transport, etc.)
Iron turner
Joiner
Laboratory assistant
Landscape gardener
Landscape gardener (employee)
Leading airman (Royal Navy)
Lorry driver (long distance)
Lorry driver (unspecified)
Maintenance fitter
Mason
Master Joiner (self-employed with employees)
Mechanic (skilled)
Metal worker (foreman)
Milliner
Miner (below ground)
Miner (foreman)
Motor mechanic
Moulder

Painter
Plater (iron and steel)
Plumber
Printer
Printing worker
Quarryman
Radio mechanic (skilled)
Railway guard
Railway signalman
Rivetter
Royal Air Force: Cpl. and L.A.C.
Rubber worker (foreman)
Saddler
Sculptor (employee)
Seedsman
Shepherd
Ships plater
Shipwright
Shoe repairer (shoe-maker)
Slater
Slinger
Spinner
Spring maker (foreman)
Steel erector
Tailor/Tailoress
Tailor's cutter
Telegraph linesman
Tenter (mill-work)
Textile worker (foreman)
Tool room miller
Tractor driver
Turner
Upholsterer
Vulcanizer
Warehouse manager
Weaver
Weigh clerk
Welder

7. Semi-skilled Manual

Agricultural worker, farm servant
Army: Private
Assembly-line worker
Boatman (rescue)
Boilerman

Bus conductor
Carter
Coal conveyor
Coal hewer
Corker

Craneman (crane driver)
Dairymaid
Delivery man
Domestic servant
Farmworker (farm labourer)
Fireman (colliery)
Fisherman
Fish gutter
Food processor
Home help
Hospital domestic
Hospital porter
Jute mill-worker
Laundry worker
Machinist
Maid
Miner (above ground)
Pipe-layer

Postman
Presser (tailor's)
Printer's assistant
Process worker
Railway linesman
Sand blaster
Seaman
Seaman (merchant navy)
Shophand: Greengrocer, butcher, fish-monger
Storeman
Tennis string maker
Ticket collector
Tracer
Waitress
Wool worker (mill)
Worker: Chemical, leather, starch, steel, rope, rubber, etc.

8. Routine Manual

Box-maker (cardboard)
Canteen assistant
Cleaner
Docker
Factory worker

Kitchen hand
Labourer
Lamplighter
Porter
Vanman

APPENDIX THREE
Comments on Interviewing Schedules and Guide to Interviewers

It is common practice to publish questionnaires, interviewing schedules and other data collecting tools as part of a research report. The advantages are considered to be the interest to the reader and the opportunity to assess answers in the light of the questions which generated them. The disadvantage of this practice is mainly economic; any additional pages raise the cost of production and may result in a research report which prices itself out of the general reader market, thereby defeating the purpose of the work.

An attempt has been made in this report to achieve a reasonable compromise. Where the respondents' answers or their interpretation of the question are obviously determined by the wording, the questions are quoted at the foot of the page. The opportunity to obtain the full schedules from the Research Unit is given to any interested reader.*

A summary of the structure, content and rationale of the interviewing schedules and guide, is given below.

Most data were obtained from personal interviews as described in Chapter 2. Three types of schedule were developed, the first being merely a predetermined selection and order of topics to be discussed in the open interviews with top managers (Chapter 4).

The other two schedules were highly structured and similar, though not identical, in content. One was used for the nursing administrators other than the top managers, the other was administered to the field workers.

The schedules began with a standard introduction, referring to the previous correspondence, explaining the study, and assuring respondents of confidentiality and individual anonymity.

The schedules fell into distinct sections designed to elicit different sets of information.

The first part dealt with respondents' current employment and career patterns to date. Emphasis was on the nurse as a woman with home responsibilities and possibly career interruption for domestic reasons. Breaks in service formed an important subsection and the longest break with the reasons for it were focused on, together with the perceived implications for the respondents' professional career.**

---

* The Director, Nursing Research Unit, Department of Nursing Studies, University of Edinburgh, 12 Buccleuch Place, Edinburgh, EH8 9JT.
** *Questions 14–26*. Asked for number of breaks of three months or more, the length of and reason for the longest break, type and level of employment before and after the break and the respondents' assessment of its effect (Chapter 7).

The next part of the schedule concentrated on part-time employment, its meaning, its extent, its acceptability and nurses' attitudes to 'part-timers'. This was followed by recording the hours worked by full- and part-time staff for the previous week. The pilot studies had emphasised the difficulty of recall, and it was finally decided that the most reliable information would be obtained by working backwards from the day before the interview.* From these answers it was possible to construct the weekly working pattern presented in Chapter 10.

Part of this section included questions on the acceptability to the respondents of their working arrangements including housing and transport. An attempt to assess and measure job satisfaction (Chapter 8), albeit crudely, was integrated. It is generally acknowledged that people do not readily admit to an error in career choice, and that there may be reluctance in admitting to dissatisfaction or boredom, as this implies, amongst other things, lack of control over one's occupation. To lend a little more weight to the validity of the answers, questions were added on respondents' hypothetical advice to daughter and friend on nursing as a career. The 'ideal occupation' has been used in the field of social psychology as a means of assessing satisfaction or frustration and Question 53** was included for this reason. It also provided a little light relief about halfway through the lengthy interview.

In the design of the study and the selection of the study population the omission of nursing auxiliaries was deliberate. It was recognised, however, that their contribution to a study of 'Women in Nursing' could not be ignored and that they might form the subject of a separate study undertaken by the Unit. Questions to learners and qualified nursing staff about auxiliaries, the extent of a working partnership with them, views on their contribution and measure of responsibility were not only considered essential to the current study but also helpful in the design of further work.

Questions designed to elicit respondents' views on patient care followed and the interview was concluded by a section of personal questions on income, home and social life and plans for the future. The reason for these questions was to find out whether earnings from nursing made an important financial contribution to the family income or whether the interest in nursing was the more relevant factor in women's efforts to pursue a dual career—housewife/mother and nurse. These questions were deliberately left to the end of the schedule in case the interview could not be concluded, either because of time pressure or because respondents refused to answer the personal questions. In the event, there were no refusals although some respondents asked for reasons.

Finally, the respondents were given the opportunity to ask questions or make comments.† They were also handed a note thanking them for their help, giving

---

* *Question 38.* Can you tell me your duty time for the last week starting yesterday and working backwards? For each day I would also like to know when you had your main meal breaks and any periods when you may have been on call?

** *Question 53.* If you were able to choose absolutely any occupation or job in the world, with a guarantee of success in this occupation, what occupation would you choose? Why?

† *Question 86.* Now I've been asking you rather a lot of questions. Are there any questions you would like to ask me or is there anything else you would like to say?

If you think of anything else at all, please don't hesitate to write. Here is our address. Thank you very much for all your help; you can be sure that your confidence will be respected.

them the name of the interviewer and the address of the Research Unit for any communication they might wish to make.

The administrators' schedules were different in two respects. They included a section of questions particularly relevant to administrative matters and excluded others. For example three questions dealt with staffing problems* and another asked for the deployment policy of part-time staff. The questions which were excluded were those relating to direct patient care (Chapter 12).

Administrators' schedules were easily distinguishable as they had a coloured cover sheet and the specific administrators' questions were alse presented on a coloured insert. This mechanism ensured that the appropriate schedule was used from the onset of the interview thereby reducing error and confusion.

After completion of the interview the basic information presented below was recorded by the interviewer.

Interviewer's Code: ☐☐   Date: ☐☐☐☐☐☐

Length of interview:		Day of week:	
Less than 30 minutes . .	1	Sunday	1
30 minutes less than 45 minutes	2	Monday	2
45 minutes less than 1 hour .	3	Tuesday	3
1 hour or more . . .	4	Wednesday . . .	4
		Thursday . . .	5
		Friday	6
		Saturday	7

The interviewer's code makes it possible to test for interviewer bias: sex, age, personality and other characteristics of an interviewer are known to influence the type of answers.

Knowledge about the length of the interviews is important not only for field-work planning but it may also suggest relationships with other variables. For example, interviews with certain types of respondents such as older people or people in specific positions, may last consistently longer than others; such information may prove to be of value.**

The recording of date and day of the week was essential for the construction of the nurses' working pattern (Chapters 9 and 10).

---

* *Question 64(a).* As an administrator do you think that there are any hours of the day or night more difficult to staff than others? IF YES (a) What are they? (b) How do you cope?

Question 64(b). Do you think there are any days of the week more difficult to staff than others? IF YES (a) What are they? (b) How do you cope?

Question 64(c). Do you think there are any particular months of the year more difficult to staff than others? IF YES (a) What are they? (b) How do you cope?

** The information, though obtained in the study, has not yet been analysed.

INTERVIEWERS' GUIDE

Each interviewer was provided with an explanatory document which was discussed in detail during the training week. It concerned itself particularly with the significance of the lay-out of the interviewing schedule, such as indented dependent questions, instruction on recording methods and rules on prompting and omission of questions. Variations of questions to meet specific circumstances were detailed as were the questions to which more than one answer could be given and those which were to be followed by probing. Technical and ambiguous terminology was explained in order to achieve a common standard of response.

For example:

Question 1 on schedule: First, how long have you been employed by the
—————————————————— hospital group/
local authority?

Guide to interviewer:

TO ALL
Phrase according to respondent's employment in either hospital group or local authority. Length of employment refers to continuous employment up to the time of interview. It should include a break only if the respondent has remained on the payroll of the hospital group or local authority. Respondent may be employed jointly by a hospital group and local authority; if so, record this and include details.

As not all interviewers were nurses, terms such as Unit Nursing Officer or 'Attachment' were explained.

Most importantly, the guide contained coding instructions and the coding key for hospitals, local health authorities and interviewers.

Instructions on recording were given as follows:

Recording
Blue or black pens should be used to record information at the interview. When you check over the interview schedule afterwards, writing in things that are not clear or expanding your personal abbreviations or translating shorthand, do this in pencil. If you ask any additional questions or use additional probes and lead-ins or even inadvertently make additional comments, record them and *underline the actual words used. Never use red,* this is what is used for coding, or *green* which is used for checking. If you run out of ink use pencil in preference to any other colour.

The ability to distinguish between recording during the interview and additions from memory afterwards were deemed important in the assessment of the data.

APPENDIX FOUR
Supplementary Tables

TABLE A4/1
Nurse staffing statistics for the research areas (hospitals)

	A Female FT	A Female PT	A All WTE	A Male FT	A Male PT	B Female FT	B Female PT	B All WTE	B Male FT	B Male PT	C Female FT	C Female PT	C All WTE	C Male FT	C Male PT	D Female FT	D Female PT	D All WTE	D Male FT	D Male PT
All hospital administrators	56	1*	63	6	0	53	0	58	5	0	7	0	11	4	0	38	0	49	11	0
Qualified fieldworkers	240	176	374	33	4	391	409	667	22	0	87	32	117	13	0	268	206	481	67	0
Learners**	361	0	388	27	0	487	0	501	14	0	31	0	41	10	0	192	0	231	39	0
Auxiliaries	207	626	599	22	3	114	605	465	0	0	41	37	66	2	2	108	238	307	9	0
Number of beds			1592					1592					428					1858		

* 36 hours per week.
** Includes student midwives and other qualified learners.
WTE Whole time equivalent.
Source: Top managers in research areas.

TABLE A4/2
Nurse staffing statistics for the research areas (local authorities)

	AA		BB		CC		DD	
	FT	PT	FT	PT	FT	PT	FT	PT
Administrators	1	0	3	0	3	0	3	0
Fieldworkers	38	2	95	30	23	9	70	15
Learners	0	0	6	0	2	0	2	0
Auxiliaries	1	2	1	13	0	4	0	18
Population size	95 000		182 000		60 600		143 000	

There were no male community nurses in these areas.
Whole time equivalents were not reported.
Source: Top managers in research areas.

TABLE A4/3
Comparison between respondents' and respondents' fathers' country of birth

	Scotland		England		Other UK		Eire		Others		Total= 100%
Respondents	599	83.3	66	9.2	6	0.8	14	1.9	34	4.8	719
Respondents' father	571	79.4	82	11.4	12	1.6	17	2.4	37	5.2	719

TABLE A4/4
Average number of one week's* working hours of full-time nurses (statutory working hours are based on an 80 hour fortnight)

Designation	Average hours for one week	No. working	No. not working	Total
Senior nursing officers	37.1	33	1	34
Unit nursing officers	37.7	76	1	77
Clinical instructors	25.8	3	1	4
Sisters	39.7	78	3	81
Tutors	36.6	6	1	7
Staff nurses	35.7	44	0	44
Senior enrolled nurses	28.5	3	0	3
Enrolled nurses	34.6	49	1	50
Student nurses	32.3	62	0	62
Staff midwives	41.0	4	1	5
Student midwives	29.1	8	1	9
Pupil nurses	42.2	49	1	50
District nurses	34.5	33	1	34
Health visitors	36.2	32	3	35
Domiciliary midwives	22.1	10	1	11
Triple duty nurses	32.6	15	2	17
District nurse/health visitor	30.5	1	0	1
District nurses/midwives	32.0	8	0	8
Health visitor/midwife	28.5	1	0	1
Student health visitors	30.0	1	1	2
Community nursing officers	35.2	6	1	7
Senior health visitors	18.0	2	0	2
Senior district nurse	30.6	1	0	1
Night superintendents	34.9	4	0	4
Triple duty and school nurse	47.0	1	0	1
District nurse/ward sister	39.0	1	0	1
Total		531	20	551
Mean average	36.1			

*Week immediately before the interview.

APPENDIX FIVE
Attitude Scales

In this study two attempts have been made to measure attitudes. First a measure of job satisfaction was used by amending the job satisfaction index constructed by Brayfield and Rothe.[1] Second, a measure of the attitudes of nurses in general, toward part-time nurses in particular, was developed especially for this study, as no suitable measure was found in the literature. This appendix describes how the measure of job satisfaction was amended and how a scale for the measurement of nurses' attitudes was constructed for use in this study.

Likert scales

Both measures took the form of a Likert scale.[2] The Likert scale consists of a number of statements or items, between half-a-dozen and two dozen, with which the respondent is asked to strongly agree, agree, disagree, strongly disagree or say whether he is uncertain of the answer. Such a scale consists of an equal number of positive and negative statements. The chief function of the scale is to divide people into a number of broad groups. Likert scales are in no way predictive of the individual's behaviour and are, therefore, not suitable for determining a single individual's attitude. The construction of a Likert scale uses a pool of statements or items in which there are neither too many extreme answers nor too many neutral ones. Ideally, a large number of statements is tested with a sample of subjects similar to those for whom the scale is being developed. Statements are chosen for their ability to discriminate favourable, unfavourable or neutral stances toward a particular object.

Inter-item analysis is then carried out to determine which statements carry sufficient statistical validity to warrant their inclusion in the final scale. The total score is calculated by summing the scores of individual items. Each statement is usually scored from one to five depending on whether the statement is positively or negatively worded towards the object of the scale. A high total score would indicate a positive attitude and a low total score a negative one. As the scale does not provide an interval measure it is difficult to determine when an attitude changes from positive to negative. In the final stages, therefore, there is a high subjective element in the interpretation of the results by the researcher.

---

[1] Brayfield, A. H. and Rothe, H. F., (1951) An Index of job satisfaction, *Journal of Applied Psychology*, 35, pp. 307–311.

[2] Likert, R., (1932) A Technique for the Measurement of Attitudes, *Archives of Psychology*, No. 140.

Reliability of scales

During the construction of the two scales used in this study, inter-item analysis was used as a measure of reliability and to determine the optimum length for each scale. Inter-item analysis should be done by correlating each item in the scale with a reliable outside measure of the attitude supposedly being measured. Such external criteria are rarely available and the scales used in the study were no exception. Inter-item analysis was carried out using methods described by Cronbach[3] and McKennel.[4] 'Alpha' is the label given by Cronbach to a particular type of coefficient which measures the reliability of a scale. A reliability coefficient demonstrates whether the scale designer was correct in expecting a certain collection of statements to yield interpretable indicators about groups of individuals. The justification for the use of 'alpha' is outlined by McKennel and in more detail by Cronbach.

'Alpha' was used to decide the optimum length of scales and their reliability in the measurement of attitudes. The testing of items for inclusion in a scale is based on the properties of the Spearman–Brown[5] formula:

$$\text{alpha} = \frac{n\bar{r}_{ij}}{1 + (n-1)\bar{r}_{ij}}$$

where n = the number of separate statements in the scale,
$\bar{r}_{ij}$ = the average inter-item correlation, and
alpha = the reliability of the total score obtained by summing the score of separate statements.

The inter-item correlations were calculated using the Pearson's product-moment correlation coefficient. It is defined by the following formula:

$$r = \frac{\sum\limits_{i=1}^{n} (X_i - \bar{X})(Y_i - \bar{Y})}{\left(\left(\sum\limits_{i=1}^{n}(X_i - \bar{X})^2\right)\left(\sum\limits_{i=1}^{n}(Y_i - \bar{Y})^2\right)\right)^{\frac{1}{2}}}$$

where X_i = ith score of item X
Y_i = ith score of item Y
$\bar{X}$ = mean score of item X
$\bar{Y}$ = mean score of item Y
$i = 1, 2, \ldots, n$

As the formula for alpha shows, the reliability of a scale will depend on its internal consistency ($\bar{r}_{ij}$) and its length (n). With perfect reliability, any one of a

[3] Cronbach, L. J., (1951) Coefficient alpha and the internal structure of tests, *Psychometrika*, No. 16, pp. 297–334.
[4] McKennel, A. C., (1968) Use of coefficient alpha in constructing attitude and similar scales, *Government Social Survey, Methodological Paper*, No. 139.
[5] Guilford, J. P., (1950) *Fundamental Statistics in Psychology and Education*, 2nd ed., McGraw Hill, New York, p. 493.

list of items measuring the same thing, would be sufficient to measure the particular attitude. For such perfect reliability alpha would equal unity.

What value of alpha is acceptable? In the measurement of personality and intelligence, psychologists aim at values of alpha of 0.9 or above and frequently use extremely lengthy tests to obtain this value. Such tests are required for accurately distinguishing between the scores of single individuals. In the survey situation, where the attitude scale is only discriminating between groups of people, one is never called upon to interpret the score of a single individual. In theory, the longer the scale, the larger the n, the higher the reliability of the scale. In practice this is not so.

In selecting statements for the two scales it was necessary to maximise reliability. The method used differs from the standard Likert method. In the Likert method the correlation coefficient is found between each item and the total score on the remaining set of items. Those items with the highest correlation values are then selected as being the best measure of whatever the total score measures. In the present study, however, $\bar{r}_{ij}$, the average inter-item correlation for an individual item and the other items in the set (i.e. the average of all the entries in the relevant row in an inter-correlation matrix), was calculated for each item. Items were then ranked according to the value $\bar{r}_{ij}$.

TABLE A5/1
Reliability coefficient alpha for attitudes of hospital administrators, hospital field-workers and community nurses to job satisfaction and part-time nurses

	Hospital administrators	Hospital fieldworkers	Community nurses
Job satisfaction	0.80	0.80	0.80
Part-time nurses	0.77	0.77	0.78
Number of nurses	125	448	146

Table A5/1 shows the values of alpha achieved in the three samples for the job satisfaction index and the attitude of nurses in general toward part-time nurses.

Job satisfaction index
As explained in Chapter 2 interview schedules and other tools were designed and tested using two pilot studies. A pre-pilot study was undertaken before the pilot studies in order to develop the two attitude scales. The original eighteen statements used by Brayfield and Rothe[6] in their index of job satisfaction were administered to a group of 48 nurses from one general hospital. The statements are:

1. My job is like a hobby to me.
2. My job is usually interesting enough to keep me from getting bored.
3. It seems that my friends are more interested in their jobs.
4. I consider my job rather unpleasant.

[6] Brayfield, A. H. and Rothe, H. F., (1951) An Index of job satisfaction, *Journal of Applied Psychology*, 35, pp. 307–311.

5. I enjoy my work more than my leisure time.
6. I am often bored with my job.
7. I feel fairly well satisfied with my present job.
8. Most of the time I have to force myself to go to work.
9. I am satisfied with my job for the time being.
10. I feel that my job is no more interesting than others I could get.
11. I definitely dislike my work.
12. I feel that I am happier in my work than most other people.
13. Most days I am enthusiastic about my work.
14. Each day of work seems like it will never end.
15. I like my job better than the average worker does.
16. My job is pretty uninteresting.
17. I find real enjoyment in my work.
18. I am disappointed that I ever took this job.

Since both scales were to be used as part of a long interview schedule one of the qualities had to be brevity, to avoid fatiguing not only the respondent but also the interviewer. The analysis of the pre-pilot study reduced the number of statements without weakening the usefulness of the scale. Values of alpha were calculated for different lengths of scale. Although the highest value of alpha, 0.88, was recorded for a scale consisting of fourteen questions, values of 0.84 and over were obtained for all scales longer than four statements.

In the first pilot study only six statements were used. Although this scale achieved an 'alpha' value greater than 0.9 it was felt that the scale was not discriminating between different levels of job satisfaction. It was decided to increase the index length to twelve statements for testing in the second pilot study. The statements used in the second pilot and the main study are:

1. I consider my job rather unpleasant.
2. I enjoy my work more than my leisure time.
3. I am often bored with my job.
4. I feel fairly well satisfied with my present job.
5. Most of the time I have to force myself to go to work.
6. I feel that I am happier in my work than most other people.
7. Most days I am enthusiastic about my work.
8. Each day of work seems like it will never end.
9. I like my job better than the average worker does.
10. My job is pretty uninteresting.
11. I find real enjoyment in my work.
12. I am disappointed that I ever took this job.

Part-time nurses scale
The development of a scale to measure the attitudes of nurses in general, toward part-time nurses in particular, was more complicated than the amendment of the existing scale measuring the attitude of people towards their job. Originally scales to measure the following attitudes were sought:
(a) Nurses' attitudes toward part-time nurses
(b) Nurses' attitudes toward married nurses

(c) Nurses' attitudes toward married nurses with children
(d) Nurses' attitudes toward married women working.

It may be that suitable existing scales were overlooked or that they are not clearly documented; whatever the reason, the search for them proved fruitless. As explained below the attempt to produce four scales was too ambitious.

After discussion with colleagues and members of the profession similar to those to whom the statements were to be administered, forty statements were collected. The statements, half of which represented a positive attitude and half of which represented a negative attitude toward the four scale objects are as follows:

1. If a nurse wants to follow her career full-time she should not have children.
2. Hospitals and local authorities should make child-minding facilities available for the children of their staff.
3. Part-time nurses can be more advantageously employed in the administrative rather than in the clinical field.
4. Patients prefer certain aspects of their personal care to be carried out by married nurses.
5. Children need the constant presence of their mother during their early years to ensure normal emotional development.
6. Some fields of nursing can be more advantageously staffed by part-time nurses.
7. Nursing is an ideal career for married women.
8. Continuity of patient care is adversely affected by the employment of part-time nurses.
9. Full- and part-time nurses should be given equal opportunities for promotion.
10. A married nurse should not take on the responsibilities of both career and child rearing.
11. Married nurses find it easier to establish professional relationships.
12. Part-time ward sisters and unit officers are not a practical proposition.
13. Women of working age should have some employment outside the home.
14. The employment of nurses with young children should be limited.
15. Nurses should make their own arrangements for care of their children and not expect their employers to provide creches.
16. Husband and wife relationships benefit if the wife has work outside the home.
17. The married nurse's obligations should be greater to her husband than to her work.
18. Part-time nurses should only be used as a reserve labour force.
19. Nurses should not marry.
20. Recruitment should be aimed at full-time rather than part-time nurses.
21. Nurses should be employed according to their skills irrespective of whether they work full- or part-time.
22. A career in nursing can become a substitute for motherhood.
23. Married nurses perform certain intimate nursing tasks better than the single nurse.
24. A training in nursing is a good training for motherhood.
25. Nurses with children under school age who so desire should be allowed to maintain their career on a part-time basis.

26. Children gain independence and maturity more rapidly if they have a working mother.
27. Married nurses have the same problems as other married working women in relation to their obligations outside work.
28. Women of working age should have some employment outside the home.
29. Married nurses are less career orientated than single nurses.
30. Mothers should always be at home when children return from school.
31. Nurses with children understand better the needs of their patients.
32. In the event of a child's illness the mother rather than the father should stay at home.
33. If a woman wants to follow a full-time career she should not have children.
34. The employment of part-time nurses in the health service should be encouraged.
35. Suitable career prospects should be readily available for a nurse returning to service after raising her family.
36. Married nurses are less reliable than single nurses.
37. Husbands and wives should be equally involved in child rearing and household duties.
38. Husbands resent the independence of a working wife.
39. Six months maternity leave should be granted to nurses without affecting their career prospects.
40. Marriage and nursing do not mix.

These forty statements were administered in the pre-pilot study along with the eighteen job satisfaction statements. Inter-item analysis was carried out to find the reliability of each scale. Table A5/2 shows values of alpha for different scale lengths in the case of each scale. The optimum number of statements included in the scales was six in the case of the part-time nurses' scale, five for married nurses' scale, five for married women and children scale and eight for attitudes of nurses toward women working scale.

The length of the whole interview schedule for the proposed study was already becoming too long. It was decided, therefore, that it would be impracticable to include all four scales. In the analysis of the pre-pilot study it was found that all four scales were reliable ($a > 0.5$). However, the two scales measuring attitudes toward married nurses and toward married nurses with children resulted in values of alpha less than 0.6. It was, therefore, decided to use just two scales, the attitude of nurses toward part-time nurses and toward women working, where the value of alpha was greater than 0.6 for six items. The following twelve statements were used in the first pilot study:

1. Children need the constant presence of their mother during their early years to ensure normal emotional development.
2. Continuity of patient care is adversely affected by the employment of part-time nurses.
3. Full- and part-time nurses should be given equal opportunities for promotion.
4. Part-time nurses should only be used as a reserve labour force.
5. Recruitment should be aimed at full-time rather than part-time nurses.
6. Nurses should be employed according to their skills irrespective of whether they work full- or part-time.

7. Children gain independence and maturity more rapidly if they have a working mother.
8. Women of working age should have some employment outside the home.
9. Mothers should always be at home when children return from school.
10. Nurses with children understand better the needs of their patients.
11. If a woman wants to follow a full-time career she should not have children.
12. Husbands and wives should be equally involved in child rearing and household duties.

TABLE A5/2
Reliability coefficient alpha for four attitude scales used in pre-pilot study

Length of scale (number of items)	Name of Scale			
	Part-time nurses	Married nurses	Married nurses with children	Women working
10	0.56	0.14	0.44	0.71
9	0.59	0.13	0.49	0.73
8	0.60	0.21	0.48	0.74
				—
7	0.61	0.31	0.52	0.74
6	0.62	0.44	0.58	0.72
	—			
5	0.62	0.56	0.64	0.73
		—		
4	0.56	0.48	0.62	0.73
3	0.51	0.62	0.63	0.59
2	0.26	0.49	0.56	0.42

Analysis following the first pilot study showed that both scales were reliable ($a > 0.5$). However, only the part-time scale returned a value of alpha greater than 0.6. Three problems emerged from these two stages. First, it was felt that nurses were not responding to five categories of answers but only to two. Their replies tended to be dichotomous—either they were in agreement with the statement or they disagreed. Secondly, the numbers interviewed at each stage, 48 and 76, produced low values of inter-item correlations, although these might have been higher with a larger number of nurses. Theoretically, at least one hundred nurses should have been interviewed to obtain more reliable results. Thirdly, it is realised that the scales may have been weak because of the wording of the statements. Oppenheim[7] writes:

'remembering that attitudes are emotional, we should try to avoid the stilted rational approach in writing attitude statements.'

The majority of the statements used in the original pool were rational statements. In stage three the following modifications were made; some new statements were

[7] Oppenheim, A. N., (1966) *Questionnaire Design and Attitude Measurement*, Heinemann Educational Books Ltd., London, p. 114.

introduced and others were re-worded to be more personal and emotive. The construction of a single scale to measure the attitude of nurses in general, toward part-time nurses in particular, was attempted.

Eighteen statements were administered in the second pilot study. They were:
1. I don't think it's a good idea for a nurse to work full-time when she has young children.
2. Most part-time nurses are only working for the money.
3. It's a shame that part-time nurses so rarely get promoted.
4. The part-time nurses I know appear to get less satisfaction from their work.
5. I think better use could be made of part-time nurses here.
6. Generally, one full-time nurse is more use than two part-time nurses.
7. Very often I find patients have more confidence in married nurses.
8. I think part-time nurses should get more responsibility.
9. Sometimes I feel we would do better with less part-time nurses.
10. It would be nice if creches and nurseries were always available for nurses' children.
11. It seems to me that part-time nurses care less about their work than other nurses.
12. Some married women are very good nurses.
13. I think part-time nurses should be able to attend more courses.
14. I don't think part-time nurses do well in positions of responsibility.
15. I don't think we could manage without part-time nurses.
16. In general married nurses seem to get preferential treatment.
17. Things seem difficult to organise with a lot of part-time staff.
18. If it were up to me I'd employ more part-time nurses.

Inter-item analysis was again carried out for the second pilot study to determine the length of the scale and the choice of statements for inclusion in the final scale.

TABLE A5/3
Reliability coefficient and length of scale in second pilot study for part-time attitude scale

Length of scale	18	17	16	15	14	13	12	11	10	9	8	7	6	5	4	3	2
Alpha	0.71	0.74	0.75	0.76	0.77	0.77	0.78	0.76	0.77	0.78	0.79	0.77	0.76	0.73	0.70	0.65	0.57

Table A5/3 shows how the optimum number of statements was reached. The optimum length of the scale was found to consist of eight statements although scales ranging from six to sixteen statements produced differences in alpha to one place of decimals only.

We were unable to use just eight statements in the scale in the main study as suggested by Table A5/3. There were two reasons for this. First, we suspected that to reduce a scale length by ten items might radically influence the responses to the eight remaining items. This was confirmed in the two pilot studies, where such a reduction in the size of the attitude scale changed the distribution of responses and produced lower reliability values. The second reason for not reducing the scale length to eight statements was that, of the eight, only two were unfavourably worded. As indicated earlier, it is necessary to have an equal number of favourable and unfavourable statements. The following twelve statements were, therefore, administered in the main study:

1. Most part-time nurses are only working for the money.
2. It's a shame that part-time nurses so rarely get promoted.
3. Generally one full-time nurse is more use then two part-time nurses.
4. I think part-time nurses should get more responsibility.
5. Sometimes I feel we would be better with less part-time nurses.
6. It would be nice if creches and nurseries were always available for nurses' children.
7. It seems to me that part-time nurses care less about their work than other nurses.
8. I think part-time nurses should be able to attend more courses.
9. I don't think part-time nurses do well in positions of responsibility.
10. I don't think we could manage without part-time nurses.
11. Things seem difficult to organise with a lot of part-time staff.
12. If it were up to me I'd employ more part-time nurses.

Treatment of inadequate answers

Many of the respondents found the change from 'normal' questions to the attitude scales difficult. At the beginning of the section on attitude scales the interviewer gave the respondent a card and indicated that she was expected to reply to the statements with one of the five options printed on the card: strongly agree, agree, uncertain, disagree or strongly disagree. Some respondents misunderstood what they had to do while others refused to answer in the way requested. Most commonly respondents felt unable to use the categories asked for. For example:

'None of these five categories fit.'

'I don't strongly agree, I don't agree, I'm not uncertain, I don't disagree and I don't strongly disagree. That question is ambiguous.'

The interviewer had been instructed to repeat the statement concerned encouraging the use of the categories provided. However, some respondents felt they were still unable to do so.

Table A5/4 shows the percentage in each of three samples who felt unable to answer one or more of the 24 statements used for the two scales. The percentage of those unable to answer individual statements is also presented in this table. Surprisingly the proportion of non-response to statements was small.

We considered two possible ways of dealing with this kind of non-response in attitude scales. Either they could be scored as uncertain answers or respondents could be omitted from any analysis which used that particular scale. The first is more contentious in that a person who refuses to answer a large number of statements would attain scores close to the mean, the score not necessarily representing an 'average attitude'. The second has disadvantages when only one or two statements remain unanswered, as a large number of individuals might be omitted in any analysis which uses either of the scales. In the original validation of the scales

TABLE A5/4
Percentage of non-response to individual statements and percentage of non-response to any one or more statements on two attitude scales

Name of scale		Hospital administrators %	Hospital fieldworkers %	Community nurses %
	1*	—	—	—
	2	9.6	0.9	4.8
	3	—	—	—
	4	0.8	0.2	—
	5	—	0.2	—
Job	6	4.8	0.4	1.4
satisfaction	7	—	0.2	—
index	8	0.8	0.2	—
	9	4.8	0.7	0.7
	10	—	0.2	—
	11	—	0.2	—
	12	—	0.2	—
	One or more	12.0	1.6	5.5
	1	—	0.4	3.4
	2	0.8	0.2	3.4
	3	0.8	0.4	4.1
	4	5.6	1.1	3.4
	5	—	—	2.7
Part-time	6	—	—	2.1
scale	7	1.6	—	2.7
	8	—	0.2	4.1
	9	—	—	4.1
	10	—	—	3.4
	11	—	0.2	2.7
	12	4.0	0.2	4.1
	One or more	10.4	2.7	8.2
Number of nurses		125	448	146

* See Tables A5/9 and A5/10 (Questions 50 and 51) for wording of statements.

non-response was scored as an uncertain answer. It was decided, however, in the analysis of attitude scale scores in the main study, to exclude individuals who made no response to one or more statements on a scale. The realiability coefficient alpha was recalculated for the three samples excluding these individuals. Table A5/5 shows that the method adopted did not reduce values of 'alpha'.

TABLE A5/5
Reliability coefficient alpha for hospital administrators, hospital fieldworkers and community nurses excluding non-response individuals

	Hospital administrators	Hospital fieldworkers	Community nurses
Job satisfaction index	0.81	0.80	0.80
Number of nurses	110	441	138
Part-time scale	0.78	0.78	0.77
Number of nurses	112	436	134

Distribution of total scores
The total score for each scale was then calculated by summing the scores on individual statements in the scales. As each scale consisted of twelve statements, respondents could get a minimum score of 12 and a maximum score of 60. To ease the burden of computation, 12 was subtracted from each of the respondents' scores so that the absolute minimum became zero and the absolute maximum 48. The distribution of total scores was then computed and standard statistics for measuring such distributions were calculated. Table A5/6 summarises these statistics.

Although most parametric tests are based on the assumption of normality of distribution in the parent population, many statistical tests are sufficiently robust to serve their purpose in cases of moderate departure from normality; with non-parametric tests, normality is not assumed anyhow.

From the data of our analysis the tested hypothesis of normal distribution in the

TABLE A5/6
Summary statistics of total scores of the two attitude scales

Statistics	Job Satisfaction Index			Part-time Scale		
	Hospital administrators	Hospital fieldworkers	Community nurses	Hospital administrators	Hospital fieldworkers	Community nurses
Maximum score	46	48	43	44	44	42
Minimum score	18	11	20	14	14	15
Range	28	37	23	30	30	27
Mean	34.69	34.92	34.96	31.52	30.64	29.67
Median	34.88	34.75	35.69	32.25	31.65	30.14
Standard deviation	4.75	4.46	4.46	5.05	5.46	5.43
Kurtosis	1.98	2.88	1.52	0.48	0.2	−0.08
Skewness	−0.75	−0.49	−0.9	−0.39	−0.5	−0.48
Number of nurses	110	441	138	112	436	134

parent population cannot be rejected; however, no other possible distributions were subjected to the rigour of statistical tests.

In the presentation of the attitude scales analysis it was necessary to group scores. This was done by dividing the combined total scores of all three samples for each scale into three groups representing high, medium and low attitude scores. The meaning of these three labels is discussed below. Although the scores did not perfectly constitute a normal distribution it was decided to determine the cut-off points of the groups by taking one standard deviation of scores from the mean score. In theory this would mean that 68.26 per cent of cases would fall under the medium scores and 15.87 per cent under the high and low scores respectively.

TABLE A5/7
Percentage of respondents with high, medium and low attitude scores

	Job Satisfaction Index			Part-time Scale		
	Low %	Medium %	High %	Low %	Medium %	High %
Hospital fieldworkers	14.3	71.7	14.1	16.5	66.5	17.0
Hospital administrators	14.5	72.7	12.7	12.5	67.0	20.5
Community nurses	14.5	73.2	12.3	20.1	67.9	11.9
All	14.4	72.1	13.5	16.6	66.8	16.6
Number of nurses	99	497	93	113	456	113

Unclassifiable: Job satisfaction index, 30 respondents; Part-time scale, 37 respondents.

For the job satisfaction scale low scores are those of less than 31, medium scores those between 31 and 39 and high scores those of 40 or over. For the part-time scale low scores are those of less than 26, medium scores those between 26 and 36 and high scores those of 37 or over. Table A5/7 shows the actual proportion of scores in each of three groups.

Interpretation of scales

Whilst statistical significance is an important concept in research it must be balanced with an appreciation of practical importance. Thus, as alluded to in Appendix 1, it is possible that an event most unlikely to have occurred by chance, i.e. statistically significant, has no practical implication and it is equally possible that a fortuitous finding raises important practical issues which merit further investigation.

Job satisfaction scores in themselves are abstract numerals and lack 'meaning'.

Although the method for the construction of the two attitude scales was object-ive, their interpretation must inevitably be subjective. It was felt, therefore, that it might be helpful to examine more closely what kind of respondents obtained high, medium and low scores respectively. The only further sources of information available were the answers to a wide range of questions recorded on the inter-

viewing schedules and these were grouped according to the three levels of job
satisfaction scores. A random sample in each group was scrutinised in some detail
in order to construct profiles of nurses who scored high, medium and low values
on the job satisfaction index. The aim was to translate the abstract numerical
concept into concrete descriptive reality.

Examples of one profile in each job satisfaction category are given below.

TABLE A5/8
Score distribution of three profile examples

Score Categories	Answers to Statements						
	Strongly positive	Positive	Uncertain	Negative	Strongly negative	Total No. of statements	Median score of corresponding category
High score	10	1	1	—	—	12	46
Medium score	4	3	4	1	—	12	35
Low score	1	3	4	4	—	12	25

The categories adopted were: High score—40 and over; Medium score—between 31 and 39;
Low score—below 31.

Table A5/8 shows the distribution of the scores in the three examples.

First, a nurse who achieved a high job satisfaction score which, as shown in
Table A5/8, implied a tendency to give positive replies.

Enrolled Nurse Appleby* worked in the chest ward of a small hospital. She
had been in the ward for less than three months. Nurse Appleby was thirty-four
and married with 3 children over ten years old.

Nurse Appleby said very little during the interview. When asked about the use
of her skills she said:

'We're getting taught a lot on the ward I'm on and getting to do quite a
bit.'**

At the end of the interview she remarked:

'I've got a stammer as you've probably noticed. Before I started nursing I
couldn't speak a word but now I'm so much better. It's because I'm happy
I think.'†

Second, Sister McMahon* whose job satisfaction score fell into the 'low'

---

* Names are fictitious.
** *Question 63.* In your present appointment do you feel that good use is being made of
your skills or not?

† *Question 86.* Now I've been asking you rather a lot of questions. Are there any questions
you would like to ask me or is there anything else **you** would like to say?

category. Sister McMahon was a theatre sister on night duty in a large general hospital. She was twenty-six and married to a merchant seaman. Of the twelve statements on the job satisfaction index five were positive responses, four negative answers and three uncertain. She was uncertain about the statement: 'Most days I am enthusiastic about my work' because:

'some nights we get nothing in or just routine cases and you feel anybody could do it.'

She gave a negative response to the statement, 'I am disappointed that I ever took this job' because, she said:

'I'm sorry I came on permanent nights, I feel I'm not getting the scope I would otherwise.'

She expressed her opinions of night duty elsewhere during the interview:

'Once I'm here I enjoy the work, but it's the eight nights on, kills everything, family life, social life. I feel the night duty hours are far too long.'

In the last seven days she had worked over 71 hours. Sister McMahon was asked whether her skills were being made use of. She replied:

'No, we don't get cold cases, we get emergencies only. There is the occasional case but not many.'*

The third example is the profile of Pupil Nurse Jones** who achieved a medium job satisfaction index score value. She had completed her training but was not yet enrolled. At the time of interview she was working day duty in a female medical ward of a large general hospital. Nurse Jones was nineteen and not married.

When Nurse Jones was asked about the use of her skills she felt that they were not being well used because she was not happy working in the ward she was in:

'Perhaps it's because I'm treated like a silly ignorant thing. The sister doesn't think her nurses can take responsibility.'*

Further comments like this were forthcoming when asked whether she had anything else to say:

'The sisters don't give the younger nurses enough tuition.'†

Nurse Jones wanted to work in the district:

'Something I've always wanted to do. The way I feel just now, getting away from the hospital environment might help. It'd be good to get round to the old folk and see how they live.'††

Any dissatisfaction which Nurse Jones has with her job appears to be related to inter-personal relationships in the hospital environment.

* *Question 63.* See footnote, preceding page.
** Names are fictitious.
† *Question 86.* See footnote, preceding page.
†† *Question 69.* Are you planning to work in the community nursing service at all? (This question was put to hospital staff only.)

Not all high scorers actually said that they were happy in their work and not all who scored low values expressed unhappiness and, as no direct question to this effect was asked, strict comparison is not possible. Nonetheless, independent readers of the interviewing schedules were agreed in their impression that the respondents conveyed satisfaction or dissatisfaction which was confirmed by their job satisfaction score values. Whilst no absolute precision in measurement is claimed comparison between the score values showed discernible differences.

All profiles suggested that satisfaction and dissatisfaction seemed to be related to professional practice irrespective of its specific type; this is in line with the generally agreed definition of the concept of job satisfaction implying an attitude to a set of factors related to one's job rather than to just one aspect of it.

Tables A5/9 and A5/10 show the percentage distributions of high, medium and low score values in the job satisfaction index and attitude test to part-time nurses respectively.

TABLE A5/9
Distribution of nurses' responses to statements on the job satisfaction index*
L=Low; M=Medium; H=High

Statements	Score	Answers to Statements				
		Strongly negative %	Negative %	Uncertain %	Positive %	Strongly positive %
1. I consider my job rather unpleasant.	L	1	9	7	68	15
	M	—	—	1	42	57
	H	—	—	1	13	86
2. I enjoy my work more than my leisure time.	L	9	76	12	3	—
	M	2	47	35	15	1
	H	1	15	40	40	4
3. I am often bored with my job.	L	2	25	16	54	3
	M	—	3	4	71	22
	H	—	—	—	19	80
4. I feel fairly well satisfied with my present job.	L	6	21	14	57	—
	M	(—)	3	5	85	6
	H	—	1	1	48	50
5. Most of the time I have to force myself to go to work.	L	—	6	6	82	6
	M	—	1	2	62	35
	H	—	—	—	9	91
6. I feel that I am happier in my work than most other people.	L	1	54	35	10	—
	M	1	16	43	39	1
	H	—	2	20	56	22
7. Most days I am enthusiastic about my work.	L	1	28	19	51	1
	M	(—)	2	7	90	1
	H	—	—	3	71	26
8. Each day of work seems like it will never end.	L	—	9	9	80	2
	M	—	1	5	74	20
	H	—	—	3	24	73
9. I like my job better than the average worker does.	L	1	42	32	24	—
	M	(—)	11	38	50	1
	H	—	—	11	65	24
10. My job is pretty uninteresting.	L	1	15	3	76	5
	M	—	(—)	(—)	68	32
	H	—	—	—	7	93
11. I find real enjoyment in my work.	L	—	15	27	57	1
	M	—	1	2	88	9
	H	—	—	1	38	62
12. I am disappointed that I ever took this job.	L	1	9	12	69	9
	M	—	(—)	1	58	46
	H	—	—	—	7	93

* Total number of nurses=719; 30 were unclassifiable.
(—)=downward rounding of a figure of less than 0.5.

TABLE A5/10

Distribution of nurses' responses to statements on the part-time scale★

L=Low; M=Medium; H=High

		Answers to Statements				
Statements	Score	Strongly negative %	Negative %	Uncertain %	Positive %	Strongly positive %
1. Most part-time nurses are	L	4	68	14	14	—
only working for the	M	1	25	18	53	3
money.	H	1	8	6	53	40
2. It's a shame that part-time	L	1	73	10	16	—
nurses so rarely get	M	1	26	21	49	2
promoted.	H	1	7	7	71	14
3. Generally one full-time	L	4	73	10	12	—
nurse is more use than two	M	—	24	18	55	3
part-time nurses.	H	—	6	4	64	26
4. I think part-time nurses	L	—	58	20	21	1
should get more	M	—	19	21	59	1
responsibility.	H	—	3	5	81	11
5. Sometimes I feel we would	L	3	62	19	17	—
be better with less part-	M	—	10	8	78	3
time nurses.	H	—	1	1	59	39
6. It would be nice if creches	L	1	14	9	68	8
and nurseries were always	M	—	5	6	76	12
available for nurses' children.	H	—	2	3	56	40
7. It seems to be that part-	L	3	30	20	47	—
time nurses care less about	M	—	3	12	76	9
their work than other nurses.	H	—	2	—	43	55
8. I think part-time nurses	L	—	10	15	72	3
should be able to attend	M	—	2	7	88	3
more courses.	H	—	1	3	75	20
9. I don't think part-time	L	1	37	31	31	—
nurses do well in positions	M	—	4	17	74	5
of responsibility.	H	—	3	4	64	29
10. I don't think we could	L	—	15	10	73	2
manage without part-time	M	—	1	2	83	14
nurses.	H	—	—	—	39	61
11. Things seem difficult to	L	9	72	10	9	—
organise with a lot of part-	M	(—)	38	15	46	(—)
time staff.	H	—	13	9	71	7
12. If it were up to me I'd	L	4	80	12	4	—
employ more part-time	M	(—)	23	34	41	(—)
nurses.	H	—	3	12	78	7

★ Total number of nurses=719; 37 were unclassifiable.

(—)=downward rounding of a figure of less than 0.5.

APPENDIX SIX
Nursing Qualifications —A Problem of Classification

Most descriptive empirical social surveys generate data which are too diverse for final presentation and use. Often it is possible to arrive at a decision about the grouping of data on the basis of the pilot work. Sometimes it is deemed desirable to retain the full array of detail until the analysis of the main study is undertaken. Whatever approach is used some information must inevitably be sacrificed at some stage of the research process.

The analysis of nursing qualifications in this study seemed a clear example of the kind of problem which survey data might pose.

As mentioned in Chapter 2, information about the qualifications held by the sample of nursing staff was obtained from interviews and it was decided to record these in full. Of the 719 respondents, 125 had no qualifications, while the remaining 574 had a total of 1289 qualifications among them. The problem lay in deciding on a suitable manner in which to show this array of qualifications.★

One possibility was a grouping of the respondents according to the number of qualifications they had. Table A6/1 shows the result of such a presentation; its drawback is the lack of discrimination about the type, relative value and combinations of qualifications, quite apart from its size.

TABLE A6/1
Grouping of respondents according to number of qualifications

One qualification					No.	Two qualifications				No.
RGN	.	.	.	.	95	RGN, DN(R)	.	.	.	12
EN	.	.	.	.	76	RGN, CMB	.	.	.	13
RMN	.	.	.	.	9	RGN, BTA	.	.	.	1
RFN	.	.	.	.	6	RGN, ONC	.	.	.	2
RSCN	.	.	.	.	3	RGN, O. Hosp.	.	.	.	12
BTA	.	.	.	.	1	RGN, O. Nat.	.	.	.	1
ONC	.	.	.	.	1	EN, RMN	.	.	.	2
O. Hosp.	.	.	.	.	1	EN, RFN	.	.	.	1
						EN, SCM	.	.	.	1
Two qualifications					No.	EN, DN(E)	.	.	.	3
RGN, EN	.	.	.	.	3	EN, BTA	.	.	.	2
RGN, RMN	.	.	.	10	EN, ONC	.	.	.	2
RGN, RFN	.	.	.	20	EN, O. Hosp.	.	.	.	6
RGN, RSCN	.	.	.	10	RMN, RFN	.	.	.	1
RGN, SCM	.	.	.	92	RMN, Foreign	.	.	.	1
RGN, RCT	.	.	.	1	SCM, RFN	.	.	.	1

★ The abbreviations of qualifications are explained in the glossary of terms, Appendix 7.

TABLE A6/1—cont.

Three qualifications	No.
RGN, EN, SCM	1
RGN, EN, ONC	1
RGN, RMN, SCM	5
RGN, RMN, CMB	2
RGN, RMN, Mangmt.	1
RGN, RFN, DN(R)	3
RGN, RFN, CMB	5
RGN, RSCN, SCM	4
RGN, RSCN, RCT	1
RGN, RSCN, CMB	1
RGN, RSCN, O. Hosp.	1
RGN, SCM, RFN	17
RGN, SCM, RNT	4
RGN, SCM, MTD	3
RGN, SCM, RCT	4
RGN, SCM, HV(cert)	22
RGN, SCM, DN(R)	26
RGN, SCM, BTA	4
RGN, SCM, ONC	3
RGN, SCM, Mangmt.	6
RGN, SCM, O. Hosp.	10
RGN, SCM, O. Nat.	2
RGN, SCM, Foreign	1
RGN, HV(cert), CMB	4
RGN, HV(cert), O. Hosp.	1
RGN, DN(R), CMB	3
RGN, CMB, BTA	1
RGN, BTA, O. Nat.	1
RGN, O. Hosp., Foreign	1
EN, SCM, O. Hosp.	1
EN, DN(E), O. Hosp.	1

Four qualifications	No.
RGN, RMN, ONC, Mangmt.	1
RGN, RFN, SCM, RNT	1
RGN, RFN, SCM, HV(cert)	3
RGN, RFN, SCM, DN(R)	6
RGN, RFN, SCM, BTA	2
RGN, RFN, SCM, Mangmt.	1
RGN, RFN, SCM, O. Nat.	1
RGN, RFN, RNT, CMB	1
RGN, RFN, RCT, CMB	1
RGN, RFN, HV(cert), CMB	1
RGN, RSCN, SCM, DN(R)	1
RGN, SCM, RNT, BTA	1
RGN, SCM, RNT, O. Nat.	1

Four qualifications	No.
RGN, SCM, MTD, BTA	1
RGN, SCM, RCT, DN(R)	1
RGN, SCM, RCT, Mangmt.	1
RGN, SCM, HV(cert), DN(R)	10
RGN, SCM, HV(cert), O. Hosp.	1
RGN, SCM, DN(R), BTA	1
RGN, SCM, DN(R), ONC	1
RGN, SCM, DN(R), Mangmt.	1
RGN, SCM, DN(R), O. Hosp.	1
RGN, SCM, ONC, O. Hosp.	2
RGN, SCM, Mangmt., O. Hosp.	1
RGN, RCT, BTA, O. Hosp.	1
RGN, RNMD, HV(cert), CMB	1

Five qualifications	No.
RGN, RMN, SCM, HV(cert), DN(R)	2
RGN, RMN, SCM, HV(cert), O. Hosp.	1
RGN, RFN, SCM, RCT, Mangmt.	1
RGN, RFN, SCM, HV(cert), DN(R)	3
RGN, RFN, HV(cert), CMB, BTA	1
RGN, RFN, RNT, CMB, O. Hosp.	1
RGN, RSCN, SCM, HV(cert), DN(R)	2
RGN, RSCN, SCM, HV(cert), O. Hosp.	1
RGN, SCM, RNT, HV(cert), O. Nat.	1
RGN, SCM, MTD, DN(R), O. Hosp.	1
RGN, SCM, HV(cert), DN(R), BTA	2
RGN, SCM, HV(cert), DN(R), O. Hosp.	2
RGN, SCM, Mangmt., O. Hosp., O. Nat.	1

Six qualifications	No.
RGN, RFN, RCT, CMB, BTA, Mangmt.	1
RGN, SCM, MTD, HV(cert), ONC, O. Nat.	1

The data could also have been presented by treating the sample according to each individual qualification, the result being Table A6/2. However, by dealing with the qualifications singly rather than in combination some important information would be lost. As 68 per cent of the qualified nurses had two or more qualifications it was reasonable to assume that particular combinations might be associated with particular attributes. Such an assumption would be justified on the frequency distribution of certain combinations of qualifications alone, quite apart from professional knowledge of statutory combinations for certain types of work.

TABLE A6/2
Frequency distribution of individual qualifications

RGN	.	.	.	.	.	475	HV(cert)	.	.	.	.	.	59
EN	.	.	.	.	.	100	DN(R)	.	.	.	.	.	79
RMN	.	.	.	.	.	35	DN(E)	.	.	.	.	.	3
RSCN	.	.	.	.	.	24	CMB	.	.	.	.	.	36
SCM	.	.	.	.	.	263	BTA	.	.	.	.	.	20
RFN	.	.	.	.	.	78	ONC	.	.	.	.	.	14
RNT	.	.	.	.	.	10	Mangmt.	.	.	.	.	.	15
MTD	.	.	.	.	.	6	O. Hosp.	.	.	.	.	.	47
RCT	.	.	.	.	.	12	O. Nat.	.	.	.	.	.	9
RNMD	.	.	.	.	.	1	Foreign	.	.	.	.	.	3

The analysis showed that the respondents had no less than 103 different combinations of qualifications among them. Table A6/3 gives the full list of these combinations in order of frequency. Although this method of classification retained most of the detail it would be unwieldy to use for the purpose of cross tabulation. After considerable thought it was decided to reduce the classification list to 24 variables using the following criteria:

1. The general basic statutory qualifications should be identifiably retained—RGN(SRN), EN(SEN).*
2. Specialised statutory qualifications giving respondents licence to practise should be identifiably retained—RSCN, RMN, RFN** (no other general qualification held).
3. The most usual combination of qualification should be identifiably retained—RGN/SCM.

Table A6/4 shows the result of the above classifications.

4. Qualifications of specific relevance to the study and/or to nursing in general were extracted. For this reason the qualifications of Registered Nurse Tutor (RNT), Midwife Teacher's Diploma (MTD) and Registered Clinical Teacher (RCT) were singled out and related to the number of additional qualifications held by the qualified teaching staff.

Table A6/5 shows the result of the above analysis.

---

* For the sake of simplicity the registered nurse is referred to as RGN and the enrolled nurse as EN.

** Although the Register of Fever Nurses is now obsolete the qualification RFN was included in the list of statutory certificates as it gave six nurses their licence to practise.

As only one respondent held the qualification of RNMD which was additional to other qualifications it was not retained as an identity.

TABLE A6/3
Each individual qualification simply listed

Qualification	Count
RGN	95
RGN, SCM	92
EN	76
RGN, SCM, DN(R)	26
RGN, SCM, HV(cert)	22
RGN, RFN	20
RGN, SCM, RFN	17
RGN, CMB	13
RGN, DN(R)	12
RGN, O. Hosp.	12
RGN, RSCN	10
RGN, RMN	10
RGN, SCM, O. Hosp.	10
RGN, SCM, HV(cert), DN(R)	10
RMN	9
RFN	6
EN, O. Hosp.	6
RGN, SCM, Mangmt.	6
RGN, SCM, RFN, DN(R)	6
RGN, RMN, SCM	5
RGN, RFN, CMB	5
RGN, RSCN, SCM	4
RGN, SCM, RNT	4
RGN, SCM, RCT	4
RGN, SCM, BTA	4
RGN, HV(cert), CMB	4
RSCN	3
RGN, EN	3
EN, DN(E)	3
RGN, RFN, DN(R)	3
RGN, DN(R), CMB	3
RGN, SCM, MTD	3
RGN, SCM, ONC	3
RGN, SCM, RFN, HV(cert)	3
RGN, SCM, RFN, HV(cert), DN(R)	3
EN, RMN	2
EN, BTA	2
RGN, ONC	2
EN, ONC	2
RGN, RMN, CMB	2
RGN, SCM, O. Nat.	2
RGN, SCM, RFN, BTA	2
RGN, SCM, ONC, O. Hosp.	2
RGN, RSCN, SCM, HV(cert), DN(R)	2
RGN, SCM, RFN, HV(cert), DN(R)	2
RGN, SCM, HV(cert), DN(R), BTA	2
RGN, SCM, HV(cert), DN(R), O. Hosp.	2
BTA	1
ONC	1
O. Hosp.	1
EN, SCM	1
EN, RFN	1
RMN, RFN	1
SCM, RFN	1
RGN, RCT	1
RGN, BTA	1
RGN, O. Nat.	1
RMN, Foreign	1
RGN, EN, SCM	1
RGN, RSCN, CMB	1
RGN, RSCN, RCT	1
RGN, CMB, BTA	1
RGN, EN, ONC	1
RGN, RMN, Mangmt.	1
RGN, RSCN, O. Hosp.	1
EN, SCM, O. Hosp.	1
RGN, HV(cert), O. Hosp.	1
EN, DN(E), O. Hosp.	1
RGN, BTA, O. Nat.	1
RGN, SCM, Foreign	1
RGN, O. Hosp., Foreign	1
RGN, RSCN, SCM, DN(R)	1
RGN, RNMD, HV(cert), CMB	1
RGN, RFN, HV(cert), CMB	1
RGN, SCM, RFN, RNT	1
RGN, RFN, CMB, RNT	1
RGN, SCM, DN(R), RCT	1
RGN, RFN, CMB, RCT	1
RGN, SCM, DN(R), BTA	1
RGN, SCM, RNT, BTA	1
RGN, SCM, MTD, BTA	1
RGN, SCM, DN(R), ONC	1
RGN, SCM, RFN, Mangmt.	1
RGN, SCM, DN(R), Mangmt.	1
RGN, SCM, RCT, Mangmt.	1
RGN, RMN, ONC, Mangmt.	1
RGN, SCM, HV(cert), O. Hosp.	1
RGN, SCM, DN(R), O. Hosp.	1
RGN, RCT, BTA, O. Hosp.	1
RGN, SCM, Mangmt., O. Hosp.	1
RGN, SCM, RFN, O. Nat.	1

TABLE A6/3—cont.

RGN, SCM, RNT, O. Nat. .	1
RGN, RFN, HV(cert), CMB, BTA	1
RGN, SCM, RFN, RCT, Mangmt.	1
RGN, RSCN, SCM, HV(cert), O. Hosp.	1
RGN, RMN, SCM, HV(cert), O. Hosp.	1
RGN, RFN, CMB, RNT, O. Hosp.	1
RGN, SCM, DN(R), MTD, O. Hosp.	1
RGN, SCM, HV(cert), RNT, O. Nat.	1
RGN, SCM, Mangmt., O. Hosp., O. Nat.	1
RGN, RFN, CMB, RCT, BTA, Mangmt.	1
RGN, SCM, HV(cert), MTD, ONC, O. Nat. . . .	1

TABLE A6/4
Final classification of basic nursing qualifications

Group	No.	%
RGN only	95	13.2
RGN+1 qualification	85	11.8
RGN+2 qualifications	26	3.6
RGN+3 qualifications	6	0.8
RGN+4 qualifications	2	0.3
RGN+5 qualifications	1	0.1
EN only	76	10.6
EN+1 qualification	17	2.4
EN+2 qualifications	2	0.3
RGN/SCM only	92	12.8
RGN/SCM+1 qualification	112	15.6
RGN/SCM+2 qualifications	38	5.3
RGN/SCM+3 qualifications	17	2.4
RGN/SCM+4 qualifications	1	0.1
RSCN only	3	0.4
RMN only	9	1.3
RMN+1 qualification	2	0.3
RFN	6	0.8
Other	3	0.4
Other+1 qualification	1	0.1
None	125	17.4
Total	719	100.0

TABLE A6/5
Classification of teaching qualifications

Respondents with RNT and other qualification	No.
RGN+2 qualifications	1
RGN+3 qualifications	1
RGN/SCM only	4
RGN/SCM+1 qualification	3
RGN/SCM+2 qualifications	1
Total	10

Respondents with MTD and other qualification	No.
RGN/SCM only	3
RGN/SCM+1 qualification	1
RGN/SCM+2 qualifications	1
RGN/SCM+3 qualifications	1
Total	6

Respondents with RCT and other qualification	No.
RGN only	1
RGN+1 qualification	1
RGN+2 qualifications	1
RGN+4 qualifications	1
RGN/SCM only	4
RGN/SCM+1 qualification	1
RGN/SCM+3 qualifications	1
Total	10

Total with teaching qualifications=26.

APPENDIX SEVEN
Glossary

Part I
A deliberate attempt was made to keep this report free from unnecessary jargon. However, as a precautionary measure, nurses not used to research language were asked to indicate which terms, if any, required definition. Part I of the glossary is the result.

Part II
Certain abbreviations had to be used especially in relation to nursing qualifications. These are presented in Part II.

Part III
In order to help the reader not acquainted with the Health Service in the United Kingdom 'Salmon' and 'Mayston' Management Structure charts are included in Part III* which also contains terminology commonly used by health service personnel. The organisational structures presented, though relevant at the time of the survey, have been superceded by the reorganisation of the NHS in 1974.

PART I

Usage of terms in the study

Bias	Distortion of the findings resulting from an undesirable influence
Data	Facts or phenomena recorded specifically in the course of the research process
Demography	Study of human populations and their characteristics
Hypothesis	Statement/explanation which is suggested by knowledge or observation but has not yet been proved or disproved
Longitudinal study	Study in which data about the same subjects are collected over a period of time
Modal value/score	Value or score which occurs most frequently
Null hypothesis	Statement/explanation which predicts that there will be no significant differences between observations
Open ended interview	Communication between interviewer and respondent

---

* The 'Salmon' chart appears as a 'pull-out' at the end of the book.

	which allows for spontaneous comments outside the constraints of a rigid interviewing schedule
Pilot study	Preliminary study intended to test the proposed method for a main study
Random sample	Result of a systematic selection of units from a population where each unit had an equal chance of being selected. A unit can be an individual, a hospital, a medical record, etc.
Research	Process of systematic enquiry for a specific purpose
Research tool	Purpose designed medium, such as questionnaire, used for the collection of research data
Response rate	Percentage of those approached who actually participated in the study
Sampling	Method of selecting a certain number of units from a total population
Statistical significance	Relating to a finding shown by appropriate statistical tests to be unlikely due purely to chance
Variable	Any factor, characteristic or attribute under study which may distinguish the units within a population from each other, such as qualifications of nurses or diagnoses of patients

PART II

Abbreviations of qualifications

RGN — Registered General Nurse (Scottish qualification)
SRN — State Registered Nurse (English qualification)
EN — Enrolled Nurse (Scottish qualification)
SEN — State Enrolled Nurse (English qualification)
RMN — Registered Mental Nurse
RSCN — Registered Sick Children's Nurse
SCM — State Certified Midwife
RFN* — Registered Fever Nurse
RNT — Registered Nurse Tutor
MTD — Midwife Teachers Diploma
RCT — Registered Clinical Teacher
RNMD — Registered in Nursing of Mentally Deficient
HV Cert. — Health Visitor's Certificate
DN(R) — District Nursing Certificate (awarded to registered nurses)
DN(E) — District Nursing Certificate (awarded to enrolled nurses)
CMB* — Central Midwives Board Certificate (Part 1 of midwifery training)
BTA* — Certificate from British Tuberculosis Association
ONC — Orthopaedic Nursing Certificate (hospital certificate)
Mangmt. — Management Certificate (any level)

---

* Qualification no longer awarded.

O. Hosp. —Other hospital certificate
O. Nat. —Other national certificate
Foreign —Foreign qualification or certificate
NO —Nursing Officer—a nurse above the grade of ward sister
UNO —Unit Nursing Officer
SNO —Senior Nursing Officer
PNO —Principal Nursing Officer
CNO —Chief Nursing Officer

PART III

Auxiliary (nursing)	Unqualified worker employed to help nursing staff, may have short in-service training
Back to nursing course	Special course provided for nurses who have had a break from nursing
Basic student/learner	Nurse trainee undertaking her/his first course in nursing leading to a recognised nursing qualification
Five day ward	Hospital ward open for five days only, usually Monday to Friday; intended for short stay patients
Formal ward report	Verbal transmission of information about patients from one shift to another
General practitioner attachment	System in which a community nurse is in a close working relationship with a general medical practice with responsibility for the practice population rather than a geographical area
General practitioner unit	Ward/unit in a hospital where the general medical practitioners care for their own patients
In-service training	Programme of training/education given 'on the job'. The person is not seconded to an educational establishment but retains his/her service responsibilities
Post basic student/learner	Nurse undertaking a course of training after the basic qualification leading to a further qualification

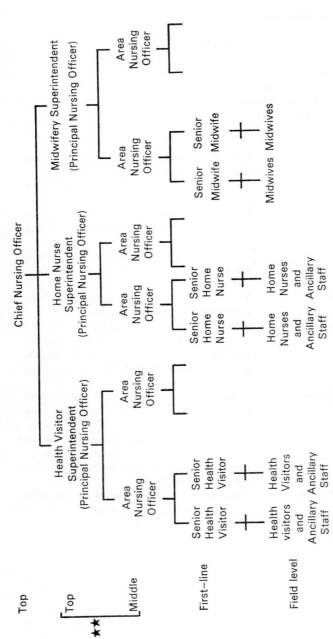

'Mayston' Management Structure (reproduced from: Department of Health and Social Security and Scottish Home and Health Department and Welsh Office, (1969) *Report of the Working Party on Management Structure in the Local Authority Nursing Services* (Chairman: E. L. Mayston, Esq.), HMSO, London, p. 20).

** In smaller authorities the functional Superintendents would be middle managers; functional superintendents would sometimes cover more than one function.

At the time of the study the Mayston management structure had not been fully implemented in all research areas; different terms for similar job description were, therefore, in use (Chapter 4).

References

Anderson, E., (1973) *The Role of the Nurse*, Series 2, No. 1, Royal College of Nursing and National Council of Nurses of the United Kingdom, London.

Auld, M. G., (1967) An investigation into the recruitment and integration of part-time nursing staff in hospitals, *International Journal of Nursing Studies*, Vol. 4, pp. 119–169.

Auld, M. G., (1974) *A Method of Estimating the Requisite Nursing Establishment for a Hospital*, M.Phil. Thesis, University of Edinburgh, unpublished.

Blauner, R., (1960) Work Satisfaction and Industrial Trends in Modern Society in Galenson, W. and Lipset, S. M., *Labor and Trade Unionism*, John Wiley, New York.

Bond, J., (1972) The role of the Married Nurse: One aspect of the staffing of the health services at socially unacceptable working hours, *Working Paper 2*, Nursing Research Unit, University of Edinburgh.

Bond, J., (1974) Knowledge and opinions of nurses—Reorganisation, *Nursing Times*, Vol. 70, No. 13, pp. 460–462.

Bond, J., (1974) The construction of a scale to measure nurses' attitudes, *International Journal of Nursing Studies*, Vol. 11, pp. 75–84.

Brayfield, A. H. and Rothe, H. F., (1951) An Index of Job Satisfaction, *Journal of Applied Psychology*, Vol. 35, pp. 307–311.

Brown, R. G. S. and Stones, R. W. H., (1973) *The Male Nurse*, Occasional Papers on Social Administration, No. 52, G. Bell & Sons, London.

Bryant, Y. M. and Heron, K., (1974) Monitoring patient-nurse dependency, *Nursing Times*, Occasional Paper, Vol. 70, No. 19.

Butler, J. R. (1968) *Occupational choice*, Science Policy Studies No. 2, HMSO, London.

Carstairs, V., (1966) *Home Nursing in Scotland*, Scottish Health Service Study No. 2, SHHD, Edinburgh.

Central Health Services Council, (1968) *Relieving Nurses of Non-Nursing Duties in General and Maternity Hospitals*, HMSO, London.

Central Statistical Office, (1972, 1973, 1974) *Social Trends*, Nos. 3, 4 and 5, HMSO, London.

Chown, S. H., (1958) The formation of occupational choice among grammar school pupils, *Occupational Psychology*, Vol. 32, No. 3.

Clark, J., (1975) *Time Out? A Study of Absenteeism Among Nurses*, The Royal

College of Nursing and National Council of Nurses of the United Kingdom, London.

Clark, J., (1973) *A Family Visitor—A Descriptive Analysis of Health Visiting in Berkshire*, The Royal College of Nursing and National Council of Nurses of the United Kingdom, London.

Clark, J., (1974) The Case for Health Visitors, *Update*, p. 602.

Cronbach, L. J., (1951) Coefficient alpha and the internal structure of tests, *Psychometrika*, No. 16, pp. 297–334.

The Dan Mason Nursing Research Committee, (1960) *The work, responsibilities and status of the staff nurse*, The Dan Mason Nursing Research Committee of the National Florence Nightingale Memorial Committee of Great Britain and Northern Ireland.

Department of Employment, (1974) *Women and Work*, Manpower Papers 9, 10, 11 and 12, HMSO, London.

Department of Health and Social Security, Scottish Home and Health Department and Welsh Office, (1969) *Report of the Working Party on Management Structure in the Local Authority Nursing Services* (Chairman: E. L. Mayston, Esq.), HMSO, London.

Department of Health and Social Security and Scottish Home and Health Department, (1972) *Report of the Committee on Nursing* (Chairman: Professor Asa Briggs), Cmnd. 5115, HMSO, London.

Department of Health and Social Security, (1974) *Report of the Committee on one-parent families* (Chairman: Sir Morris Finer), Cmnd. 5629, HMSO, London.

Department of Health and Social Security, (1974) *Report of the Committee of Inquiry into the pay and related conditions of service of nurses and midwives* (Chairman: the Earl of Halsbury, FRS), HMSO, London.

Edwards, G., *Men in Nursing*—The Society of Registered Male Nurses: An Era of Nursing History and Development (unpublished).

Fogarty, M., Allen, A. J., Allen, I. and Walters, P., (1971) *Women in Top Jobs*, George Allen and Unwin, London.

Fogarty, M. P., Rapoport, R. and Rapoport, R. N., (1971) *Sex, Career and Family*, PEP, George Allen and Unwin, London.

Franklin, B. L., (1974) *Patient Anxiety on Admission to Hospital*, Series 1, No. 5, Royal College of Nursing and National Council of Nurses of the United Kingdom, London.

Gilmore, M., Bruce, N. and Hunt, M., (1974) *The Work of the Nursing Team in General Practice*, Council for the Education and Training of Health Visitors, London.

Ginsburg, E. et al., (1951) *Occupational choice: an approach to a general theory*, Columbia Press, New York.

Goldthorpe, J. H., Lockwood, D., Bechhofer, F. and Platt, J., (1970) *The affluent worker: industrial attitudes and behaviour*, Cambridge University Press.

Grant, N., (1975) The Nursing Care Plan 2, *Nursing Times*, Occasional Paper, Vol. 71, No. 13.

Guildford, J. P., (1950) *Fundamental Statistics in Psychology and Education*, 2nd ed., McGraw Hill, New York.

Hall, J. and Caradog Jones, D., (1950) The Social Grading of Occupations, *British Journal of Sociology*, Vol. 1, No. 1.

Hayward, J., (1975) *Information—A prescription against pain*, Series 2, No. 5, Royal College of Nursing and National Council of Nurses of the United Kingdom, London.

Hobbs, P., (1973) Aptitude or Environment, The Royal College of Nursing and National Council of Nurses of the United Kingdom, London.

Hockey, L., (1966) *Feeling the Pulse—A Survey of District Nursing in Six Areas*, Queen's Institute of District Nursing, London.

Hockey, L., (1972) *Use or Abuse? A study of the state enrolled nurse in the local authority nursing services*, Queen's Institute of District Nursing, London.

Hunt, J. M., (1974) *The Teaching and Practice of Surgical Dressings in Three Hospitals*, Series 1, No. 6, Royal College of Nursing and National Council of Nurses of the United Kingdom, London.

Hunt, M., (1972) The Dilemma of Identity in Health Visiting, *Nursing Times*, 68, Occasional Papers, pp. 17–20, 23–24.

Hutchinson, A. S. and Kane, J., (1967) Short stay on 5 day ward, *District Nursing*, 10, p. 145.

ILO, (1963) An international survey of part-time employment, *International Labour Review*, Vol. 88, No. 4.

Institute for Operational Research, (1975) *The Movements of Hospital Nursing Staff in Scotland*, IOR/834, IOR, Edinburgh.

Janjic, M., (1972) Part-time work in the Public Service, *International Labour Review*, Vol. 105, No. 4.

Jefferys, M. E. P., (1966) *Women in Medicine*, Office of Health Economics, London.

Katz, F. E. and Martin, H. W., (1962) Career choice processes, *Social Forces*, Vol. 41, No. 2, pp. 149–154.

Kemp, I., (1969) Health Visiting in Scotland, *Health Bulletin*, Vol. XXVII, No. 2.

Kramer, M., (1974) *Reality shock: why nurses leave nursing*, Mosby, St. Louis.

Likert, R., (1932) A Technique for the Measurement of Attitudes, *Archives of Psychology*, No. 140.

Marris, T., (1971) *The work of health visitors in London*, Greater London Research Department of Planning and Transportation, Research Report No. 12, Greater London Council, London.

Miller, D. and Form, W. H., (1956) *Industrial sociology*, Harper, New York.

Ministry of Education (Kelsall, R. K.), (1963) *Women and Teaching*, HMSO, London.

Ministry of Health and Scottish Home and Health Department, (1966) *Report of the Committee on Senior Nursing Staff Structure* (Chairman: B. L. Salmon, Esq.), HMSO, London.

Moser, C. A. and Hall, J. R., in D. V. Glass, ed., (1954) *Social Mobility in Britain*, Routledge and Kegan Paul, London.

Mulvey, M. C., (1963) Psychological and sociological factors in prediction of career patterns of women, *Genetic Psychology* Monographs, 68.

McGuffin, S. J., (1958) Factors influencing the choice of careers by boys in two Belfast grammar schools, a summary in *British Journal of Educational Psychology*, Vol. 28, No. 2.

MacGuire, J. M., (1969) *Threshold to Nursing. A review of the Literature on Recruitment to and Withdrawal from Nurse Training Programmes in the United Kingdom*, Occasional Papers on Social Administration, No. 30, G. Bell and Sons Ltd., London.

McIntosh, H. T. and Reid, M., (1974) A Study of Wastage in Health Visiting, *Health Bulletin*, Vol. XXXII, No. 2.

MacKay, G. A., (1907) *Practice of the Scottish Poor Law*, William Green and Sons, Edinburgh.

McKennel, A. C., (1968) Use of coefficient alpha in constructing attitude and similar scales, *Government Social Survey, Methodological Paper*, No. 139.

Nie, N., Bent, D. H. and Hull, C. H., (1970) *Statistical Package for the Social Sciences*, McGraw Hill, New York.

Office of Population Censuses and Surveys, (1970) *Classification of Occupations 1970*, HMSO, London.

Office of Population Censuses and Surveys, (1971) *The Registrar General's Decennial Supplement, England and Wales, Occupational Mortality Tables*, HMSO, London.

Oppenheim, A. N., (1966) *Questionnaire Design and Attitude Measurement*, Heinemann Educational Books Ltd., London.

Osipow, S. H., (1968) *Theories of Career Development*, Appleton, New York.

Oxford Regional Hospital Board, (1967) *Measurement of Nursing Care*, Operational Research Unit, Oxford Regional Hospital Board.

Rhys Hearn, C., (1974) Evaluation of patients' nursing needs: prediction of staffing 1–4, *Nursing Times*, Occasional Papers Vol. 70, Nos. 38–41.

Roe, A., (1956) *The psychology of occupations*, John Wiley, New York.

Rogoff, N., in Merton, R. K., et al., (1957) *The Student Physician*, Harvard University Press, Cambridge, Mass.

Rosenberg, M., (1957) *Occupation and values*, Free Press, Glencoe.

Ross, S. K., Munsin, B. J., Ireland, J. T. and Adams, J. F., (1969) Home for the Weekend, *Health Bulletin*, Vol. XXVII, No. 4, pp. 38–39.

Scottish Home and Health Department, (1970) *Duties and Training of Nursing Auxiliaries and Nursing Assistants*, SHM, No. 70/1970, SHHD, Edinburgh.

Scottish Home and Health Department, (1972) *Nurses in an Integrated Health Service*, HMSO, Edinburgh.

Scottish Home and Health Department, (1973) *Towards an integrated Child Health Service*, HMSO, Edinburgh.

Scottish Home and Health Department, (1974) *Review of the Senior Nursing Staff Structure (Salmon Report)*, SHHD, Edinburgh.

Scottish Home and Health Department, (1974) *Nursing Manpower Planning Report No. 1*, Re 34884 TBL(3), SHHD, Edinburgh.

Scott Wright, M., (1968) *Student Nurses in Scotland, Characteristics of Success and Failure*, Scottish Health Service Study, No. 7, SHHD, Edinburgh.

Siegel, S., (1956) *Non parametric Statistics for the Behavioural Sciences*, International Students Edition, McGraw-Hill, Kogakusha Ltd., Tokyo and London.

Stockwell, F., (1972) *The Unpopular Patient*, Series 1, No 2, Royal College of Nursing and National Council of Nurses of the United Kingdom, London.

Super, D. E., (1957) *The Psychology of Careers*, Harper, New York.

Woelfel, M., (1975) Geriatric Care: opinions of a sample of nurses, *Nursing Times*, Occasional Paper, Vol. 71, No. 26.

World Health Organisation, (1966) *Report of the Expert Committee on Nursing*, World Health Organisation, Geneva.